Touching Bellies,
Touching Lives

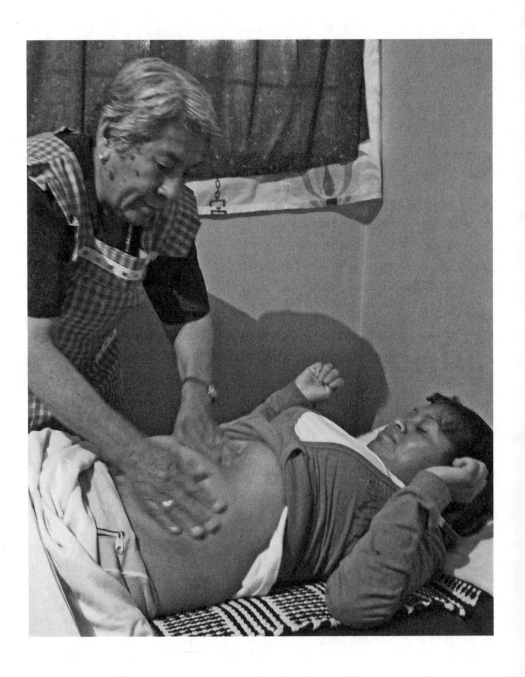

Touching Bellies, Touching Lives

Midwives of Southern Mexico Tell Their Stories

Judy Gabriel

Long Grove, Illinois

For information about this book, contact:
Waveland Press, Inc.
4180 IL Route 83, Suite 101
Long Grove, IL 60047-9580
(847) 634-0081
info@waveland.com
www.waveland.com

Cover: Filiberta Quijano Tun (profiled in chapter 9) massages her granddaughter Lidia's belly.

Frontispiece: A midwife in Tlaxcala, Isabel Perez Juarez, massages a pregnant woman's belly.

Copyright © 2016 by Waveland Press, Inc.

10-digit ISBN 1-4786-2710-7
13-digit ISBN 978-1-4786-2710-4

All rights reserved. No part of this book may be reproduced, stored in a retrieval system, or transmitted in any form or by any means without permission in writing from the publisher.

Printed in the United States of America

7 6 5 4 3 2 1

To the midwives of Mexico

Contents

Preface xi
Acknowledgements xv

1 How It Began   1
The First Birth 1
Becoming a Doula 3
Oaxaca 9
Congreso in Oaxaca 15
The Rebozo Club 19

2 Oaxaca   20
Huesera, Healer of Joints:
  Ignacia Cruz Rivera (Nachita) 21
Poop on the Face:
  Paula Pérez Martinez (Abuelita Paulita) 25
Still Finding Romance:
  Francisca Silvia Moreno Martinez (Silvia) 29
Sidelined and Sad: Marcelina Antonio Felix 32
Widow of a Doctor: Marta García 35
The Hospital 37
Reviving a "Dead" Baby:
  María Magdalena Hernandez Rosario (Lena) 38

3   Huajuapan   47

Stern Teacher: Delfina Morales Diaz   48
Daughter of a Great Midwife:
   Juana Graciela Cruz Lopez   54
A Failed Seamstress:
   Margarita Mendoza Zamora   57
Saving the Unborn: Jovita Loyola Cortez   63
Mourned on the Day of the Dead:
   Casilda Marin Garzón   65
A Pinard Changes Hands: Isabel Rangel Cruz   67
Successful Outcomes in the Traditional Setting   69
Fundal Pressure   72
Nettles: Eduiges Mendez Jimenez   73
Home Again   76

4   Zihuatanejo   78

Ay, Qué Susto: Isabel Valadez Mulina   79
Saved by a Baby Chicken:
   Bricia Jimenez Hernandez   82
Busier than Ever: Lorenza Torres Hernandez   85
The Belly Massage   88
The Old Scolder: Mariana Oregón Lopez   90
Birth in America:
   María de Jesús Rosa Ruiz (Chucha Rosa)   93
Isabel Gives a Massage   93
An Angel in the Hospital:
   Sara Castro Mondragón   94

5   The Hospital in Zihuatanejo   97

Toco   101
How to Get a Pregnant Woman Upside Down:
   Silvina Rosas Villegas   102
A Chance, Almost, to Help a Woman in Labor   104
A Birth in the Night   105
A Reluctant Midwife: Alvina Salas Valdorinas   106
Un Aparato for Isabel   107
Birth on a Rock: Mariana Gomez Sanchez   108

Loved and Missed:
  María de Jesús Vandolinos León (Doña Chucha)   109
Cesarean or Vaginal?   110
Mother and Daughter: Antonia Alonso Vargas (Tonia)
  and Norma Hilda Jaime Alonso   111
The Birth of Saira's Baby   112
Last Class and Goodbye   116

6   Chiapas and Tabasco   117
Quadruplets: Emiliana Ruiz Mazariegos   117
El Congreso   119
Why Are There So Many Cesareans in Mexico?   121
Birth by the River:
  Ana María Moren Hernandez   123
Do Storks Deliver Babies?:
  Francisca Orduño Armenta   124
Born, Not Made: Francisca Catalina García   125
Tenejapa Midwives   126
Adoption   128
A Proper Courtship:
  María de Jesús Pérez Torrez   129
Not Very Friendly, Luisa   132
Recent Widow: Lucía Jiménez Mendes   134
Rattlesnakes in the Kitchen:
  Laura Aguilar Landero   139

7   Yucatán Peninsula   143
Mayan Mother and Daughter:
  Antonia Echeveria and Elena Uk Kupul   143
Blond Mayan Midwife: Sabrina Speich   150
A Breech Great Granddaughter:
  Filiberta Quijano Tun   151
Paciencia: Francisca Montantez Aldana (Panchita)   156
Indentured by Her *Don:* Feliciana Cocom   159
Campeche: Feliciana Cocom May   161
Touched by a *Don:* Leonisa Trujeque Fuentes   164
The *Congreso*   166

8 Vera Cruz, Puebla, and Morelos — 171
The Birth of Rosa's Baby:
  Socorro Espinosa Sanchez   172
The Birth of Lucita's Baby:
  Angelina Martinez Miranda   177
Musing on the Bus   178
Congreso in San Cristóbal   180

9 Oaxaca and Home — 181
A Family of Doctors   183
Silvia Hears Her Story   184
Lena Gets a New Dress   185
Daughter and Granddaughter   187

Epilogue: Hope for a New Midwifery in Mexico — 192

References   195

Preface

A Brief History of Childbirth in the United States (As Experienced by One Midwestern Family)

My grandmother had her babies at home, in the 1920s on a farm in Kansas, with her own mother, my great grandmother, serving as midwife. I presume all the women of my ancestry, until then, had their babies at home, attended by the women of their families or by midwives. I can hear their voices, traveling down through the ages, whispering *"you can do it,"* woman to woman, since the beginning of time.

My grandmother didn't say "you can do it" to her own daughters. By the time my mother and her sisters were having babies in the 1940s, the transfer of childbirth from home to hospital had reached even rural Kansas. The medical system had convinced women that they couldn't do it—or shouldn't. The new message was that women could leave everything to the doctors and nurses of the new maternity wards.

The procedures used in those wards were typically quite invasive, but my mother and my aunts never complained about the treatment they received—because they didn't remember. They would have been given, along with other drugs, Scopolamine, a drug that induces amnesia. Where the memory of childbearing should have been, there was a void: not remembered pain, not joy, and not a sense of accomplishment. Birth had become something that people with specialized expertise did for women.

By the late 1970s, when I became pregnant, things were beginning to change. The epidural allowed women to have relief from pain while still remaining conscious. Lamaze classes were being taught, and many hospitals allowed husbands to enter the labor room. Brave women were pioneering a revival of midwifery in our country. I didn't happen to hear much about these changes myself—my husband and I were working in Iran when my son was born and he was delivered by Cesarean—but back home in the United States there were *beginning* to be more options for the few women who knew to look for and fight for them.

Now, four decades later, the dominant model of childbirth is still very high-tech, but it is (to varying degrees, depending on the hospital and the caregiver) more respectful of women, and alternatives are more readily available. Women can have their babies at home or in a birth center or in a hospital, with a doctor or midwife, and with or without pain relief. Books and the Internet now give women access to information about their options and explain the benefits and risks of all the various interventions that are used.

An Even Briefer History of Childbirth in Mexico (As Experienced by the Midwives of the Rural, Southern Part of the Country)

The midwives I met in my travels (which took place between 2001 and 2015) were almost all, like me, born during the middle of the last century. They had also seen tremendous changes in the birthing practices of their culture. When they were born, at a time when childbirth had become medicalized and depersonalized in my country, it was still, in their *ranchos* and villages, a natural process that took place in the home with the help of experienced women.

During our lifetimes, while my culture moved toward more respect for women and more options in the birthing experience, the midwives have seen their culture give ever *less* respect to birthing women as it has adopted high-intervention medicine as the preferred model for childbirth. Nearly half the births in Mexico are now by Cesarean. In the 1970s over 40 percent of the births in Mexico were attended by midwives (and the percentage would have been a great deal higher in rural southern Mexico, which was the last part of the country to be reached by modern medicine). The number had fallen to 15 percent by 2007, and to 2.1 percent by

2012. The dominant view in Mexico today, among the most progressive, most educated, most wealthy, and in most circles most respected, especially in the north and in large cities, is that midwifery is an ignorant vestige of the past.

Two Changing Cultures Meet

My search for traditional midwives took me to the twelve southernmost states of Mexico (which has a total of 32 states): Oaxaca, Puebla, Tlaxcala, Veracruz, Guerrero, Chiapas, Tabasco, Quintana Roo, Yucatán, Campeche, Morelos, and Michoacán. I focused on the south because that was the part of Mexico I had previously visited and come to love and because midwifery has survived more nearly intact there than in the northern part of the country. (In 2011, over 90 percent of the midwife-attended births in Mexico took place in the twelve states I visited [*Estadísticas Demográficas* 2013]). There, in rural, southern Mexico, I was able to find traditional midwives who were still active in their profession and others who no longer worked but who remembered *the way things were*.

We found that we had much in common, these traditional midwives and I. Our differences felt trivial in comparison with what we shared. We had passed much of our lives sitting with laboring women, attending to them: witnessing their pain, willing and coaching them to be strong, holding their hands, wiping their brows, cleaning up their vomit and other body fluids, and rejoicing with them when the hard work of labor was done. The cries of all those laboring women—cries of pain and cries of joy—had seeped into our hearts.

What I brought to my meeting with traditional midwives, what they most appreciated about what I brought, was great respect for their accomplishments and their wisdom, a respect their own culture has, for the most part, withdrawn. Few of them had met anyone of the modern world (of the world where access to things like education, computers, and cars can be taken for granted) who respected their ways and wanted to learn from them. That respect was my primary gift to them.

What they gave me cannot be so easily summarized. As people say, "It would take a book . . ." It has taken a book. You hold that book in your hands.

Stories Can Be Lost

One of my cousins remembers hearing that our great grandmother, the one who helped our grandmother give birth, helped other women in labor too, not just her own daughters, so she may have been a lay midwife of sorts. We don't really know. We never heard anything about that part of our great grandmother's life, because no one talked about such things when we were growing up. She's gone now, and her daughters and their daughters, our mothers, are gone too. Her stories have been completely lost.

If I could meet my great grandmother now, now that I've become involved in childbirth myself, as a doula and a childbirth educator, now that these subjects are no longer taboo, I would ask her, "What did women know when knowledge about childbirth came not from specialists, not from books that tell us what to expect when we're expecting, but from instinct and experience and from the women who came before?

"What was it like to give birth in your time? Did women walk during labor, or did they 'take to their beds'? Did you give them food and drink? Did you give them herbs? Did women sit or squat or lie in bed when they were pushing? Did you receive any babies that were breech? Any twins? Were you ever afraid? What were the circumstances that led to you attending a birth for the very first time?"

I never had a chance to ask my great grandmother these questions, but I have asked other midwives, women who are rooted in the ways of the past as she would have been, women who learned about childbirth from instinct, from each other, from experience, from dreams, and from God.

I've asked, "How did you become a midwife?"

But I've asked in Spanish.

Acknowledgements

The gratitude and love I feel for the women whose stories appear in these pages cannot be expressed in a few lines. The entire book is a love letter to them. And I am equally indebted to other traditional midwives whose stories are not included because of space constraints. Their pictures and names appear after the Acknowledgements.

I want to thank those who taught me to support women in labor: Penny Simkin, the mother of the doula movement and my teacher when I trained to become a doula in 1996; my friends/mentors in the Rebozo Club, Judith Lienhard, Mary Tippin, Mary Purdy, and Susie Happ, who taught me so much and helped fund one of my trips; and the doctors, midwives, and obstetrical nurses I've worked with in hospitals in Oregon who shared their knowledge with me. I want to especially acknowledge the nurses. Their job is demanding in so many ways and yet they find time to be the doulas when there is no doula. I've shared many challenging, tender, and triumphant moments with them, and they have taught me much.

I also want to express my gratitude to the women who honored me by allowing me to be at their side during their journey toward motherhood. You, most of all, were my teachers.

Thank you to anthropologists Robbie Davis-Floyd and Brigitte Jordan, who knew and loved Mexican midwives before me. Your work inspired me.

For help with the book, I thank: Judy Bowker who gave me my first trip to Oaxaca and who shared her wisdom and perspective as I struggled to find a shape for the book; Jan Tritten, president of Midwifery Today, who (informally) polled her colleagues whenever I needed the perspective of American midwives; Cris Alonso, president of the Asociación Mexicana de Partería, and Sabrina Speich, founder of Parteras Tradicionales Unidas Tumben Cuxtal, both of whom advised me on many details; friends who ran errands for me in Mexico, Joe Craig, Bonnie Barr, and Christy Cozby; and the women who read early drafts (too early; I'm sorry) and gave advice and encouragement, Doctora Heather Diaz, midwife Kate Davidson, writer Rebecca Jaynes, and Marjorie MacKeown. Thanks also to Jeni Ogilvie and Tom Curtin of Waveland Press, who were the midwives for the final push that birthed this book after a 14-year period of gestation. I give love and thanks to fellow traveler and writer Marsha Jacobson, whose encouragement meant so much, and to my dear friends Judy Lundell, who was my staunchest supporter, and Annie Karlson. I can never repay Annie for the many hours she spent going through the manuscript—with a fine-tooth comb in one hand and a magic wand in the other.

Finally, I thank my husband, Jim Gabriel, who believed in this project from the moment it was a tiny and tentative hope in my heart. His love and support have been boundless.

Author Note

I've tinkered a little, but really very little, with the chronology of events when it helped smooth the ride for the reader. I used the first name only, maybe not the true name, for a few people—women in labor primarily—either because I didn't get or didn't remember the full name, and I changed identifying details of a few people I met in hospitals, primarily in adherence to hospital confidentiality protocols. I've given full and correct names for all the midwives (except one in Chiapas who refused to tell me her name) and have translated and related their words as accurately as I could. I consider their stories to be sacred.

Dolores Madalina Urbina Trujillo,
Victoria Salazar Acazar,
Vauldelia Mendosa Rosas,
Margarita Mendosa Rosas

Adela Landeros Aguila,
Cipriana Vellis Marques,
Delfina Garcia,
Eustolia Roque Cruz

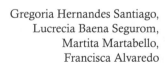

Gregoria Hernandes Santiago,
Lucrecia Baena Segurom,
Martita Martabello,
Francisca Alvaredo

María Victoria Tomas Cecilio,
Serafina Saguro Tomas,
Mirna Edith Amaya Valladares,
Concepción Martinez Escamilla

Esperanza Perez,
Isabel Juan de la Cruz Mendoza,
Margarita Cernas,
Natalia Montiel Aguirre

Juana Morales Mendoza,
María del Carmen Duran Moreno,
Sobadora Ema María Cocom Flores,
Agustina Lopez Lopez

Chapter 1
How It Began

I started by asking, "*¿Cómo se hizo partera?*" (How did you become a midwife)? Some midwives answered, "My mother was a midwife," or "My grandmother [or my aunt or my mother-in-law] was a midwife." But others hesitated, unable to answer. It seemed that midwifery had chosen them, not the reverse. There had been no plan, no intention, no effort to prepare. A woman didn't think, after attending one birth, *now I am a midwife*, nor did she think it after a second or a third. They hadn't reflected on the process, not in a way that would have prepared them to answer my question: *How?*

And so I found a better question, a more concrete one that led more surely into the midwives' stories. I asked, *Can you tell me about the very first birth you ever attended on your own?*

The First Birth
Hermila Diego González

Hermila, a midwife from Oaxaca wearing a long cotton gown embroidered at the neck and hem, said she was seventeen years old the first time she attended a birth.

> One day the village priest asked me to help a woman in labor. I asked why the midwife Lupe couldn't help her, and he said Lupe was getting too old to work. He said I would know what to do because my grandmother had been a midwife.
>
> I didn't know anything about childbirth. I'd never been with my grandmother when she attended a birth, and I hadn't had any babies myself. But the priest was insistent, so I went to the woman's house.

> She told me what to do. I just made a tea and fetched things for her and, when it was time, I held my hand under her skirt to catch the baby. When the placenta came, I thought it was her insides, but she explained what it was. She said I had to tie something around the cord, so I tore a strip of fabric from the bottom of my slip and used that. I was afraid to cut the cord; she had to do that herself.
>
> Two weeks later I was called to attend another birth. And then there was another. . . .

A Midwife in Chiapas

A midwife from Tenejapa in Chiapas, a somber, tiny woman with purple ribbons woven into her braids, said the first birth she attended was that of her own baby.

> My grandmother attended the births of my first two babies. When I was pregnant for the third time, I dreamed about the birth. I dreamed that the baby was sitting [breech] and that I pushed him into the head-down position. In the dream I knew everything I needed to know about how to attend the birth. A woman dressed in beautiful robes appeared to me in the dream. She said, "You're going to help my daughters. You must never deny a woman who needs your help."
>
> When I woke up, I massaged my belly, trying to feel the position of the baby, and I found that his head was at the top. I pushed him into a good position, knowing how to do it from the dream. When it was time for the birth, I leaned against the bed and bore down, and he was born; then I cut the cord and bathed him, all just as I'd done in the dream.
>
> Since then I've helped many other women have their babies. If there's going to be a problem, I'm always told what to do ahead of time in a dream.

María de la Paz Puebla Alvear

María de la Paz, a modern-looking woman from Morelos, said she was eleven years old when she first became involved in a birth.

> I was walking down the road on my way to school when a pregnant woman standing at the side of the road called out to me, "¡Ayúdame! ¡Ya viene!"
>
> I asked, "What's coming?"
>
> The woman said, "The baby."
>
> Her baby was born then, right there beside the road. I spread my sweater out on the ground and put the baby on it. When the placenta came out, I thought it was the woman's guts. I put it on the sweater too.

Then I hurried off to school, because I didn't want to be late. I left the woman standing there—with the baby and the placenta still lying on my sweater. I was living with my grandparents at the time, and they were mad at me for losing the sweater, but I never told them what happened.

I got involved in another birth when I was thirteen. My neighbor was having a baby by herself, without a midwife, so I offered to help her. It was her sixth baby, so she knew what to do. I just brought her the things she needed and watched. After that I helped other women in labor whenever I could. As I gained experience, women started asking me to be with them. I never told my grandma what I was doing, but I told my grandfather. He was a *curandero* [traditional healer]. When I told him I was helping women have babies, he gave me some herbs I could use to make a tea that would help if I ever had a situation where the placenta failed to come out.

I feel that being a midwife was my calling. Being asked to help that woman when I was eleven years old was a sign that God wanted me to do this work.

It was a calling: the call of family tradition, the call of sacred duty, the call of God speaking in a dream, or the call of a woman in labor crying for help. The midwives of Mexico are the courageous, compassionate women who couldn't say no to the call.

Becoming a Doula

¿Y cómo me hice yo acechadora de parteras? How did I happen to become a person who wandered around southern Mexico asking such questions? My story, the story of how I became a doula (a professional who provides physical, emotional, and informational support to women in labor), a childbirth educator, and a stalker of traditional midwives, began in 1964, when I traveled by train from my home in Minnesota to Mexico to spend a summer in a village in Puebla working as a volunteer with the American Friends Service Committee. I was nineteen, eager for love and adventure.

I found adventure and I found love, too, but not the kind of love my friends were finding at that age. I fell in love with village life in southern Mexico: with the quiet pace, with the landscape, with the sense of accomplishment that comes from being understood in a second language, and with the children who came to our courtyard to play American games like Drop the Hanky and who walked with us to the neighboring village where we got our mail and bought chocolate bars.

Chapter One

Judy with girls at a picnic in Santa Cruz Analco, Puebla, 1964.

I learned, years later when I returned to the village, that there were four midwives there in 1964, but I didn't meet them. I wasn't interested in babies then, not in babies, not in birth, and not in midwives. Many years would pass before I would become interested in matters related to childbirth. I would return to Mexico to study Mexican sociology at a university in Mexico City. I would finish college, travel to other continents, pursue a career designing computer systems, marry, raise my own children—a son born by Cesarean in a hospital in Tehran and a daughter adopted from a Russian orphanage—and move to a small town in Oregon. Then it would be time for my mind and heart to turn to matters of birth.

The small town in Oregon is in the Willamette Valley, a lush, fertile area that grows Christmas trees, grass seed, hops for the beer industry, and a large variety of fruits and vegetables, all with the help of workers from southern Mexico. In 1996, looking for a way to help the women among those workers, I became a doula and began helping Spanish-speaking women in labor at a local hospital. Soon I was busy. Nurses would call me: "The patient is all alone," they'd say, or "The woman is really scared," or "She's having back labor." I became a certified childbirth educator and started teaching childbirth classes and parenting classes in Spanish; I was certified as a translator.

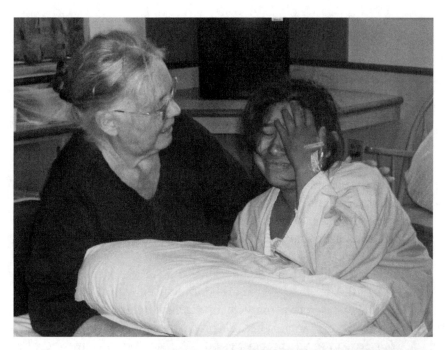

Judy helping a woman in labor in a hospital in Oregon.

Five years after I started working with Mexicans in my community, a friend, also named Judy, a professor at a nearby university, asked me to help her with a project that required travel to Oaxaca. She wanted to photograph people there who had family members living in Oregon. My job would be to identify families for her study and then travel with her to serve as guide and translator. Thirty-five years after that first trip, I finally had a chance to return to southern Mexico!

Judy and I visited and took pictures of the Oregon members of each family before we left on the trip. One young woman, Francisca, a former student who'd become my friend, said her first baby was born in Oaxaca, but the rest of her four children were born in Oregon. Her mother Isabel had never seen her Oregon-born grandchildren. For some reason Francisca had never even sent pictures. Judy took dozens of photos for us take to Isabel.

Francisca said she'd married her husband Gabriel when she was fifteen years old. After they were married, they lived with Gabriel's grandmother Julia, who was a midwife in a *rancho* (cluster of farms) near Francisca's village. Francisca became pregnant right away.

"We were so young!" Francisca said. "We didn't even know where the baby was going to come out. We talked about it, trying to figure it out."

"But you lived in the country," I said. "Surely you'd seen animals giving birth."

"Yes, we had a general idea, but we weren't sure which hole was involved."

"Couldn't you have asked Gabriel's grandmother?"

"No, we would have been too embarrassed."

Francisca told us about the birth.

> I felt like pooping, so I was going back and forth to the toilet [typically a hole in the ground hidden behind bushes or a cane fence], but nothing was happening. Gabriel's grandmother asked me what was going on, but I was too embarrassed to tell her. She figured out that it was time for the baby to come, so she had me sit on a special chair she used for births and she had me push. Gabriel helped me by pushing on the top of my belly with his hand. Soon they told me to push, and I did, and the baby was born.

"Just like that? Didn't you have contractions?"

"Not that I can remember. I just had that feeling that I needed to poop."

Francisca said Julia had massaged her belly during the pregnancy. The massages were deep and probing and felt *muy rico* (very delicious). A few days after the birth Francisca was given a bath in a little enclosure made of poles and leafy branches with a fire inside heating a pot of herbal water.[1] Julia poured the aromatic water over Francisca's body and threw handfuls of it onto hot rocks to make steam. Francisca remembered the bath as also being *muy rico*.

I asked Francisca to describe the special chair Julia used. She said it was made of wood and it was low. That was all she remembered.

"Did Gabriel's grandmother use her fingers to check how your labor was progressing?"

"No! She didn't look at my private area at all. I was wearing a big skirt that covered everything. She didn't touch me either. She treated me with respect. Birth is more dignified in Mexico than it is here."

"Here women have to do this," Gabriel said. He leaned back in his chair, lifting his legs and spreading them wide. Gabriel and Francisca both laughed.

"The nurse in the hospital even suggested I look in a mirror!" Francisca said.

"Were the births you had here as fast and as easy as that first one?"

"No. They took longer and were more painful. Why is birth easier in Mexico than it is here?"

I pointed out that every birth is different, so it can't be assumed that being in Mexico was the reason why her first birth was the easiest. I reminded her that she'd been more physically active when she lived in Mexico. She had no car; she walked everywhere. Physical activity, especially walking, makes labor easier. And fear inhibits labor. The hospital setting, so sterile and foreign, with caregivers who spoke only English, must have been frightening. In Mexico she'd been in her own home, being cared for by a woman she knew, who viewed birth as a natural process. That would have made it easier to ignore the sensations of labor. And maybe—I didn't voice this thought to Francisca, but I wondered—maybe there had been something else, something we lost when we turned childbirth over to modern medicine. Gabriel's grandmother would have been rooted in the old ways. Maybe she had some insight or knowledge, passed down to her through the ages, that helped ease labor.

That evening, after we took pictures of Francisca's family, I was called to the hospital to help a woman, Angelina, in labor. The nurse told me that Angelina didn't speak Spanish; she spoke only Zapoteco (the language of an indigenous group, the Zapotec, of southern Oaxaca). The nurse had been trying to get Angelina up out of bed, to move, to walk, but Angelina refused—or she didn't understand.

I sat beside the bed and tried to coach Angelina through a few contractions, speaking in Spanish, assuming, hoping, she understood at least a few words and knowing that a soothing tone mattered more than the meaning of my words. I wasn't sure I was going to be able to connect with her enough to help—she scarcely looked at me—but then a familiar head-tilting-back grimace made me think she was having back pain with her contractions, so I put my hand on her lower back and asked "Does it hurt here?" She didn't answer, but her back curved into my touch. I pressed against her lower back during the next contraction (countering from the outside a pressure the baby's head was making from the inside) and asked, when the contraction was over, "Did it help when I pressed with my hand like that?"

She looked directly at me then, appeal in her eyes, and said *sí*. So she did understand Spanish. She began to trust me because my hands had known how to help.

It seems that the most common cause of back pain during labor ("back labor") is some awkwardness in the position of the baby's head. If the baby's head isn't well aligned with the mother's pelvis, labor will be slower and more painful. I suggested some ways Angelina could move her own body to help the baby move into a better position, and she worked hard to follow my directions. After about an hour, the back pain suddenly disappeared and the pace of labor picked up. When Angelina seemed to display an urge to "push" (to bear down with her diaphragm as we do when we try to force a bowel movement) the nurse performed a vaginal check (she inserted two fingers into Angelina's vagina to feel the cervix) and said Angelina was fully dilated; it would be alright for her to push if she felt like it. I helped her get into a squatting position on the bed, arranging a bar for her to hold onto. She looked confused and afraid, so I tried to reassure her, explaining what was going to happen next, but suddenly Mother Nature explained it for me. With the next contraction, a grimace smashed across her face and she made a grunting push. When the contraction ended, she fell back against the bed to rest. I wiped her brow and gave her water and then helped her back up into a squat to resume her hard work with the next contraction. The nurse called the doctor. The baby was born after only half an hour of pushing.

I had always been particularly interested in working with women who were having back labor. I'd had back labor myself during twelve hours of labor (lying flat on my back the whole time) in an Iranian hospital when I was giving birth to my son. I'd learned since then that lying on the back is the worst possible position for labor, especially when there is back pain; what is needed is *movement*. I knew many positions and exercises that helped, but I was always on the lookout for one more "trick" to add to my arsenal of things to try. It occurred to me that the midwives of Mexico might have found something and that, if they had, Gabriel's grandmother might be able to tell me about it.

Judy and I visited Francisca and Gabriel again before we left for Oaxaca and showed them the pictures Judy had taken of their children. Tears came to Francisca's eyes as she imagined her mother seeing the pictures. "Be sure to bring them back to me," she said. She explained that there are jealousies and grudges in a small village. If the pictures were to fall into the hands of someone who wanted to harm her family, that person could take them to a *brujo* (witch or shaman) who could use them to cast a spell. So that explained why she had never sent pictures to her mother. We promised we'd bring them back.

I asked Gabriel about his grandmother, the midwife Julia. Was she still alive? Could we visit her? He said she was still living but she was old and no longer worked as a midwife. Still I wanted to meet her. Even though it didn't seem likely that we'd have time for another visit while we were in Oaxaca, I wrote down her name, Julia Reyes, and the name of her *rancho* and had Gabriel give me rough directions.

During the days that followed, as we prepared for our trip, I kept thinking about the chair Francisca had mentioned, the "special chair for birth" Julia had used. I wanted to see it. I'd seen pictures of birthing chairs from other cultures, but I'd never heard of any special kind of chair being used in Mexico. That didn't mean there wasn't such a thing; all I knew about childbirth in Mexico was what I'd heard from Francisca. I imagined a craftsman in a village in the mountains carving a beautiful chair according to some design passed down through generations. I saw him polishing the wood, making it smooth. Maybe I could find such a craftsman. Maybe I could bring a chair like that back to Oregon.

Oaxaca

Our first outing, once we'd unpacked our bags in Oaxaca, was to the *zócalo* (the big park in the center of town), where children played, lovers embraced, and balloon sellers paraded with their wares. I sat on a bench under one of the tall, graceful trees that shade the park, my heart bursting with impressions and memories and happiness to be back in Mexico.

We found a driver, Arturo, to take us to Francisca's village. Sitting three abreast in his big Chevy pickup, we headed south on a two-lane highway toward the municipality of Zaachila. Arturo had to ask directions more than once, but eventually we found the gravel road that zigzagged through the mountains to the village. When we got there, Arturo parked his truck next to the school and settled down in the shade of a building to wait. A young boy volunteered to show us the way to Francisca's mother's home.

Isabel was arriving home, carrying buckets of water, just as we reached her small adobe house. We gave her the photos of her grandchildren and then waited quietly while she leafed slowly through them. Tears slid down her cheeks. She touched one of the photos with the tip of a finger; she kissed it. When she was done, I mentioned that Francisca wanted the photos back. Isabel held them to her chest. "Tell her I'll take good care of them," she said. Judy and I looked at each other. We had *promised* to return them.

Oh well.

Isabel led us to the homes of other families we wanted to visit. We gave each family gifts we'd been asked to deliver and photos Judy had taken of their relatives in Oregon, and Judy took hundreds of pictures. As we moved from house to house through the village, our group grew. The longing everyone felt for their loved ones in faraway Oregon spilled over onto us. By the time we rejoined Arturo in the center of the village, we had a crowd of friends who hugged us and wished us well. "Come back soon," they all said. Arturo must have wondered what could have happened to make us the objects of so much affection. He couldn't know that we were standing in for the children and grandchildren the people of the village prayed for every day.

We were exhausted. The heat, the altitude, the bright sun, the intense socializing, and a day without food had all taken their toll. We dug granola bars and water bottles out of the bottom of our bags and settled back in the bench seat of Arturo's truck for the ride down out of the mountains.

And I began to think about Julia, the midwife who lived somewhere at the base of those mountains. "Do you think we could try to find Julia?" I asked Judy.

It seemed impossible—we were so drained, and we had only the vaguest idea how to find her—and yet, how could we not try?

Julia Reyes

When we reached the outskirts of Zaachila, we asked directions to Julia's *rancho* and were directed to a rough dirt road that stretched out over flat, open land covered by scrubby brush toward the mountains. "Just follow that road," we were told. After traveling for about half an hour, making arbitrary choices at every fork and watching the road deteriorate into ruts in the dry grass, we came upon two children in school uniforms who said they were on their way to the *rancho*. They climbed into the back of our truck and guided us the rest of the way.

Julia, a stout woman, less than five feet tall, her brown leathery skin webbed with fine wrinkles and her grey hair braided into two plaits, was sitting with her granddaughter Paula under a little tree. Both were barefoot. As soon as we introduced ourselves, Julia jumped up and disappeared into her adobe house, returning a few minutes later, still barefoot but now wearing a frayed pink satin dress. She was so excited to see us she could barely speak. She was shaking with excitement.

She didn't respond to my questions about her life and work as a midwife. That was all so long ago; she was too old to remember. She only wanted to talk about her grandson, Francisca's husband Gabriel. We had no photos to show her—we'd given them all to Isabel—but we told her about her great grandchildren in Oregon. She wasn't interested in them; it was Gabriel she longed for. When would he be coming home? He had a house waiting for him, she said, pointing to a partially completed structure made of cement blocks about half a block away.

When I asked her about back labor, she gave me a blank look. Pain is pain. Labor hurts. She had apparently never considered back pain to be a special issue. And when I asked about the chair, she looked confused.

"What chair?" she asked.

"The special one you used when a woman was pushing out her baby."

She didn't remember having had a special chair.

My fantasy, the one about the craftsman polishing the wood, dissolved into the dust that surrounded us. Looking around me, at the starkness of the landscape and the sparseness of possessions, I realized how silly the fantasy had been. Of course, the "special" chair had been an ordinary wooden chair; what had been special about it was that it was the one, among the various chairs of the household, that Julia liked to use for birth.

We gave her some money, telling her it was from Gabriel, and she gave us each a handful of raw peanuts. Her last words to us were, "Tell Gabriel to come home." She watched us and waved as we drove away, looking, even in a pink satin dress, like part of the landscape.

***

The next day, in a village to the south, I asked about midwives and was told that the last one had died just six months before. Women in another village said they'd had four midwives just a decade ago, but they were all gone. Three had died, and one had gone to live with her son in Puebla. A German woman who lived in the city of Oaxaca said she'd tried to find a midwife when she was pregnant, but there were none at all in the city. (She was wrong about that, I later discovered, but I believed her at the time.)

It seemed the midwives of Mexico were fast disappearing. And Julia could not or would not remember. I felt like a child who arrives at a much anticipated party only to find that she's late and the party has already ended.

Francisca Jimenez (Doña Chica)

And then, on the last day before we returned to Oregon, in the town of Nejapa in the muggy lowland area of southeastern Oaxaca, we met the midwife Francisca Jimenez, known to everyone as Doña Chica, a beautiful woman with smooth dark skin and intelligent eyes, fifty-five years old. She told us she'd gone to Mexico City for a six-month course in midwifery when she was young.

Doña Chica.

I asked how much she was paid for her work, and she laughed. "Whatever the people can afford," she said. "Sometimes just a bag of corn."

She said there hadn't been any doctors in the village when she started working as a midwife, but since then a Center of Salud ("Health Center": a government-subsidized clinic) had been built. The clinic was staffed by a series of recently graduated doctors, whom she called *practicantes*, who were performing their *servicio* (a year of service, required of all newly trained doctors in Mexico, during which they work in a clinic or hospital in some area where there's a shortage of doctors). She said that the *practicantes* typically had little or no experience in obstetrics before they came to the village. There had been a few over the years who looked to her for advice and support, but most dismissed her as an ignorant vestige of the past. She cringed when she spoke of the misguided practices women of her village had been subjected to in that clinic.

For example, one *practicante* gave a laboring woman an injection that was supposed to strengthen her contractions and then sent her home, telling her to come back when the contractions were stronger. The woman returned the next day, but the doctor just gave her another injection and sent her home again. After four days of that—four trips to the Center of Salud and four injections—her family brought her to Doña Chica.

> They showed me the packaging from the medicine the doctor had been using, and I saw that he'd been giving the poor woman the medicine we use to *stop* labor. I gave her an injection of Pitocin [an artificial form of the hormone oxytocin used to induce or strengthen contractions] and soon she was in active labor. The baby was born that night.

When I asked about back pain in labor, Doña Chica offered to show us a technique she uses. One of her neighbors, Amalia, who was also visiting, helped with the demonstration. Doña Chica stretched a rebozo (traditional shawl) across the bed and had Amalia lie down with her lower back and buttocks over it. Then Doña Chica took the two ends of the rebozo and started pulling up, first on one end and then on the other, rolling Amalia from side to side.

This technique would become well-known in the United States in the years that followed my visit to Oaxaca. I would learn to use it myself and would come to value it as a very effective way to help shift babies into a more favorable position. But I didn't see that potential when Doña Chica showed it to me. It was obvious later, when I saw the procedure being used on a *pregnant* woman, her belly sloshing from side to side as she was rocked, how the baby might be freed up to find a better position. But because Doña Chica's "patient" Amalia was slender, with no belly at all, I didn't consider how the movement would affect a baby in the uterus. I saw the technique as a "mere" ritual, like the lighting of a candle, and I didn't imagine I might ever use it myself.

Judy and I hugged Doña Chica and thanked her and returned to the city. Although Doña Chica hadn't shared any ancient wisdom about childbirth and I'd failed to recognize the value of what she had given me (knowledge of the rebozo procedure), I took away from our visit a hopeful sense of possibility.

Maybe the party wasn't over quite yet.

***

Back in Oregon, a few days later, we gave Francisca copies of the pictures Judy had taken of her mother and we confessed that we'd left the pictures of her children in Oaxaca. She understood. "I know my mother will be careful with them," she said. "She'll bury them under her bed."

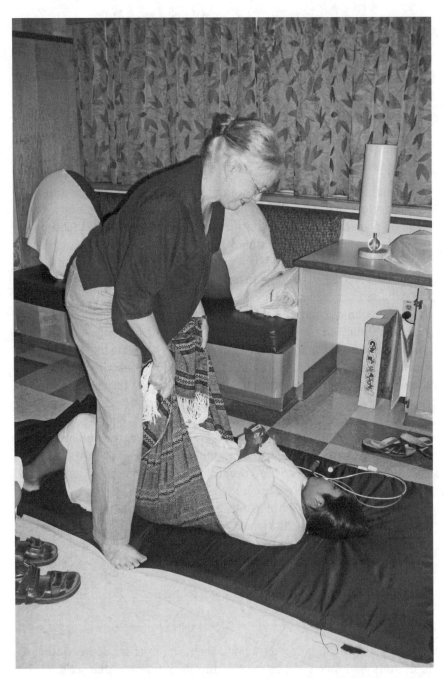

Judy using a rebozo to rock a woman from side to side, a technique that often helps improve the baby's position.

Congreso in Oaxaca

I returned to Oaxaca two years later for a *congreso* (conference) co-sponsored by the Oregon-based organization, Midwifery Today, and the Mexican branch of MANA (Midwife Alliance of North America). There were 275 attendees, about half from Latin American countries and about half from the United States, Canada, Europe, and Australia. Most were midwives. Others were doctors, nurses, doulas, and educators. All but a few were women.

On the first day of the *congreso*, which was held in the annex of a beautiful old church, the organizers had those of us who came from economically privileged countries assemble in the courtyard. They reminded us that people from our cultures had often come to Mexico for the purpose of conquering and exploiting and emphasized that we, in contrast, were coming with humility and respect, and that we were being welcomed. The traditional midwives formed a receiving line and welcomed us as we entered the church, hugging us or kissing our cheeks, squeezing our hands, murmuring words of welcome. It felt like a homecoming to me. My heart was very full.

The party is not over, I thought. But it was ending. Later that morning, during a general session of the *congreso*, anthropologist Robbie Davis-Floyd told us that 85 percent of the midwives remaining in Mexico were over the age of sixty-five. She said that in the early 1970s (when Mexico first started gathering such statistics), 43 percent of births in the country were attended by midwives. Now, in 2003, the rate was 15 percent. And while the rate of midwife-attended births was falling, the Cesarean rate in Mexico had risen alarmingly—to 40 percent.[2]

Cesarean section is a valuable tool that saves lives, but unnecessary use of the procedure adds significant risks to both mother and baby, including, for example, nearly tripling the risk of maternal death due to childbirth (Wagner 2006, 44). An excessively high Cesarean rate can be seen as evidence that there's an unhealthy dependence on technology in childbirth and that the prevailing attitude fails to understand and does not value the natural process of birth. (The World Health Organization [WHO] had advised, "There is no justification for any region to have [Cesarean] rates higher than 10–15 percent" [1985, 436–437].) A rise in the Cesarean rate can be seen as a measure of the acceptance of attitudes and policies that are achieving the demise of midwifery in countries like Mexico.

Four of my friends from back home, three labor and delivery nurses and a midwife, were also at the *congreso*. Together we attended a session about using the rebozo to help women in labor. There, in that session, we saw Mexican midwives demonstrate the procedure Doña Chica had shown me two years before. This time, surrounded by midwives from all over the world who were taking notes, nodding their heads, and making plans to try it themselves, I saw the potential of the technique.

Between sessions, the attendees mingled in the courtyard, chatting in English and Spanish. We were a colorful sight, wearing our embroidered dresses and blouses. I asked the traditional midwives how they'd learned about childbirth. One midwife said, "I learned what I know about birth thanks to all the women who honored me by allowing me to attend their labors." Another said, "We learned about birth from birth." I loved how those statements showed respect for birth, how they characterized birth as a teacher rather than as a process to be managed. I saw that the passing on of wisdom went both ways. Midwives guided women in labor, but they also learned from them.

When the *congreso* was over, I went to the bus station for the first leg of my journey home. After I bought a ticket, I recognized three women from the *congreso* waiting for the same bus. I talked to them while we waited and sat next to one of them, Delia Lima Barcenas, for the four-hour trip to Puebla. As we left the congestion of the city and headed into the dry empty hills of northeastern Oaxaca, she told me about her life.

Delia Lima Barcenas

She was no longer working as a midwife, she said. She had allowed her business to dwindle down to nothing when women started going to doctors, but her husband had died two years before, and now she needed more income. She wanted to resume her work, but to do that she would need a delivery table—the kind that has leg supports—and she couldn't afford one.

No, I thought, *not a delivery table with leg supports!* I'd heard nightmarish stories of women in Mexican hospitals laboring and pushing for hours in the unnatural position imposed by those tables.

I told her that back home we were encouraging women to assume more natural positions during delivery. I told her about a birth I'd recently attended in a hospital in Oregon. The patient, who had

Delia.

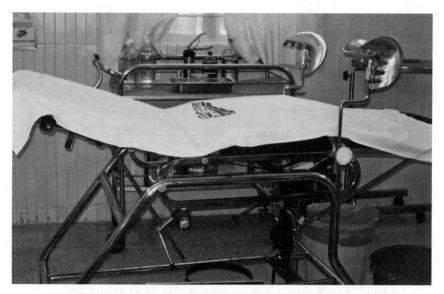

A delivery table in a Center of Salud in a small town in Oaxaca. Photo by Richard Schorr.

already had three babies with a midwife in Mexico, didn't like being in the bed. She wanted to give birth as she had always done, kneeling on the floor, and the doctor was willing to oblige her. When it was time for the birth, the woman knelt on a sterile pad and had me kneel facing her. She put her arms on my shoulders and clasped her hands behind my neck so that I could bear her weight as she leaned forward and pulled down during contractions. The doctor sat on a low stool behind her and caught the baby from there.

"Indigenous women in the mountains near my home give birth like that too," Delia said. "But my patients live in town. They expect a delivery table." It seemed that a delivery table was a necessary symbol of professionalism in Delia's world.

I wished her success, but I was lamenting the role my culture has played in leading her to believe that this modern device was a necessity. *Don't follow us*, my heart cried. *We overshot. We lost too much.* I later read an account by Robbie Davis-Floyd (2014) of a midwife who used her delivery table mostly "for show," to satisfy the expectations of patients and their families who "believe in the efficacy of the hospital and its procedures." That midwife said she tried to keep her patients *off* the delivery table as long as possible—or even altogether. Perhaps Delia would do the same.

I asked her about the first birth she had attended on her own.

She began, "I fell in love with my mother-in-law when I was a little girl. . . ." And I settled back in the comfortable seat of the first-class bus to listen to her story.

> My family lived next door to a midwife when I was a child. She was a wonderfully kind woman who always dressed in white. My mother used to take me to her when I was sick or when I had an injury that needed to be bandaged. I thought she was the most beautiful woman I'd ever seen. I thought she was an angel. I told my cousins, "When I grow up, I'm going to marry the midwife's son so the midwife will be my mother-in-law."
>
> As I grew older, I forgot about my plan to marry the midwife's son. My family moved, so the midwife was no longer my neighbor. But then, one day when I was eighteen years old, attending a party with my cousin, I noticed a handsome young man I didn't recognize. I asked my cousin, "Who's that guy?" and she said he was the son of the midwife who used to live next door to me. So I met him, and we fell in love and got married. That's how I got my wish to have the midwife as my mother-in-law.
>
> My husband and I lived with his parents after we were married. My mother-in-law took care of patients in her own bedroom. She would pull a curtain across the door when she was with a patient, but I could hear what was going on and occasionally I caught a glimpse. She noticed my interest and asked me if I'd like to help her. I started attending births with her, and I also went with her to classes for midwives offered by the Center of Salud in a neighboring town. She could read and write, but it was a slow process for her. She liked having me along to take notes.
>
> One day she said, "I think you're ready to attend a birth on your own."
>
> I said, "No, I don't want to. I like helping you, but I don't want to work alone."
>
> She just smiled as if she thought she knew more about it than I did.
>
> A few days later, when my mother-in-law was away from home attending a birth, a woman came to the door in labor. When I told the woman she'd have to go somewhere else because the midwife wasn't home, she said she knew I'd been working with my mother-in-law and she trusted I could help her myself. Her contractions were strong; she didn't feel she had time to find another midwife. So I had to do it. It was an easy birth; everything went smoothly.
>
> When my mother-in-law came home that evening, she heard the baby crying and saw the dirty linens from the birth. "Well," she said, "I see you were ready after all!"

I said goodbye to Delia and her friends in the bus station in Puebla and continued on to the airport in Mexico City.

The Rebozo Club

Back in Oregon, I, and my friends who had been at the *congreso* (we later dubbed ourselves the Rebozo Club), started using the rebozo technique and showing it to others who worked in the same hospital. I used a beautiful red rebozo I'd bought during my first trip to Mexico in 1964. The technique often produced dramatic change. A patient who'd been having back labor would say, after a period of being rocked from side to side, "My back pain is gone." Then often she would add, "Now it really hurts *down there*." And we (nurse and doula) would smile. Once, when a doctor and I had been rocking a woman for a few minutes, the patient suddenly called out, "I want to push!"

***

I continued to work as a volunteer doula helping Spanish-speaking women in labor and teaching parenting classes and childbirth classes in Spanish. I was invited to Mexican baby showers, weddings, *quinceñera* parties (a celebration held when a girl reaches the age of fifteen), and funerals for babies born too early to survive. Some days I spoke more Spanish than English. It wouldn't seem that I needed to travel to Mexico again—Mexico had come to me—but the stories I'd heard echoed in my mind. It was as if I'd started to read a wonderful book and had then misplaced it. There was a sense in me of something unfinished. And there was a sense of urgency.

The last midwife died six months ago . . .

We used to have four midwives, but they're all gone now . . .

There aren't any midwives at all in the city of Oaxaca . . .

The midwives of Mexico were disappearing. It wasn't too late for me to hear their stories, but it would be soon.

Endnotes

1. The enclosure Francisca described was a makeshift version of the *temazcal* (traditional Mexican steam bath), which is similar to the sweat lodge of Native Americans. See Horacio Rojas Alba's article (1996) for a detailed description.
2. The rate was also high, 27.6 percent (CDC 2005) and still climbing, in the United States at that time.

Chapter 2

Oaxaca

It was market day in Etla. Stalls with their brightly colored tarps and mounds of luscious produce filled the plaza next to the *zócalo* and lined the narrow streets that led up the hill beyond. Taxis, most of them *mototaxis*, (three-wheeled motorcycles with benches in back for passengers) were lined up along one edge of the plaza. The drivers lounged on park benches and leaned on their vehicles, waiting for fares.

I approached a small group of drivers and asked, "Are there any *parteras* in Etla?"

"*¿Cómo* [huh]? *Parteras?*"

"Yes, *parteras.*"

"*¿Parteras?*" The drivers looked at each other. "*¿Parteras?*"

"Yes, you know, the women who used to help women in labor before there were clinics and hospitals."

"Oh, you mean *¡parteras!*"

"Yes, *parteras*. Are there any?"

The drivers discussed this question. One remembered a Matilda, but another said Matilda had died. They reached a consensus: there were no midwives in Etla. Another driver, a little older than the others, came to see what the discussion was about. I asked if he knew of any midwives in Etla, and now I had the other drivers helping me explain that by *"parteras"* I meant *"parteras."*

Did I mean the women who massage the bellies of pregnant women?

Yes. Soon I was on the back of the man's *mototaxi* heading for the home of the woman who had massaged his wife's belly during both her pregnancies.

Huesera, Healer of Joints: Ignacia Cruz Rivera (Nachita)

Nachita was a tiny woman, but her regal bearing and air of authority made a big impression. I thought of her as tall; I was surprised, later when I developed my pictures, to see that she barely reached my shoulder, which meant she couldn't have been more than about four and a half feet tall. She was seventy-five years old, she said, and had been a widow for eighteen years. Her aunt had been the midwife for the births of all her children.

Nachita.

> I had eleven babies, but four of them died as infants. There were no doctors in the *rancho* where we lived, and we were far from the nearest town, with no cars and no buses, so we did the best we could on our own. My husband would come home from working in the fields with some injury, and I would do what I could to cure him using herbs and massage. I did the same for my children.
>
> One night I had a dream in which a group of old women with soft faces and soft voices wearing flowing white robes told me I was supposed to become a healer.[1] They gave me herbs I was supposed to use to cure people. After having that dream I was more confident. I became skilled at massaging bones and joints and also at using herbs. Neighbors started coming to me when they had problems.
>
> I gave belly massages to pregnant women, but I didn't want to attend births—that scared me—until one day, about twenty-five years ago, I had to help my own daughter-in-law in labor. We'd asked my son to take her to the doctor when the contractions first started, but he was busy and he thought it was too soon. Then, all of a sudden, it was too late. I received the baby and the placenta, and cut the cord myself.
>
> After I saw how easy it was, I agreed to help other women in labor. I'd been at a few births with my aunt when I was a little girl, and I remembered how she took care of me when I was having my own babies, but I had no real training. I just learned by necessity. I have faith in God. He is always with me, guiding me.
>
> Once I was called to help a girl who was in labor six weeks early because of a fall. She'd been in the hospital for three days, but the doctors hadn't been able to stop the contractions. They decided she

would have to have a Cesarean. The family was afraid of that, so they brought the girl home. When I got to her house, I found the poor girl on the floor in the middle of the room, still having contractions and crying. She couldn't get up onto the bed—it was too high—so I had the family put a mattress on the floor. Two doctors, one of them a relative of the family, arrived just as I was starting to work. They said nothing could be done. They didn't think the baby would live.

I said, "I'm going to massage the girl's belly. Don't worry. This baby is not going to be lost."

The mother-in-law said, "This woman knows more than you doctors. You may have gone to the university, but, excuse me, for you doctors it's always *puro cuchillo, puro cuchillo* [just knives, just knives]. Leave the midwife to work in peace, and you'll see what can be done without knives."

So I did my work. I rocked the girl in a rebozo and massaged her belly, moving the baby up. The contractions stopped.

The doctors asked, "How did you do that?"

I said, "You were standing right there watching. I did it in front of you. I'm not hiding anything. You saw me rock her; you saw me massage her."

"Is that all you had to do?" they asked.

I said, "Yes, that's all I had to do. What else would I have to do?"

The girl started to feel the baby move. She was very happy. She said, "What good are all these doctors? What did they do? Nothing, nothing."

Six weeks later, when the girl began to have contractions again, they sent for me to receive the baby. It was a boy. When he was born, I said, "Look, here is the baby that was going to be lost. Look at this precious, beautiful baby boy."

I asked her about the use of herbs in labor, and she began a discourse on the subject, addressing me as if I were a student, speaking quickly, naming a few herbs I'd heard of and many I had not. I tried to get her to slow down. I wanted to know the purpose of each herb, which part of the plant was used, how much was needed, and how the tea was prepared, but she breezed on, not relating to my questions *when, how, how much,* and *why.* I began to feel uncomfortable with the question, *why,* and I would learn to use it carefully as I continued on my quest. It could too easily seem to demand that the midwives *justify* their actions to me—so I could judge for myself whether they made sense or not.

When I was back home, I read about the use of herbs in traditional healing and realized that my questioning of Nachita had been based on a superficial understanding of the subject. I had always thought herbs were used for their chemical properties, like prescription medicines. But now I learned from writer/healers and healer/scholars, such as Patrisia Gonzales (2012) and Elena Avila (1999), that there is a spiritual component to the healing power of herbs. Avila says,

> Many cultures believe you can only use the herbs that have come to you in a dream or a vision, forming an alliance with you. . . . There is always an exchange of energy between plants and the people who use them because plants are as alive as we are. (1999, 71)

I had hoped to learn about some herb that would magically ease labor, but I began to see that it would take a great deal of study before I could appropriate such a practice for use outside its authentic context.

Nachita was more open when she talked about the use of a drink she called *chocolate espiritual*. "You add two raw eggs to a cup of hot chocolate," she said in her teaching voice. "Only use a little water, and don't add any sugar at all. The drink needs to be strong and bitter. The woman drinks that when she's nearing the end of labor, and it makes the baby come quickly." She said that the *chocolate espiritual* may make the woman vomit, which apparently she saw as a good thing.

I'd seen, in my own work, that nausea is common in late labor and that it usually seems to be an indication of progress, but I'd never heard anyone suggest that vomiting should be induced on purpose in order to *promote* progress. I imagined, extrapolating from what Nachita said, that the heaving diaphragm pushes the baby downward and stimulates the woman's urge to push.

Nachita added, "Another way to make a woman vomit is to put her braid in her mouth."

I'd seen in the hospital in Oregon that sometimes, when labor became intense, a Mexican patient would put her braid, or a strand of her hair, into her mouth—or, more often, an older female relative would put it in her mouth for her. I'd speculated about the possible reason, thinking perhaps it was meant to help the woman cope with pain, and had read that one observer thought it was supposed to help the woman avoid crying out (Goldsmith 1990, 29), but Nachita was clear; the purpose was to *provocar vómitos*. "You have to push the braid into the back of the mouth," she said, again the teacher.

When I asked Nachita about the best position for pushing, she replied decisively, "Lying on the back." That surprised me. I'd been under the impression that traditional midwives favored more upright positions. I mentioned that in the hospitals where I worked in the United States we'd found it was often helpful to have the woman kneel, squat, sit, or lie on her side while pushing, and Nachita immediately agreed with me—as if she hadn't just declared the opposite. She described an arrangement similar to the one my friend Francisca in Oregon had described: The woman is on her knees with her husband sitting on a low chair behind her. The woman leans back against him, and he wraps his arms around her torso above her belly. The midwife is in front, ready to receive the baby.

In the years to come, I would hear other midwives be equally evasive and contradictory on this subject. It seems that the forces that made Delia feel she needed a delivery table had made other midwives, like Nachita, feel reluctant to talk about their use of upright positions during labor. Apparently their contact with the world of modern medicine had made them wary about revealing their true practices. I had to let them know that I was aligned with their point of view, not with the point of view that disparaged their ways. It was easy for me to do given that I was in awe of their skills and I shared their respect for the natural process of birth. I had, like the midwives, spent thousands of hours supporting women who wanted to avoid unnecessary interventions in labor, and I was genuinely skeptical about the direction of modern medicine when it came to childbirth.

I'd told Nachita, when I introduced myself, that I dreamed of someday writing a book telling the stories of Mexican midwives. Now I asked her to sign a slip of paper giving me permission to include her name and story if I ever realized that dream. I read the paper, which was in Spanish, aloud—so as not to embarrass her if she couldn't read—and indicated where she should sign. She took the pen I offered and bent over the slip of paper to write her name; then she handed the paper back to me ceremoniously, as if it were the sealing of a pact. She kissed me on both cheeks and then, as I was leaving, reminded me, "Be sure to tell them about the girl who almost lost her baby." I promised I would.

All the midwives I met in the years to come (all except one in Chiapas, and I didn't even ask her) willingly signed that slip of paper. Some signed with an "X" and some signed so laboriously that I suspected their own name was the only thing they'd learned to write, but all proudly signed. They wanted their stories to be told.

***

Two and a half years had passed since the *congreso* in Oaxaca: two and a half years of thinking about the stories I'd heard and dreaming of hearing more. I thought of the midwives' stories as treasures scattered around Mexico in the hearts and memories of amazing women who would share them with me if only I could find them. I was encouraged by the ease with which I'd found Nachita. I wasn't sure if she actually considered herself to be a *partera*—she'd emphasized that she was a *huesera*, and she'd been evasive when I asked how many births she'd attended. Still, she was knowledgeable about the customs of childbirth of her region. I would learn there was a continuum of knowledge and authority. Some women helped only their own daughters-in-law in labor. Some helped other family members and occasionally a neighbor. Some of these women would go on to gain significant experience and eventually be identified by their communities as *parteras*.

The next midwife I met was clearly known, esteemed, and loved by her community as *una partera*. I'd heard about her from the cleaning lady in my hostel. Paulita, who was known by everyone as "Abuelita Paulita," lived in the cleaning lady's village, Ánimas Trujano, south of the city.

Poop on the Face: Paula Pérez Martinez (Abuelita Paulita)

When I asked the first person I saw in the village, a woman selling sodas, if she knew where I could find the midwife Paulita, she pointed to a blue metal gate across the highway. I had, by chance, gotten off the bus almost directly in front of Paulita's home. I crossed the highway and knocked at the gate—and Paulita answered.

She was a short, motherly-looking woman with narrow shoulders and a soft rounded body. She stood, deeply composed, with her hands clasped at her waist, while I told her of my interest in midwives; then she invited me in and led me across the courtyard to a small bedroom where we sat facing each other, each on one of the two narrow beds that almost filled the room. She was seventy-three years old, she said, and her kidneys were failing. She gave herself dialysis four times a day with the help of her daughter, using supplies given to her by the local Center of Salud.

She answered my questions thoughtfully in a soft, clear voice.

> I lived in a *rancho* as a child, but my parents died when I was twelve, so then my brothers and sisters and I went to live with our grandparents in the city of Oaxaca. I was the oldest, so I had to work to help my grandparents support us. I found a job cleaning for a lady doctor. Sometimes, when her other workers didn't show up, she would ask me to help her with her patients, so I had a chance to observe her work. I learned a lot by watching her.

Then I got a job working for another doctor, a man this time, cleaning for him too. He taught me to give injections, and he explained what he was doing when he was attending a birth. He said, "This knowledge will support you when you're old."

One day, when he had a patient in labor, the doctor said to me, "You attend this birth." So I did—with him watching and telling me what to do. He told me to clean the vaginal area with soap and to shave her, so I did that. He told me to perform *el tacto* [literally "the touch," but in this context, a vaginal exam: the insertion of fingers into the vagina to see how open the cervix is]; I did, and I told him her cervix was eight centimeters dilated. He checked and said I was right. According to him, a woman had to be thirteen centimeters dilated for the baby to be born. I don't know if that was right [it wasn't; ten centimeters is considered to be full dilation], but it's what he said. The doctor used gloves, but I never did. I just washed my hands with soap.

The woman pooped when she was pushing, and there was quite a bit of blood. Also, the amniotic fluid was dirty [containing poop from the baby]. None of that had ever bothered me before, but now that I was the one receiving the baby, it made me feel sick. I thought I might throw up. When the doctor saw my reaction, he scooped some of the woman's poop into his hand and wiped it on my face. I was shocked,

Paulita.

but I kept working. I cleaned the baby with a rag, then I cleaned my own face, and finally I clamped and cut the cord. I guess smearing poop on my face was the doctor's way of teaching me not to get sick when I was attending a birth. It worked. I never felt sick again.

I continued to work for him, helping when he needed me, until I met my first husband and moved here with him.[2] The people here soon learned that I knew how to help women in labor.

The first birth I attended on my own turned out to be twins. Fortunately they were both head-down and the birth went smoothly. One was a boy and one was a girl. They're forty-eight years old now and live in Mexico City. They recently came to visit me.

I've attended births of five more sets of twins since then. In some cases the second twin was coming feet first, and that always made me a little nervous, but all the births went well and the babies were fine.

Women expected me to know things that I hadn't learned from the doctor, like how to massage their bellies and lift their organs, how to use the rebozo, how to adjust babies in the womb, and how to close up the pelvis after birth. I learned those things from a *curandero* who lived in a nearby village. He didn't attend births, but he knew many of the techniques I needed to learn.

There weren't any doctors here when I first came, so midwives took care of all the births. I used to go to all the surrounding villages and *ranchos*. There were no cars. I would walk or go by horse or burro. Sometimes I had to walk through rivers up to my armpits.

I had bad luck with husbands. My first husband left me, and then there was another one, and he left me too. I had seven children altogether, but only four lived. Two died as infants. One died of pneumonia at the age of three while we were on our way to the hospital in the city. Life was hard after my second husband left. I had my work as a midwife and also I washed clothes for other people and made and sold tortillas. My children would go early every morning to the mill to buy dough for my tortillas.

The government started a clinic here in 1977 with a lady doctor. My patients used to tell me that the *doctora* scolded them for continuing to come to me. One day the *doctora* sent for me, asking me to come to the clinic to talk to her. I didn't want to go, because I thought she was going to be mad, and anyway I was very busy, but I went, and it turned out she was nice. She arranged for me to go to a one-month government-sponsored *curso* [course] for midwives in the city of Oaxaca.[3] There were about fifteen women in the *curso*. There was a room full of cots, where we slept, and they gave us breakfast each day and water for bathing. My children brought me food and clean clothes from home. I don't remember much about what they taught except that they did mention *el tacto*, but I already knew about that. They gave us each a diploma at the end.

I was a midwife for almost fifty years. It was hard work. There were so many nights without sleep, always with the usual work to catch up on afterward. But it was a blessing too, to see all those babies come into the world.

Paulita and other Mexican midwives I met didn't claim to "deliver" babies. They used the Spanish word *atender* ("to pay attention to, to keep in mind, to heed, to wait on, to attend to, to attend, to be present at") to describe their role in childbirth, or they used terms I've heard American midwives use: They "received" babies (*recibir*) or "caught" them (*agarrar*). I liked how these terms honor the women and the baby as the main actors in the drama of birth, giving credit to them, not the midwife, for the achievement.

The key to a good labor, Paulita said, is to "walk, walk, walk" and to drink cinnamon tea. When a woman has three contractions in five minutes it means she has about an hour or an hour and a half yet to go. When the woman says "*no aguanto*" (I can't take it), it means it's time for her to have her baby.

I asked about the doctor who smeared poop on her face. Didn't she think he was a bit sadistic?

No, he was just trying to help her learn.

I asked how many births she thought she'd attended, but she had no idea. "Sometimes as many as four a week," she said. So she'd probably averaged at least one per week—which would mean she'd attended over two thousand births in her fifty years as a midwife.

"What was the biggest problem you ever faced as a midwife?" I asked.

She thought for a minute. "Occasionally the placenta would be stuck in the uterus and I would have to send the woman to the doctor. I would tie the cord to the woman's leg so it wouldn't disappear up inside her uterus while she was on her way."

"Did you ever lose a woman or a baby?"

"No. No women ever died. Some babies were dead, sometimes even decomposing already, before the woman came to me, and some babies were born so severely deformed that they died shortly after birth, but if the baby was healthy before labor began, I was successful. The saints always helped me in difficult cases. I never lost a baby or a mother, *gracias a Dios*."

When it was time for me to leave, Paulita kissed my cheek and wished me well on my travels. I told her I hoped to return to Oaxaca someday. I hoped to see her again.

"I'll be gone," she said simply. "My time is almost over."

Still Finding Romance:
Francisca Silvia Moreno Martinez (Silvia)

The cleaning lady who'd told me about Paulita had been talking about my quest with her friends and relatives and had learned of a midwife named Silvia who lived in San Martín Coyotopec, a town famous for its black pottery. I went by bus to see her.

It was a long hot walk on unpaved streets from the highway to Silvia's house. There weren't many people out, but I managed to find someone to give me directions whenever I was in doubt. Everyone knew Silvia. She answered when I knocked at her gate and invited me into her kitchen; then she rinsed her hands and offered me her wrist, as Mexican women do when their hands are wet or dirty, apologizing for stains on her fingers. The stains were from peppers, she said. She'd been roasting and peeling peppers, preparing to make *chiles rellenos*, which she sold in the market. She looked younger than her fifty-nine years: lean and muscular, with a strong, angular face and without a trace of gray in her long braids. She was proud and opinionated and apparently happy to have an excuse to take a break from her work.

Silvia.

My mother-in-law was a midwife. She'd attended the birth of my first baby, and I expected her to attend the birth of my second baby, too. On my due date, which happened to be the Day of the Dead, I prepared cinnamon tea for when I went into labor and then I started to get ready for the holiday. I made *mole* [a thick chile sauce] and then went out to get the special bread and candles we use on the Day of the Dead. When I came back, as soon as I stepped inside, I felt a strong contraction. With that one contraction, my bag of waters broke and water came gushing out onto the floor. The pain was so strong I fell to my hands and knees, and right then the baby was born!

I picked him up and crept across the room to a chair. My husband came into the kitchen, drunk, and then staggered off in search of his mother. It took him a while to find her. By the time they came back, the placenta had come out and I'd cut the cord. The baby got dirt in his eye when he fell out, so I'd cleaned him up, using the cinnamon tea that was supposed to have been for me to drink during labor.

My mother-in-law was really too old to be working as a midwife, so after I'd managed the birth of my own baby by myself, women started coming to me instead of to her. All I knew about attending births was what I'd learned when my own babies were born.

Being a midwife is a *don* [pronounced "dohn": an aptitude given to a person as a gift from God; an inner strength a person is born with]. God gave me the *valor* to do this work. I never feel afraid.

Years ago doctors from the Center of Salud asked me to go to a *curso*, but I couldn't be away from home that long. I have a disabled brother to take care of. I did go to a program in the city of Oaxaca offered by Mexfam, an agency that promotes birth control. They showed us how to give injections and had us practice by injecting oranges. I went there once a month to get condoms and birth control pills and syringes filled with birth control medicine. They sold these things to me inexpensively, and then I would sell them to the people in the village.

I'm not as busy as I used to be, but I still attend about ten or twelve births a year, and women still come to me for belly massages, even if they're going to have the baby at the Center of Salud. They come when they're having premature contractions, too. I give the woman a special tea and massage her belly, lifting the baby, and that stops the contractions every time. I can't tell you how many times I've done that.

To find out if she used the rebozo, since I didn't know the word in Spanish for what we called "rebozoing" back home, I demonstrated what I meant by making pulling motions with my hands, and she immediately understood. She said yes, she started every belly massage, including the massage that stops premature labor, with a little rocking from side to side in a rebozo.

I later read that the official word for the rebozo procedure is *la manteada* (the noun form of the verb *mantear*, which means "to toss in a blanket"), but the midwives never used that term. They would say they "rocked" a woman (*mecer*) or they "shook" her (*sacudir*), and I would ask, "You mean in a rebozo?" and they would say yes. Many of the midwives seemed to think of the procedure as part of the belly massage, a way of "loosening things up" before the massage, not as something separate that needed its own name.

Silvia, like Paulita, said she'd dealt with miscarriages and babies that had died in the womb before she became involved, but she'd never lost a healthy baby. I asked how she knew a baby in the womb was no longer living.

"You can tell by touching the woman's belly," she said. "A live baby reacts to your touch. Even if he's sleeping, you can feel life."

She said she gives women *chocolate espiritual* and various teas, including one that eases the pain of contractions and another that induces labor.

I asked her to tell me about a particularly challenging birth, but she couldn't remember one.

A birth during which she'd felt afraid?

There had been none. She said she prayed, "God help me. Help this poor girl." God always helped her. He never failed.

I asked about breech births, using the terms the midwives used: Had there been any babies that were "standing" (breech with the feet coming first) or "sitting" (breech with the bottom coming first)?

Oh yes, there had been quite a few of those.

Weren't some of those a bit challenging?

> Well.... Once when I went to help a woman in labor, I found the baby's foot was sticking out, dark and lifeless. The baby was dead. The woman had been like that, with the foot sticking out, for several hours. I went to see the *presidente* of the village to ask him what I should do, and he said I should save the woman if I could.
>
> The woman wasn't having contractions, so I gave her an injection of Pitocin. Still there were no contractions. I checked to see if the second foot had come down into the vagina, but it hadn't. I saw that the cervix was completely dilated, so I put on gloves, smeared Vaseline on them, and reached up into her uterus to find the second foot. It took me over half an hour to get the baby out; then it took me another half hour to get the placenta out. The *presidente* thanked me,

but no one paid me. Who's going to pay for a birth like that? Only God knows how hard I worked. I can just hope that He'll give me a little extra time at the end of my life to reward me.

And there had been another, similar birth.

> Again there was a foot sticking out, but this time the foot was wiggling. The woman was lying on the floor, naked. A doctor and nurse were there, just standing there, looking worried. They asked me, "What should we do?"
> I stuck my hand into the uterus, as I'd done in that other case, and found the second foot. This time the woman was having contractions, so it was easier. I guided the baby out, pulling carefully on the two feet. He was fine.
> The doctor said, "*Ay, señora,* we could never have done that."

I would have the same experience again and again as I talked to midwives in the years to come; they had nothing to say about normal, routine birth. Babies come out. The midwife ties and cuts the cord. What could they tell me about that simple process that I didn't already know? And so I ended up asking about births that were not routine. Women who had attended hundreds or even thousands of normal births could tell me little about those normal births, but some of the breech births and twin births and births that had confounded doctors did stand out in their memories.

Silvia had four children, she said, adding, "I would have had more if I could have, but that's all God gave me." She had been a widow for six months. She said that her husband had been a "good man" who "treated her well," but then on reflection she added that he had been overly fond of alcohol and was sometimes *latoso* (a nuisance) and yelled at her a lot, and she had wasted a lot of time going around the village looking for him. Life had not been easy.

There was another man in love with her now, she whispered. She had kissed him on the cheek, but he wanted more. She didn't know what to do.

I advised her to enjoy the attention, regardless of what she decided to do about it. "We don't get enough of that at our age," I reminded her, and we both laughed.

Sidelined and Sad: Marcelina Antonio Felix

It was market day when I went to Zaachila, a town near my friend Francisca's village. I approached an old woman selling squash to ask if there were any midwives in the town.

¿Parteras?
Yes, *parteras*.

I would have the same need to explain what I was looking for many times as I continued on my quest. It wasn't that people couldn't understand me; it was that they couldn't *believe* they had understood me. It didn't make sense that an American tourist would be wandering around looking for a midwife. Older women were always a good source—they remembered—and the belly massage turned out to be the key. "You know," I would say, "the women who massage the bellies of pregnant women."

The woman I was talking to would rub and press on her belly and look at me inquiringly. You mean like this? You mean *parteras*?

I would rub and press on my own belly to show that yes, that was what I meant. Yes, *parteras*.

Sometimes I would be in a group, in a store or on a sidewalk. Members of the group would consult with each other. "I think she means *parteras*," one woman would say, rubbing her belly. "Yes, I think she does," another would remark, and she would rub her belly too. *Parteras*. Rub, rub, rub.

Marcelina.

Ah, *parteras*! The woman in the market in Zaachila finally understood. Yes, there was a midwife named Marcelina.

Marcelina was wearing a pale blue pinafore decorated with flowers and peacocks she had embroidered herself. I happened to be wearing a blouse I had embroidered myself, so we compared our stitches, hers forming pretty images, mine a border of intricate little repetitions, and felt the comradery of a shared interest. An electric sewing machine dominated the small cluttered room where we sat while she told me about her life as a midwife.

> I worked for my cousin when I was young, cooking and doing the housework. He was a bachelor, and I was unmarried, too, so I lived in his house. He was a doctor. He had nurses who helped him, but sometimes they didn't show up. On those days he would say to me, "Hurry up and finish the housework so you can help me with my patients."
>
> We didn't have ultrasounds and pain medications in those days, and a woman would have had to go to the city of Oaxaca for a Cesarean. We just worked in the way we called *al valor Mexicana* [with Mexican courage]. Sometimes we would start with a birth at six in the morning and work all day until late in the evening. We would stay with the woman until she triumphed. Today's doctors aren't patient like my cousin was when he was alive.
>
> My cousin died in a car accident after I'd worked for him for about five years. After his death, people started coming to me with their medical problems. Salesmen from the drug companies sought me out. They said, "You know about these things because you used to work for the doctor." They sold me medicines for common problems like diarrhea and vomiting and fever. I took care of people, and I was successful. There were only a few kinds of infections in those days. Everything was cleaner then. We used to wash and reuse things. Now it's "disposable this" and "disposable that." People can't be bothered to clean up after themselves.
>
> I worked for many years like that, treating common illnesses and helping women in childbirth. The government built a clinic in the town, but women still came to me. I was very busy. Sometimes I attended three or four births a day. People would come to get me in the middle of the night. I would just barely have lain down my head after a birth when someone else would knock at my door. I had four beds in my house. There were times when they were all full, and I would have patients in my neighbor's house, too. Everyone knew me because I went all over town attending births.

Marcelina said she had learned traditional practices from other midwives she met in the *cursos*.

> One midwife showed me how to give belly massages. She said, "You just do this and the woman gives you five pesos! [A peso has been worth about eight to ten U.S. cents during most of the last sixty years.] I had seen one of my aunts give belly massages, but I hadn't thought about doing it myself, since the doctor never did. That other midwife was right. Women liked the massages and were happy to pay five pesos for them. There's a tendon between the pubic bone and the hip that gets sore during pregnancy. The massage relieves that pain. Women stand up after the massage and say "It doesn't hurt anymore!"

She said she learned the use of the rebozo from midwives in the *cursos*, too. And they told her about the drink called *chocolate espiritual*.

"Did the doctors who were teaching the *cursos* realize that you and the other midwives were exchanging ideas like that?" I asked.

No. She laughed. It had obviously not occurred to the organizers of the *cursos* that by bringing midwives together they were helping to spread practices they would have liked to eliminate.

Marcelina had never married; she had no children. She said she always wished someone would give her an unwanted baby.

> I tell the single mothers, "If you don't want your baby, you can give it to me; I don't care if it's a boy or a girl; I'll take it." I work hard for the birth, too. I would be happy to raise the baby. But no one has ever given me one.

As I was preparing to leave, when I told her how much I valued the work she'd done in her lifetime, her eyes filled with tears. She said she wasn't ready for her career as a midwife to be over. She'd gone many times to the Center of Salud, begging them to help her find something she could do that would be useful, but they didn't see any value in her experience.

Widow of a Doctor: Marta García

Marta, in the town of Ocotlán, was younger than other midwives I'd met, about fifty, with hair cut short in a modern style but still wearing the traditional pinafore. She'd learned about childbirth by helping her husband, who'd been a doctor, serving as what sounded like combined nurse and doula for his patients. After he died in a car accident, when her children were still young, women continued to come to her. "They liked the way I'd treated them when I was helping my husband," she said.

While Paulita and Marcelina had gone on to learn traditional midwifery practices after an initial period of learning from a doctor, Marta

Marta.

never did, and she dismissed the midwives who used traditional practices as being *muy rústica*. She didn't use the rebozo, she didn't massage bellies, and she didn't value the use of herbs. "I give women chamomile tea if they ask for it, but other than that I don't use herbs. Sometimes a woman's family wants to give her a drink called *espiritual* made of hot chocolate and raw eggs. They say the drink makes a woman sweat and speeds labor. I don't believe in that—it's not my custom—but I don't mind if they drink it. They think it helps."

I'm not sure she even thought of herself as a midwife—she was more like an unofficial doctor—but to me and to her patients she was a midwife. She revealed a midwife's loving heart, patience, and trust in the process of birth when she said, "I allow birth to unfold at its natural pace, and I give women emotional support. Women feel weak when labor drags on for a long time. They scream; they despair. Sometimes they want to die. I speak to them softly, telling them everything is going to be fine. I say, 'Be calm; relax; don't give up.' I remind them to breathe. 'Breathe deeply,' I say. 'Your baby is going to come. You can do it.'" And she had a *partera*'s reliance on the help of God. "I pray for His guidance when I'm attending a birth," she said, "and He helps me. He never fails. I couldn't do this work without Him." She had helped the most humble of her neighbors, even when they couldn't pay, and she'd traveled great distances on foot, as midwives did when cars were scarce, sometimes with a child clinging to each hand and a baby on her back in her rebozo.

She was still busy when I met her, attending about thirty births a year. I asked why women continue to seek care from midwives, and she said, "Some women come to me because I charge less than the clinics,[4] and some come because they feel more comfortable with me than with a doctor, but more and more often it's because they don't want a Cesarean. Either they've been told they have to have one or they're afraid that's what they will be told when they get to the hospital. Doctors get impatient if a birth takes too long. They can perform a Cesarean in an hour, and they make more money with Cesareans."

I asked Marta if husbands are involved in the births of their babies.

"Well, they can stay if they want to, but what use are they? They usually leave during the birth and then come back when the baby is cleaned up."

I was surprised to hear her voice a stereotype I would have expected to hear from my own compatriots, one that in my experience was inaccurate. I had seen Mexican men who wouldn't leave their laboring wife's side for a minute, refusing to sleep, often even unable to eat while their wife was working to birth their baby.

As I continued my travels, I found that many midwives do expect a husband to participate in his wife's labor. I was often told that men should be present because "they need to see how women suffer" (not because they could be of any use). When men were expected to help, it was during the pushing stage. The man would sit behind the woman, and she would lean back against him. He would put his arms around her midriff under her breasts to give her "something to push against."

Marta had three children, two sons and a daughter, all young adults when I met her. One of her sons was in the military; the other had just finished his studies to become a doctor and was performing his *servicio* in a small town in the state of Yucatán. The daughter was in her first year studying medicine at the University of Oaxaca. I wondered if her children, the son who was a doctor and the daughter studying medicine, would be influenced by their mother when they had their own practices. Would they remember their mother saying *you can do it* to all those women? Would they truly believe, as their mother did, that women can?

The Hospital

Watching out the window from the bus as I returned to the hostel after the visit with Marta, I saw the five-story government-subsidized hospital for people without insurance. I was curious to see the obstetrics department in a public hospital in Mexico. Mexican women I'd met in Oregon had talked of impersonal, even unkind treatment they'd received in hospitals like that. "I was all alone," they said. Some said they were made to feel ashamed or were told to "shut up" when they cried out. A few said they'd been forced to walk nonstop until they were fully dilated, but most had been restricted to bed for the entire labor. They had been left, often naked, exposed to the eyes of a steady stream of nurses and doctors at various levels in their training and had been subjected to frequent vaginal exams performed by any of these who was curious or wanted to practice.

I had formed a picture in my mind, based on such remarks, of what the obstetrical ward of a Mexican hospital would be like, and I'd allowed myself to fantasize about working in one as a volunteer doula helping women in labor. My efforts (in the fantasy) were wildly successful and were noticed by the doctors and nurses who were working around me. These imagined doctors and nurses whispered to each other, "Look at that. Look at what a difference it makes when a woman is given support."

The next day, I went to the hospital. I asked for the Obstetrics Department and was directed to an elevator in a drab hallway at the far end of the building. A young man wearing what looked like a military uniform was standing in front of the elevator holding a rifle across his chest. He told me I couldn't go up to Obstetrics without a pass. To get a pass I had to see the social worker.

Why did they need an armed guard in front of the elevator? I wondered. I imagined hordes of distraught family members, carrying flowers, tortillas, and soup, storming the elevator, worried about their loved ones. *Has the baby been born? Is he okay? Is my wife (or daughter or granddaughter or niece) okay?* These hordes would not be sterile, and there would be women among them who had old-fashioned ideas about how babies should be born.

I found the social worker's office, but other people who also needed passes told me it might be hours before she returned. Impatient, and thinking that the idea had probably been a hopeless long shot anyway, I gave up and left.

Reviving a "Dead" Baby: María Magdalena Hernandez Rosario (Lena)

Yaxe, in the foothills beyond Ocotlán, looked like the village I'd stayed in when I came to Mexico in 1964—with adobe houses, adobe walls, adobe-colored dirt roads, tattered cane fences, and dusty cactus, all stretched out under a dazzling blue sky with mountains in the background. I'd made my way to Yaxe because a woman working as a cook in a *lonchería* in Ocotlán had told me there was a midwife named Lena living there.

I asked an old man who was walking along the side of the road if he could direct me to the home of the midwife Lena. "You mean *Tía* Lena (Aunt Lena)?" he asked. Apparently Lena was called "aunt" by everyone in the village.

Lena's grandson, who was sitting in front of her house, went in to tell Lena she had a visitor. Soon she came out, with arms

Lena. Photo by Richard Schorr.

outstretched, reaching for a hug before she even knew who I was or why I'd come. She was so short that her hug came around me at the waist. She had a body like a child, with no breasts, no hips, and no fat at all, just muscle and bone, and she moved with a child's quick energy too, but her hair, which was twined into short braids, was white. She was eighty-four years old, she said. She was barefoot, wearing a handmade green cotton dress and a pink pinafore. Her eyes sparkled with pleasure at the prospect of having company (whoever I might turn out to be). She invited me into a cluttered, dusty courtyard surrounded by cane fencing, with a small lean-to for goats in the corner. We sat on wooden chairs with chickens pecking the ground at our feet.

> I got married when I was eighteen years old and had a baby about a year later. I had nine babies altogether, all born about a year apart, but only one survived. One little boy lived to the age of three; the others died when they were a few months old. Only God knows why my babies died. It was because of fever or vomiting or diarrhea or something like that. We didn't have doctors then, and there were no cars to take us to Ocotlán.
>
> When my best friend Camila became pregnant, she asked me to attend the birth. I didn't think I would know what to do. My mother was a midwife, but she hadn't taught me anything about her work.[5]
>
> Camila's husband told Camila to go to the real midwife, Josefa, but Camila insisted on having me. So I massaged her belly every month. I massaged her the way I'd seen my mother massage women, the way she massaged me when I was pregnant. When it was time for

> the baby to be born, Camila sent for me, and I went to be with her. I helped her get on her knees at the end, and then her little girl was born. The baby was *privada*.

Lena pronounced the word *privada* gravely and then paused, apparently expecting a reaction. I asked her, "What does *privada* mean?" (The only meaning I knew for the word was "private.")

Lena thought about it for a minute and then said, "You know . . . not breathing. Dead."

Oh. As I took in this sad turn of events, Lena continued, cheerful and animated, pleased with the drama of her story.

> I was so scared. Camila's husband wasn't home, but I knew how mad he'd be if the baby didn't live. He was a mean man, and he'd wanted the real midwife Josefa to attend the birth. I tried everything to revive the baby. I patted her bottom, but she didn't breathe. *Diosito, Diosito* [dear God, dear God]. I kept praying to God to revive the baby, to let her live. I put the baby on the family's altar and prayed for her. *Virgencita, Virgencita* [dear Virgin, dear Virgin]. I blew cigarette smoke on her face.[6] Still she didn't breathe.

I was confused. Lena's tale about her efforts to revive the baby seemed to go on and on, punctuated with appeals to *Diosito* and *Virgencita* and *Mariacita* that would have been useless if the baby really was dead. Maybe I'd misunderstood: maybe the baby wasn't really dead. Or, I hoped, maybe she wasn't going to stay dead.

> Camila's husband came home and asked what was happening. I told him the baby had been born and it was a girl, but she was *privada*. He said, "Why didn't you get Josefa? We're going to send for Josefa so she can come and take care of this!"
>
> I told him to hold the baby. The godmother and godfather of the baby came, and I told them to hold the baby. I never stopped praying, but the baby didn't breathe or cry, and Josefa never showed up. Someone was sent to get holy water, because it didn't look like the baby could be revived.
>
> You can imagine what a terrible situation it was; it was my first birth, the mother was my best friend, there was supposed to have been another midwife there, the baby was *privada*, and the father was furious!
>
> I put the baby in Camila's arms and covered her with a blanket. I said, "Put your breast in the baby's mouth. Maybe God will revive the baby." Then I went to the river to wash the things that got bloody during the birth. When I came back, everyone was smiling. They

said, "Look, Lena, look at the baby." The baby was alive and was nursing at Camila's breast. Oh how I gave thanks to the Virgin Mary for letting that baby live! I gave Camila chamomile tea with sugar.

After that, other women asked me to attend the births of their babies. That's how I became a midwife.

Camila's baby died six months later, but she had three more babies and they all lived. Her husband trusted me after the first birth, so I was Camila's midwife for the births of all her babies.

I asked Lena if she had used *el tacto*.

Not normally—that was not our custom—but I did have to touch a woman once. The baby was already three days old when the people called me. They'd managed the birth themselves without a midwife, but now, according to the husband, whenever the woman peed, "a piece of her insides was coming out." They didn't want me to look, but I had to insist. When I checked her, I saw that what was coming out was a piece of the placenta. I washed my hands and pulled carefully until it came out.

When I asked if there had been any particularly challenging births, Lena covered her face with her hands, laughing.

Once I was called to help a woman who had been in labor for three days. Oh how she was screaming when I got there! She was crying, "Don't touch me!" There was another midwife there already. The other midwife thought the baby was coming head first, but I thought it was coming bottom first. I could tell by feeling the woman's belly. There were a lot of people there. Someone had gone to Ocotlán to find a doctor and had been told that the doctor charged six hundred pesos to attend a birth. I told them, "Give me an hour. If I can't get the baby out in an hour, then you'll have to go to the doctor."

Even I didn't believe I could cure that woman, but I had to try. I prayed for God and the Virgin to help me. I have a lot of faith. The woman was lying on her back and wouldn't get up. She'd been like that for three days. I gave her a drink made of chamomile tea, castor oil, and beer, all mixed together; then I massaged her belly to move the baby into the head-down position. The castor oil stopped the pain and made the woman poop. She slept for about half an hour, and then, when she woke up, she was ready to push. The other midwife and I helped her. [They applied pressure to the top of the woman's belly while she pushed.] The baby was a girl. After the birth, we gave the woman warm beer. That was the customary drink we always offered after a birth. They paid me thirty pesos.

Lena said she hadn't worked for four years. She'd stopped after having eye surgery when a doctor told her that long nights without sleep weren't good for her.

> My friend Camila died a long time ago, and I miss her. It was because of her that I became a midwife. I told Camila I couldn't do it, but she knew I could. She had faith in me. I learned for her.

I wondered about Camila's baby, the one that came back to life while Lena was at the river. I asked Lena if she really thought the baby went for such a long time without breathing and was then revived. She laughed (at my gullibility, I imagine) and replied, "The baby must have been breathing all along, just so softly that we couldn't see it!" (Back home later, after looking in many dictionaries, I found one that said *privado* can mean "stunned" or "knocked unconscious.")

I asked Lena about the use of the rebozo in birth, and she offered to show me. We went into the house, which was a one-room adobe structure with a dirt floor. It was dim inside; there was no electricity, and there were no windows. She took a straw mat (her bed) which had been leaning rolled up against the wall, and laid it out on the floor; then she spread a rebozo across it.

I was to take the role of pregnant woman. Lena had me lie down on the straw mat with the rebozo under my hips and took her position standing over me, one foot on each side of my hips, holding an end of the rebozo in each hand. She gave one end a tug.

"*Ay*, you're heavy!" she cried.

Yes. And Lena couldn't have weighed more than eighty pounds. She gave up. She could have done it when she was younger, she said. She decided she would massage my belly instead. She knelt beside me and began her work, kneading and probing with callused hands, feeling for the shape and position of an imaginary baby, nudging him into a good position for birth. How many times she must have performed those same movements on bellies that held real babies!

When I asked her what I would do when it came time for me to push, she said—a little evasively I thought—"You lie on your back." I reminded her that she'd mentioned her friend Camila being on her knees for the birth. I told her, as I'd told Delia and Nachita, about the trend in the United States toward more natural positions for pushing. And she changed her answer, as Nachita had done. "Yes!" she said quickly. "Women should be on their knees or they should be sitting."

"But," she added, "I know some people say it's better to have the woman lying on her back."

She looked at me sharply, now emboldened by my respect for her traditional ways, and held up a gnarled finger to emphasize her point: "And don't cut the cord too soon."

So she'd heard about that, too, about the practice in hospitals of clamping and cutting the cord as soon as the baby is out. There were a few voices in the United States advocating for "delayed cord clamping" (waiting a few minutes or until the cord has stopped pulsing), and this idea made sense to me—I could imagine that important exchanges were still taking place between the baby and placenta as long as the cord was still pulsing—but the norm still was to clamp and cut the cord immediately after the birth. Lena insisted that I should wait not just a few minutes but until after the placenta had come out. "Put the baby on one side of the woman and put the placenta on the other side while you massage her belly. Then you can cut the cord."

"Well, I don't actually cut the cord myself—that's not my job," I said. "But I agree that it does seem like a good idea to wait."

"Yes," Lena agreed. "Doctors don't have any patience. That's why they like to operate—because it's faster."

As I continued my travels, I found that waiting until after the placenta had come out before cutting the cord was common practice among the midwives of Mexico.

I hadn't seen French obstetrician Frederick Leboyer's book, *Birth without Violence*, which first came out in 1975, in which he says that "to sever the umbilicus when the child has scarcely left the mother's womb is an act of cruelty whose ill effects are immeasurable. To conserve it intact while it still pulses is to transform the act of birth" (2002, 41). That message had barely made a ripple in the American practice of obstetrics, at least as far as I had seen, but during the years that followed my visit with Lena, Leboyer's voice began to be heard and was joined by a multitude of other voices, many of them from respected health organizations. There had never been any reason to clamp and cut the cord quickly, except habit and efficiency, but now we learned that there were important reasons to wait. Delaying the clamping of the cord allows 20 to 40 ml more blood to pulse from the placenta to the newborn, carrying with it an additional 30 to 35 mg of iron (Hutton and Hassan 2007) and more hemoglobin (Andersson 2011).

Lena said women who'd had their babies in clinics and hospitals had told her afterward about how the doctors clamped and cut the cord as soon as the baby was born. It worried those women. They came to Lena for reassurance that no harm had been done, but Lena was as uneasy about the practice as they were. She might not have been able to explain why it was better to wait, but it seemed to her that it was wrong to intervene in nature's process.

Lena had me get into position for birth: the position she really used, not the one she'd been told was better, both of us kneeling, facing each other. My husband would be in a low chair behind me, she explained.

"*Bueno*," she said. "Your baby can be born now." She looked as if she were really waiting for something to happen.

I grunted a little, pretending to push, and Lena laughed, clapping her hands. I grunted again and cried, "*No aguanto; no aguanto.*" I'd heard those words so many times from Mexican women, at the end of labor when contractions are at their most intense, and no doubt Lena had too.

She laughed and clapped again. Then she looked up at me and said in a serious tone, gently, "You can do it, child. You're almost done."

With one more prolonged grunt I birthed my imaginary baby. Lena held it up triumphantly, and we both laughed. Looking at our beaming faces, an observer might have thought we'd brought a real baby into the world.

When I told her I wanted to take pictures, she jumped up to change her dress. I watched her select a dress from two that lay folded on a shelf against the wall, and then I stepped outside to wait. She appeared a few minutes later, having changed from the green dress, which had been old and frayed, to a pink dress that was slightly less frayed.

I took pictures and said goodbye, with more hugs and a feeling of great affection, as if I were saying goodbye to a beloved grandmother. I promised I would come again.

And if I come back, I vowed, I'll bring Lena a pretty new dress.

***

I was already mentally shopping for that dress as I looked down over the snow-capped mountains of central Mexico from the plane that took me home a few days later. The dress would have to be in a child's size but of a style that would suit an older woman. I might have to alter something.

I worried that Lena might not be there if I returned someday. She was eight-four years old and so thin and frail she looked as if her own energy might consume her. And what about Paulita? She had seemed sure she would be gone.

I prayed: Wait for me. Be there still.

Endnotes

1. It is common in many traditional cultures throughout the world that dreams serve as the vehicle by which healers are called to a profession and are given instruction regarding methods employed in that profession. Anthropologist Brigitte Jordan points out that, in addition to being called and instructed in dreams, healers also derive status and authority from having had such dreams. She says the stories healers tell about such dreams "serve as culturally recognized claims to expert status" (1993, 196).
2. The word *esposo*, which the midwives used to refer to their partners and which is translated as "husband," may mean that a civil marriage ceremony or a church ceremony has taken place, but it often meant that the couple had formed what my world would call a "consensual union" or a "common-law marriage." These informal unions, which were based on precolonial norms, were very common when Paulita was a young woman, especially among the poor, who often couldn't afford to host a wedding. (See Pérez Amador 2012, 42, and Castro Martin 2002, 36).
3. Mexican health agencies started offering training courses, which the midwives referred to as *los cursos*, in 1974 in an effort to upgrade the skills of traditional midwives. I wondered if the instruction in those *cursos* was relevant to the circumstances of the midwives, but the midwives couldn't tell me. They would have accepted the authority of the doctors who taught the *cursos*, because they were men, they were from the city, and they were educated. But regardless of the quality and relevance of the instruction, it seems the midwives were pleased and honored to attend, and they learned from the interaction with each other. They received more respect in their communities after attending the *cursos*: they came back with certificates and other symbols of professionalism, sometimes even white lab coats.

   Jordan (who actually attended one of these *cursos* in 1979) suggests that the teaching methods used produced only "minimal changes in the behavior of trainees, while, at the same time, providing new resources for *talking about* what they do. In particular, midwives learn how to converse appropriately with supervisory medical personnel, so that when the public health nurse visits to check on them, they can give all of the appropriate responses to her questions" (179).

   The midwives trusted what they had learned from birth itself more than what they were told by the doctors who taught the cursos.

   It may not have been hard to qualify for the certificates midwives were given at the end of the *cursos*. Jordan says that the staff "helped" the midwives fill out the questionnaire that served as a test and that, in the *curso* she attended (and, as far as I could tell, in all the *cursos* I ever heard about), "all of the midwives passed" (1993, 182). She suggests that the trainers were held accountable for the *number of midwives certified*, not for the quality of the information absorbed by the midwives.
4. Although midwife care had been the most inexpensive option for birthing women during all of Marta's life, the Mexican government had recently inaugurated a program, called Seguro Popular, which aimed to make health care free to the uninsured poor. The Seguro Popular, which would make childbirth free in government-subsidized clinics and hospitals, was not yet universally available when I met Marta, but its implementation has become more widespread and has accelerated the demise of midwifery in Mexico since then. See Malkin (2011) for more information about Mexico's universal healthcare program.

5. I heard such statements many times during my travels in Mexico: "My mother (or mother-in-law or grandmother or aunt) was a midwife, but she didn't teach me anything." Jordan explains that while the didactic way (Western culture's preferred way) of transmitting knowledge involves *talking about* a subject, the apprenticeship model of transmitting knowledge involves *doing*. She points out "a curious phenomenon in apprenticeship learning: it looks like there is little teaching going on" (1993, 194). The midwives who told me they hadn't learned anything from the older midwives in their lives may not have been aware that teaching did, in fact take place, or they might have discounted the instruction they received when discussing the subject with me—since I was from a world that values only didactic teaching. Lena may have absorbed a great deal while accompanying her mother and helping her in ways that seemed incidental at the time.
6. Tobacco has been used for medicinal purposes in the Americas since pre-Colombian times. Many sources mention blowing tobacco smoke at the afflicted person, for example into the ear to cure earaches (Hajdu 2010) or over a child to protect him during the night (Drywater-Whitekiller 2011), and Gonzales (2012, 27) learned from her teacher, Nahua midwife Doña Filo, that tobacco smoke can be used to advance labor. Several of the midwives I met mentioned blowing cigarette smoke in a baby's face to revive him.

Chapter 3

Huajuapan

"Remember when Matilda had Señora Martinez's neighbor drink pee?" Leonora asked her aunt. The aunt did remember, and both women laughed. They explained that Matilda, a midwife in their village, had given a woman urine to drink when the placenta refused to come out.

"Did it work?" I asked.

Oh yes. The placenta came sliding right out.

"Where did they get the pee? Whose was it?"

They said that Matilda had the woman's husband pee into a cup, and then she had the woman drink from the cup while the pee was still warm.

"How was it supposed to work?" I asked. Is there a chemical in urine that causes a placenta to be expelled? Does it have to be male urine? Does it have to be the husband's? Does it have to be warm?

They didn't know; they'd heard the story for years, but they'd never thought to question it.

I was visiting Leonora, a former student of mine, in preparation for a trip to her native area, Huajuapan (wah-HWAH-pahn), in northern Oaxaca. When I asked the two women if they thought I'd be able to meet Matilda while I was in Huajuapan, they said no, Matilda had died several years ago, but there was another midwife, Delfina, who was still working in the village.

"Delfina is a great midwife," Leonora said. "She knows how to give belly massages and attend births and she can cure all kinds of childhood illnesses."

There was also a *tío* (a male midwife) in the village, Leonora said. He was old—he might not be practicing any longer—but he was still alive the last they'd heard. He was a *curandero* primarily, but he also attended births. People trusted him. Leonora and her aunt described how he would have a woman sit on his lap facing away from him and how he would somehow reach around the woman to catch the baby without seeing anything a man isn't supposed to see.

I couldn't quite picture that, but I took their word for it that it was possible.

But Delfina was the greatest midwife in the village. She was the one I must meet. Delfina had attended the births of all seven of the aunt's babies. In fact, the aunt had traveled all the way from Oregon to Huajuapan for the birth of her last child, just so she could have Delfina as her midwife. "I wasn't going to let some doctor stick his fingers up me!" she said.

Leonora wrote down the name of the village for me, Santa María Xochixtlapilco, and told me how to reach it; she gave me money to take to her mother, who still lived there.

Six months had passed since my last trip to the city of Oaxaca. I'd chosen Huajuapan because I wanted to see other parts of Oaxaca, away from the capital, and I'd heard about the region from the many Huajuapeños I'd met—in my classes and in the hospital—who had come to the Willamette Valley for work. I would enjoy being able to say to those I met in the future, "Oh yes, I've been to Huajuapan."

The bus trip from Mexico City to Huajuapan de León, the principal city of the district of Huajuapan, passed through fields of marigolds, all in full bloom, spread across the landscape like giant orange blankets. Workers bent over the long rows, cutting the flowers, and then loaded them onto waiting trucks. I asked the other passengers on the bus why Mexico needed so many marigolds, and they told me it was for the Day of the Dead. Of course! It was only a week away. The bright colors of marigolds—placed along paths and on crosses and home altars—would help the souls of the departed find their way home.

Stern Teacher: Delfina Morales Diaz

I met Leonora's mother, Luisa, in her village the day after I arrived in Huajuapan. She explained that the old *tío* had died, but Delfina was alive and was expecting my visit. I followed Luisa along dusty streets to Delfina's home, a cluster of small buildings hidden behind a tall adobe wall. A grandson let us into the compound, and Luisa led me to a cinder-block building inside. She called out, and Delfina came to the door. She looked like a warrior, with wide cheek bones and a regal nose, less than five feet tall but still imposing: confident, proud, seeming to be grounded like a mountain. She was busy bathing a woman who had recently given birth, but I could join her if I didn't mind that she'd be working while we talked. I didn't mind!

The patient, Angelina, sat in a large copper tub full of hot water with bundles of herbs floating around her, scenting the air. I explained about my interest in Mexican midwives, pointing out that Delfina's fame had reached all the way to my own village in Oregon, and got Angelina's permission to watch Delfina bathe her. Delfina returned to her seat on a little stool at one end of the tub, facing Angelina. I positioned another stool behind her, so that I wouldn't be facing her naked breasts, not that she seemed to mind.

The building we were in, a two-room structure with concrete floors, was Delfina's house. Delfina said there'd been a big earthquake in Huajuapan in 1980, just after the house was built. Hundreds of people had been killed, and many buildings had been destroyed, but her brand new house had not been damaged.

Using metal tongs, Delfina took a bundle of herbs from the water and held it over the younger woman's head, allowing the hot water to run into Angelina's hair and down her shoulders. Angelina took a bundle into her own hands and used it to daub herbal water onto her breasts.

Angelina said her baby had been born in the hospital in Huajuapan. She'd gone to a doctor for prenatal care, but she'd also come to Delfina for belly massages and for reassurance that all was well with the pregnancy. And now she was receiving the traditional postpartum bath. She hadn't told the doctor she was seeing a midwife.

I asked Delfina about the purpose of the bath, and she explained: "The purpose of the postpartum bath is . . ." She paused, looking point-

Delfina heating herbal water for a postpartum bath [left]. Delfina giving a postpartum bath [right].

edly at the notebook in my lap, and I dutifully opened it. She said the bath "closes" the woman's body after birth so she won't bleed too much, and it stimulates her milk supply. "Women are often pale after having a baby," she said. "The bath improves their color." I wrote this all down.

I asked what herbs were in the water, and she replied officiously, echoing, I imagined, the tone of doctors in those *cursos* years ago: "Herbs to be used in the preparation of water for the postpartum bath . . ." There was another pause, another stern look at my notebook, and I prepared once again to take notes. She began naming herbs. Her list, with translations I was able to find later, included *sauco* (Mexican elderberry), *pirul* (pepper tree), *romero* (rosemary), *salvia* (sage), *rosa de castilla* (Gallic rose), *pericón* (Mexican tarragon), *laurel*, *ojas de naranjo* (orange leaves), and *manzanilla* (chamomile). I didn't think there really were that many different herbs in the water she was using that day, but I assumed that any and all of them might be used when they were available.

When the bath was over, Delfina wrapped a sheet and blanket around Angelina and had her lie down on a bed in the other room. She said it was important for the woman to sweat and sleep after the bath.

She talked about how she had bathed women in the past, before there was a copper tub, when women had their babies at home. The family would prepare a little enclosure, like the one my friend Francisca had described, made of bamboo poles covered with animal skins or blankets or tarps. When it was time for the bath, they would build a fire inside the enclosure, with rocks to hold heat and with a pot of herbal water kept warm on the rocks. The midwife would dip water from the pot and pour it over the woman's body, and she would splash water on the rocks to create more steam.

Delfina said she'd hated giving baths the old way. The smoke was supposed to be directed outside, but how well that worked depended on the skill of the people who prepared the enclosure. There was usually smoke. The smoke and steam and heat were suffocating. The copper tub was better.

When I asked how she had become a midwife, she settled back in her chair, relaxing a little but still managing to look imperious.

> My childhood was difficult. We were poor, and my father drank a lot. I got married when I was fifteen and went to live with my husband's family, so life was better for a while, but then my in-laws died, leaving my husband and me on our own. Life was a struggle again.
>
> I had six children. I had a midwife with me for the first four births, but she didn't get there in time for the last two. She had to

come on foot from Huajuapan de León, and my babies came fast. I was on my own for those last two births.

One day my sister-in-law went into labor when she and I were the only two at home. Our husbands were off working in the mountains. She would have been all alone if I'd gone for the midwife, so I stayed and helped her myself. I did everything a midwife would do. I cut the cord and tied it with thread and bathed both her and the baby. When her husband came home, he said, "Where's my wife? How is she?" and I said, "There she is with her baby."

After that, other women asked me to help them in labor. I didn't have any tools or materials. I would sterilize the stub of the umbilical cord by burning it with a *vela de sebo* [a homemade candle made of animal fat] and then tie it with thread. I cleaned the mucus out of the baby's nose and mouth by sucking with my own mouth.

I didn't make much money attending births, just a few *centavos* (a fraction of a U.S. cent) for each one, so I also worked washing clothes.

One day a man came to my house to tell me there was going to be a *curso* in Huajuapan de León starting the next week. He said he knew I was attending births. I denied it, but he obviously knew. I told him I couldn't attend, but he insisted. Finally I told him he could sign me up if he wanted to, but I was still thinking about it and I had to ask my husband. I knew my husband would be against it.

I went to see one of the families I washed clothes for in Huajuapan de León. The husband was a doctor. When he saw me at the door, he said, "What are you doing here? It's not your day to wash our clothes." I told him I'd come to see his wife.

I explained to his wife about the *curso*, and she said I should go. "You can be a midwife," she said. "You won't have to wash clothes for the rest of your life."

When I told my husband I wanted to go, he was angry. He said, "If you want to go wandering the streets, go ahead and do it, but don't expect any help if something happens to you."

That made me mad, so I decided to attend the *curso*. I got up every day at five in the morning to cook and clean and bathe the children, and then I walked five miles to the *curso*. I had four children then. My oldest daughter took care of the younger ones while I was gone. The sessions ended at 8:00 in the evening. I would stop at the doctor's house on my way home, and the doctor's wife would give me food, all prepared and ready to eat, to take to my family for dinner. She did that for three months until the *curso* was over.

That first *curso* was in 1969. I went to two more in Huajuapan during the seventies, and then in 1979 I went to one that lasted three months in the city of Oaxaca. It was six hours away by bus, so I had to stay there the whole time. My husband was furious when I left. I had six children then, and the youngest was only eight months old.

I learned a lot from other midwives in the *cursos*. They told me how to use various herbs, and they taught me how to massage women's bellies and how to rock women using a rebozo. They also talked about how to encourage women in labor and how to bathe them afterward.

Giving encouragement is the most important thing a midwife does. I recently had a patient who was only thirteen years old. She was so little it seemed impossible for her to have a baby, but she did well. I gave her a hot bath to make her sweat, I had her walk, and I encouraged her with loving words. That was all she needed.

I never went to school, but I've accomplished a lot in my life. I've helped many women and children. I thank God for giving me the strength and courage I need for my work.

I asked if there had been any especially challenging births. Had she ever been afraid?

No, all the births had gone well.

Any cases when the baby came feet first or bottom first?

Yes, of course, there had been many of those, but none had posed any particular problems.

Any really fast births?

She smiled. Yes. Once when she responded to a banging at her door she found that a baby had just been born right there in her courtyard. Delfina helped the woman come inside and then received the placenta.

And one baby had come "sliding out like a slippery worm," without any effort at all. Delfina thought he was dead because he wasn't moving, but his color was good and he began to cry when she patted his feet.

"He must have been asleep," she said. "The birth was so easy it didn't even wake him up!"

And once a woman in labor with her thirteenth baby had come to Delfina after being turned away at the hospital. The doctor there had told her she wasn't really in labor; he'd said she should come back the next day.

By the time Delfina got the woman into bed, the baby's head was crowning (starting to emerge)!

"The doctor should have believed her. A woman having her thirteenth baby knows when it's time for the birth."

I visited Delfina twice more while I was in Huajuapan and each time found that she had attended a birth during the previous night. Both times she had me peek into the other room, where the new mother lay curled up with her baby, wrapped in a cocoon of blankets, asleep. Delfina was busy cleaning up, preparing for a normal day of work after a night without sleep.

The last time I was there, I took pictures of Delfina standing next to her altar. I noticed an aluminum pinard horn (a device used by midwives throughout the world for listening to the fetal heartbeat; it looks like a tube that's been compressed in the middle to form an hourglass shape). It was on her altar, tucked between a clock and a nativity scene. Delfina said she'd been given the pinard at one of the *cursos*. She didn't seem to think it was very useful. Later I saw that other midwives also had pinard horns, which in all cases they'd been given in the *cursos*. I saw a few midwives use the pinard, but most seemed to rely more on what they could learn through touch, observation, and intuition for knowledge about the wellbeing of the baby. Still, even if they didn't use their pinards, they displayed them. As Jordan points out, "The gadgets [she mentions scissors, clamps, and suction bulbs] become increasingly important to [the traditional midwives], if not for their actual use value, then definitely as visible symbols of their expertise" (1993, 180).

I picked the pinard up and studied it. I coveted it. I could imagine it on my mantel at home, a souvenir of my visit with Delfina and of my quest. She might have given it to me without a thought—she didn't seem to value it—but I didn't ask.

As I was leaving the compound I met a group of smiling family members who were coming to see the new baby. They greeted me cheerfully and accepted my congratulations without seeming to question why a gringa would be visiting their beloved midwife.

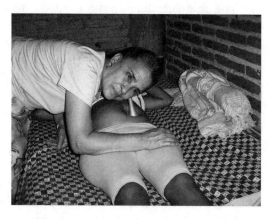

Lorenza (profiled in chapter 4) using a pinard horn to listen to the fetal heartbeat.

Daughter of a Great Midwife: Juana Graciela Cruz Lopez

When I'd been planning the trip, studying a map of Oaxaca and looking at the small dot that represented Huajuapan de León, I'd imagined a sleepy little town or at least one that was less congested than the city of Oaxaca, but it turned out to be bustling and noisy, with crowded sidewalks and the usual snarl of cars, trucks, and motorcycles. Near the center of all that activity stood a stately cathedral. Next to the cathedral was a large *zócalo* shaded by tall, spreading trees. One afternoon, as I escaped the sun under those trees, two children approached me, giggling and shouting "treekotreet!" reminding me that Halloween was only a few days away. I gave a few coins to each of them, and they ran triumphantly back to their parents.

A statewide teachers' strike was in progress in Oaxaca. Every evening at about sunset, as an army of squawking birds settled into the trees above, teachers met in the *zócalo* to discuss strategies for the strike. One of the female teachers told me about the strike, about the unfair treatment of teachers, and about the general situation of social injustice in Oaxaca. She also told me about her experience with a midwife. She said all four of her children had been born in the hospital. The first three births had been routine, but the last baby had been "sitting." When the doctor discovered the problem, a few weeks before the baby was due, he told the teacher she'd have to have a Cesarean.

The teacher's mother-in-law said "No. No Cesarean." She took the woman to see a midwife.

The midwife, Juana, massaged the teacher's belly. When she was done, she said, "Everything is fine now. You can have a normal birth."

The next time the teacher went to the doctor, he was surprised to see that the baby had shifted into the head-down position. He said she was lucky. "I didn't tell him I'd seen a midwife," the teacher whispered to me. "I didn't want to make him mad."

She gave me directions to Juana's home, and I went to see her the next day. A tired looking woman with dark circles under deep-set sad eyes, she seemed reserved and suspicious as she talked to me from the doorway of her house, which was a narrow one-room dwelling jammed between two larger buildings. I thought she was preparing to close the door in my face if I turned out to be proselytizing or selling something, so I quickly told her why I was there, mentioning my visits with Delfina.

Ah, I knew Delfina. She also knew Delfina. It wasn't clear whether they were friends or rivals, but, in any case, my connection with Delfina seemed to legitimize my visit. She invited me into her house and offered me a seat on a padded bench just inside the front door. She was sixty-eight years old, she said. She'd been a midwife all her adult life.

Juana.

> I learned my skills from my mother, who was a great midwife, loved and respected by everyone. One of the doctors in town used to ask her to help him when he performed surgery. I went to *cursos*, starting in the eighties, but I was already experienced by then. I had learned from my mother. My husband went to the United States looking for work when the youngest of my three daughters was eight years old and never came back, so I raised my daughters alone with the income I earned by working as a midwife.
>
> The roof of my house collapsed during the earthquake in 1980, and a beam fell on my mother's head. She had a big gash that needed to be stitched. Getting medical attention after the earthquake was a problem—the hospital had been destroyed, and there were so many people injured—but there was one doctor I knew would come. He loved my mother; she had attended the births of two of his children while he was in Mexico City studying. I sent for him, and he came right away. He didn't charge us a single *centavo*.
>
> Later they set up tarps and tents in the *zócalo* and doctors treated patients there. One of my former patients was due to give birth at that time. She'd been planning to have the baby in the hospital, because she wanted to have her tubes tied, so when her labor began she went to the *zócalo*. When she got there, a nurse gave her a hospital gown and started an IV, but then the nurse disappeared and no one came to help the woman. After waiting as long as she could, she pulled the needle out of her arm and found a taxi to bring her to my house. The baby was born in the taxi on the way here. I got her into what was left of my house and received the placenta and cut the cord. I washed her and the baby, and then I went out and cleaned up the taxi. The woman was worried about getting the gown back to the people in the *zócalo*, but I told her, "If they want their gown, they can come and get it."
>
> I used to be busy—sometimes I attended three or four births a day—and I've attended so many twin births and so many births of babies that were sitting or standing that I can't even count them. God has always helped me; I never had to send a woman to the hospital. I

don't attend births anymore because my knees are bad, but I still give belly massages. Sometimes, when a doctor in the hospital tells a woman she's going to need a Cesarean, the woman will leave the hospital and come to see me. I give her a massage, and then she returns to the hospital and has a normal birth. On two different occasions after I did that, the baby was born in the car on the way back to the hospital.

I told Juana I would like to see her massage a pregnant woman's belly. "You should have come last week," she said. "There was a new moon last week. I give most of my belly massages during the new moon."

"Is there some reason for giving the massage then?" I asked, expecting to hear some belief about the relationship between lunar cycles and fetal position.

"No, it's just a way to help women remember to come once a month."

I asked the usual questions about her practices. She had women lie on their backs for the birth, she said. I assumed she'd learned that from her mother who would have learned it from the doctor. She said women used to lie on a straw mat on the floor, but most have beds now.

I had stopped asking midwives if they used gloves or not. Everyone knew what the answer was supposed to be, so I risked embarrassing those who didn't use them, and I wasn't sure I could trust the answer of those who said they did. But Juana told me, without being asked, that she didn't use gloves. "I wash my hands ten times," she said.

A few years later, at a *congreso* in Tulum, I heard her policy endorsed by Dr. Marcos Leite, an obstetrician from Brazil, who told a roomful of traditional midwives, "You probably feel safe walking in your own neighborhood without a weapon—you know the cats and dogs in your own neighborhood—but if you go into a cage full of tigers and lions, you may want to carry protection. Likewise, when you're receiving a baby in the home, simple hand washing is enough. But if you're in a hospital, you need gloves. The germs we have in hospitals are tigers and lions." And doctors who have done extensive research on tribal childbirth add, "The fact that the mother is cared for within the family in an environment where most of the bacteria have previously been encountered may account for the surprisingly low incidence of puerperal sepsis seen in the most primitive circumstances" (Jelliffe and Bennett 1962, 71).

Juana told me about a tea made from an herb she called "Santa María" that she gave to women in early labor. If the woman was in real labor the tea made the contractions stronger, but if it was still too early, the contractions stopped. She gave women hot chocolate (no egg) during labor and an injection of Pitocin just before the baby was born.

Why did she use Pitocin? Again, the question *why.* Again, the risk of sounding judgmental. And again, the risk of forcing a midwife to manufacturer a cause-and-effect answer when none existed. The true reason may have been that she and her mother had learned to use Pitocin from their doctor friends and hadn't questioned why, or maybe it was because "everyone else uses it" or because "patients expect it." It seems that the use of Pitocin, like the use of the delivery table and the IV, is an important element in what is perceived as "good professional care."[1]

In my further travels I learned that the use of Pitocin "at the end of labor" (at some point between about seven or eight centimeters dilation and crowning) is widespread among midwives and doctors in Mexico. The midwives had learned the practice at one time from doctors and then had passed it to each other. Although the original purpose apparently was to prevent postpartum hemorrhage (which it would do, but for that purpose it's better to wait until after the baby is born) most of the midwives and their clients had come to think of it as a way to *speed* labor. I always wanted to protest when I heard them talk about using Pitocin for that reason. Labor is *already* speeding along at the point when they give it. It seems that the drug is getting credit for what nature would do quite nicely itself if left to proceed on its own.

Juana mentioned that once a doctor had asked her why women kept coming to her, and she'd told him she didn't know. The doctor thought she must have some special trick, but she told him, "No, I don't do anything special."

I pointed out that her skill in giving belly massages and repositioning babies might be considered "something special," and she laughed. Really, there was nothing mysterious about that!

A Failed Seamstress: Margarita Mendoza Zamora

The directions I'd been given to Margarita's house were vague, but once I was in Margarita's neighborhood I found that everyone knew her and could point the way. I recognized the house when I reached it by the hand-lettered sign in the window announcing *Se atienden partos* (Births attended).

Margarita welcomed me into her house and invited me to sit on a bench in the living room while she cared for patients who were waiting. She was treating a baby who was suffering from the folk illness *empacho*,[2]

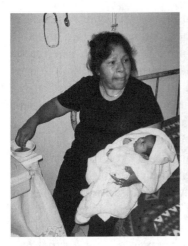
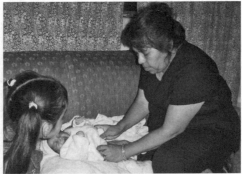

Margarita treating a baby for *mollera caída* [left].
Margarita treating a baby for *empacho* [above].

massaging the baby's belly and back, pinching his back, patting the bottoms of his feet, and giving him something that had been a staple of home medical care during my own childhood, castor oil.

The next baby, which was just a few days old, needed to have the dressing changed on his umbilical cord. Another was treated for a folk illness called *mollera caída* with massage and some kind of manipulation performed with Margarita's finger inside his mouth.

I wondered if the women had taken their babies to a doctor before bringing them to Margarita. I imagined they might do both: They might go to the doctor first and then to the midwife "just to be sure" or to satisfy a worried grandmother. But the midwife might be the first recourse. She would be the least expensive and in most cases the most convenient option. I didn't ask. Asking if they'd taken the baby to the doctor seemed too likely to convey the judgment, *I think you should have.*

The women waiting to be seen by Margarita chatted with each other and with Margarita's two adult daughters, who were sitting at a table by the kitchen. Everyone asked about the health of everyone else's family. Margarita's three-year-old granddaughter made herself available for any attention the grown-ups might pay her, and Margarita's husband passed through the room now and then. I told them about my interest in traditional midwifery, and they told me about their labors.

Margarita chatted with everyone, including me, but she became quiet and focused when she was working with a baby. Occasionally she disappeared into the kitchen to fetch an ingredient she needed for a treatment or to stir a pot of beans that was bubbling on the stove.

Her husband, on one of his passes through the living room, told about an incident that had occurred many years before. A woman had come to the house in labor while Margarita was visiting a friend a few blocks away. He sent one of his children to get her, but Margarita didn't believe there really was a woman in labor—she thought her husband was just trying to get her to come home—so she stayed where she was. When the birth seemed imminent, Margarita's husband decided to go himself to get his wife, but the laboring woman insisted that her own husband go instead. She thought Margarita's husband would be the more useful of the two men if she needed help before Margarita got back. Sure enough, the woman started to push soon after the husband left. When Margarita's husband seemed reluctant to get involved, the woman said, "Don't be a coward; you can do it," and so he did. She showed him how to hold her around her torso when she was pushing and how to tie and cut the cord after the baby was born. When Margarita got home, she found her husband smiling proudly, holding a bucket with the placenta in it. The woman was holding the baby wrapped in her rebozo.

One of Margarita's daughters said, "My dad used to love liver prepared in this special way we called *hígado salsa macha*, but after that birth he never ate *hígado salsa macha* again."

"Remember the time the woman's skirt caught on fire?" the younger of the two daughters asked. Her sister and Margarita remembered.

I asked how that could have happened, and Margarita described a practice called *ensomada de humo* that was supposed to speed labor. "You build a fire and let it burn down until all that's left is smoldering embers, and then you sprinkle herbal water on the embers to make steam. The woman stands over the embers wearing a poncho or blanket to capture the heat, smoke and steam." Margarita said she doesn't normally employ the practice, but "sometimes women insist." In that one case, the *ensomada de humo* appeared to be working. The woman's labor became intense. In the excitement of the impending birth, the younger daughter, who was just a girl then, was the only one to notice that the woman's skirt had caught fire. She was the one to throw water on the flames.

When the patients had gone, Margarita sat with me, her granddaughter in her lap and told me about her life as a midwife.

> My mother was a seamstress. She wanted me to become a seamstress, too, but she wanted me to have training—which she'd never had. When I was fourteen years old, there was a priest from Puebla living here with his two aunts who were both seamstresses. My

mother arranged for me to go with them when they went back to Puebla. I was supposed to live with the aunts and learn sewing and clothing design from them.

Unfortunately I didn't like sewing; I wanted to become a midwife. So the aunts enrolled me in a private midwifery school in Puebla. I don't know how they talked the school into accepting such a young girl, but somehow they did.

When I finished my training at the school, I came back to Huajuapan and told everyone I was a midwife. I was only fifteen years old! I didn't have any clients of my own in the beginning, but the older midwives used to call me to give injections [of Pitocin] for them. When I was called to a birth to give an injection, I would race to get there as quickly as I could so I could watch what the older midwives did. That's how I learned about the use of herbs and about other traditional practices. The patients got to know me. They were impressed that I knew how to give injections, so they started calling me instead of the older midwives.

By the time I got married, when I was twenty-three, I was busy as a midwife. My husband and I lived with my parents instead of his after we got married, because I was already established as a midwife in my own neighborhood. [The norm throughout Mexico has traditionally been for married couples to live with the husband's family.] My husband was a great help to me. He would take care of our children when I was busy with a client, even after working all day at his own job in an office, and he helped me in any way he could. For example, if a patient left the placenta here, he would bury it.

People used to bury the placenta in their courtyard—doing that is supposed to ensure that the child will love his family and stay close to home—but there were a few patients who didn't want to be bothered with the placenta. If they left it here, my husband would bury it in our own courtyard. He would put a candle or rock on the ground above it to make sure no one stepped on it or accidentally dug it up. When there wasn't room for more placentas here, he buried them on some land we have in the country. Two of my grandsons' placentas are buried on that land, and those are the two grandchildren, more than any of the others, who love the outdoors. They love animals, and they love going to the country with my husband.

The Mixteco people (an indigenous group who live in Oaxaca, Guerrero, and Puebla) have their own customs. They wrap the placenta in a basket or in a straw hat and hang it from a tree. One Mixteco man said that if you bury the placenta the child will have a closed-up intellect, but if you hang it from a tree the child will have a free intellect.

I was busy as a midwife. Sometimes I attended six or eight births in a month. Once I attended three in one day. All the beds in my house would be filled with women who were in labor or who were recovering after a birth. Sometimes I would send my children to sleep at their grandparents' house because their beds here were occupied. Once two brothers both brought their wives here at the same time and the two babies were born five minutes apart. We put the two women, each holding her baby, side by side in the bed for a photo.

Once, when I went to attend a birth, I found that the woman was all alone and the baby was crosswise. I worked hard to reposition the baby, but when he finally shifted, he went into the sitting position! I tried to move him again, but he was stubborn, so I told the woman she'd have to go to the hospital. She refused. She said, "I'm staying here. I'll die like a dog if you won't attend me, but I'm not going to the hospital."

My grandmother and my little sister were with me. My grandmother told me I had to attend the birth. She said, "Midwives don't say 'no.' This is your job. You have to do it."

I told my grandmother, "Okay, I'll do it, but you have to help me."

When the baby's bottom started to emerge, I called for my grandmother to come help, but she didn't answer. She'd gone to the temple of the Virgin of Guadalupe to pray that the baby would be born safely. So that was her way of helping!

The baby came out small and dark, looking lifeless, like a hairless rabbit. I slapped him and cleaned the mucus out of his mouth and nose, and then I breathed into his mouth. I called to my sister to come help, but when she saw the baby, she fainted. I had the patient take over for me, breathing into the baby's mouth, and I ran, stepping over my sister, to get two buckets of water: one hot and one cold. I dunked the baby into one of the buckets and then the other until he started to cry.

Another woman with yet another baby was arriving as I said goodbye to Margarita. Walking back to the hotel, I thought of all the worried mothers back in Oregon who had said to me: *I took him to the doctor, but the doctor didn't do anything.*

Margarita always *did something.*

Margarita had said she thought the big *farmacia* next to the town market might sell pinard horns, so I stopped there on my way back to the hotel to see if they did. Since I didn't know how to say "pinard horn" in Spanish, I tried to describe what I wanted by explaining how it was used. Several employees and two customers became involved in the attempt to figure out what I was talking about, but it seemed hopeless, until finally I made a sketch. One of the employees said, "Oh, you mean the thing they use for listening to the baby's heartbeat" (which was exactly what I'd been saying all along), and then everyone congratulated everyone else for the success of their group effort. They did not have a pinard, but they could order one from Puebla. I was to come back in a few days.

Preparations for the Day of the Dead were increasingly evident. Bundles of marigolds were being sold from temporary stalls along the sidewalk, from the backs of trucks, and in flower shops. When I asked a sidewalk vendor if I could buy just a single bloom, she gave me one as a gift. I put it in a plastic water glass but couldn't find a single horizontal surface in my tiny hotel room, not a table, not a shelf, not even a window sill. I finally put it on top of the toilet tank, making it my Day of the Dead altar.

Day of the Dead altars were being assembled in every home I visited. People used tables, not toilet tanks, covering them with candles, crosses, holy water, pictures of saints, photos of departed loved ones, cans of beer and soda, mounds of oranges, and other food offerings. The tables were decorated like parade floats with hundreds of marigolds and a red tropical flower with big floppy petals.

I went to see Margarita again on the morning of the Day of the Dead. Her family was busy preparing for the trip to the cemetery, where they would spend the day picnicking and communing with the spirits of dead loved ones. Margarita told me her granddaughter had been talking about "the grandmothers" all morning. The girl's mother had asked her, "What grandmothers?"

"The grandmothers over there by the altar," the girl had replied. Everyone understood that she was referring to the souls of her dead ancestors. She was only three years old, Margarita reminded me. No one had explained the significance of the altar to her. No one had explained the meaning of the Day of the Dead. It had to be that she could really sense the presence of the spirits. This awareness by an innocent child made the world of the departed seem close and real. Even I could feel it.

Margarita asked if I'd like to go with them to the cemetery, but I declined, thinking it would be an intrusion. In spite of mounting evidence to the contrary, I persisted in my idea that the Day of the Dead was a solemn holiday about loss and grief. Later, having decided to go on my own, I set out on foot for the trip of about two miles to the cemetery. There was little traffic on the usually congested main streets and none at all once I moved away from *el centro* (the business district). Stores were closed; the town was quiet. There was no music, no chatter of children playing behind the walls that surrounded each yard, and there were only a few other pedestrians. There was a sense around me of life suspended. For a few hours at least, Mexico was still.

Through the open gate of the cemetery I glimpsed a festive scene of brightly painted monuments, flowers, music, and Mexicans in party clothes; then I headed back through the quiet streets toward *el centro.*

Saving the Unborn: Jovita Loyola Cortez

I was a bit disappointed when I picked up my pinard horn at the pharmacy to see its shiny newness, but still I was glad to have it. I tucked it into my suitcase; it was time to leave Huajuapan.

I headed north, crossing into the state of Puebla, and stopped in the town of Chila. A woman I'd helped in labor back home had told me there was a midwife named Jovita living in Chila.

Jovita talked to me from behind the counter of the little food store she and her husband owned. She said she was no longer working as a midwife, because women now had their babies at the Center of Salud, but when she was young it had been *pura partera, pura partera.*

> It was important to my husband that our first baby be a boy. I worried when I was pregnant. *What if the baby was a girl? What if my husband didn't want me anymore?* My parents told me not to worry. They said that if I had a girl and my husband didn't like it, I could live with them, so I stopped worrying about the sex of the baby. I was still scared about the actual birth of course. People said I would "see the devil dressed as a horseman," which meant I was going to have a horribly painful experience.
>
> Fortunately the baby was a boy.

Jovita and her husband behind the counter in their store.

I decided after having that baby that I wanted to become a midwife. I talked some older midwives into letting me go with them to births so I could see what they did, and a nurse who was spending a few months in Chila showed me how to give injections. After a while women started coming to me. The older midwives didn't like that—they wanted all the business for themselves—so I made a deal with them. I told them they could do all the midwife work, things like cutting the cord and bathing the woman and doing the laundry afterward, and I would just give the injections. They were happy with that plan, but it didn't really work out the way they wanted because women still came to me. After having one baby with me a woman would come for the next and the next. One woman had twenty babies, all with me as the midwife.

I didn't want a midwife for the birth of my last baby. My mother wanted to send for one, but I felt I could manage on my own. My husband had tied a rope to one of the rafters in preparation for the birth. I just gave myself an injection of Pitocin, grabbed the rope, squatted down, and had my baby.

I always gave an injection of Pitocin when the baby was crowning. The only other injection I might use was *ergotrate* [ergot] if a woman bled too much after the birth.[3] Other than that, I just used herbs and maybe a cup of *chocolate espiritual* with a little *ruda* [the herb rue] to give the woman energy and strength. If the cervix was hard, I would put the woman's braid in her mouth to make her vomit and that would speed things up.

If the woman looks up at the ceiling and starts shaking, that means she's dying. When that happened I would stroke her eyes to close them so she couldn't look up, or maybe I would hold alcohol under her nose. I had women breathe camphorated oil if they fainted. Once a husband fainted, but I didn't give him camphorated oil. I just told the family to get him out of the way.

She said she gave injections of progesterone to women who were threatening to miscarry. (Doctors also give progesterone for this purpose.) And then she added that if a woman came to her asking for an abortion, she would tell the woman she was giving her medicine to get rid of the baby, but what she really gave the woman was progesterone "to make the pregnancy stronger." She said, "I wouldn't be able to sleep if I helped a woman kill her baby. I'd be thinking about the child who never had a chance to cry!"

Mourned on the Day of the Dead: Casilda Marin Garzón

My next stop was Acatlán in western Puebla, a town famous for its beautiful hand-painted pottery. I was browsing among stalls that sold the pottery and talking to the vendors, when one of them mentioned a midwife, Casilda, who lived on a hill beyond the market. I went on foot to find her.

Members of her family, including her husband, a thin, white-haired, eighty-four-year-old man, were sitting in the small yard in front of the house around a huge mound of uprooted peanut plants, stripping peanuts from the roots and dropping them into buckets at their feet. They told me that Casilda had died seven months earlier. Two of her daughters, Ana and Guadalupe, invited me into the house. Guadalupe had come from the city of Puebla for the holiday. They told me Casilda had become a midwife after the Virgin of Guadalupe appeared to her *en una revelación* (in a vision) telling her to cure people and telling her what herbs to use. She went to a *curso* once, but she was already experienced by then; she knew the traditional ways. She'd known how to cure fevers and intestinal worms and many other ailments, using nothing but herbal remedies. Once when Ana was suffering from menstrual cramps because she'd eaten too much squash (which, they told me, you should never do while menstruating), Casilda prepared a special tea that cured her.

To treat a baby with a protruding bellybutton, Casilda would massage the baby's belly, pushing the bellybutton in with her finger, and then she would insert a bullet-shaped plug she'd made using a mixture of an herb called *epazote* and resin from the copal tree. Once the plug was in place, she would wrap a strip of fabric around the baby's belly to hold the resin and cotton in place.

Casilda had been able to predict how many babies a woman would have by studying the *nudos* (knot-like lumps) in the umbilical cord. If the cord had six *nudos* then the woman would have six more babies. The spacing of the *nudos* indicated the spacing of the babies. If two were close together, then two of the babies would come one right after the other. If they were really close together, that might indicate there would be twins. Both women remembered seeing Casilda bent over a bowl full of glistening placenta, examining and counting the *nudos* in the cord.[4]

If the placenta didn't come out promptly, Casilda would poke the umbilical cord with a needle or she would have the woman chew fresh mint and salt. Once, when no other method worked, Casilda had someone wake up a boy in the house and had him pee into a cup. She had the woman drink the pee, and then the placenta came out.

Another woman had drunk pee!

I asked the questions Leonora and her aunt had been unable to answer: Does pee, or male pee or *warm* male pee, have some property that expels a placenta? No. Once again the goal was to *provocar vómitos*. Casilda didn't tell the woman what was in the cup until after she drank from it. The woman threw up when she was told, and that (again I presumed it was the heaving of the diaphragm) made the placenta come out.

Once, when Casilda went to a party at another midwife's home, she found a woman in labor there. The labor had been stalled for several hours. Casilda broke the amniotic sac (bag of membranes that surround the baby), using a sharp edge of a lump of salt to cut it, and the baby was quickly born. He was very dark. It had been almost too late. (I later heard midwives in other parts of Mexico mention using salt in the same way.)

The young women remembered one harrowing experience Casilda had told them about. A man came late at night seeking help for his wife, and Casilda went with him, walking several kilometers and crossing a river to get to his home, which was a pathetic little bamboo structure in the middle of nowhere. The man's wife was alone, lying on the dirt floor on a straw mat with the baby's hand sticking out of her vagina. Casilda told the man the baby couldn't be born with the hand coming first like that.[5] She said she couldn't help the woman; he would have to take her to a doctor. He left, supposedly to find a taxi.

The woman cried out to Casilda, "Don't leave me; don't let me die."

Casilda stayed, of course, but the man didn't return that night. At some point, when it didn't seem safe to wait any longer, she decided she had to proceed on her own. She pushed the baby's hand back up into the uterus, and then the birth proceeded normally. The baby, a girl, was born with her two hands in front of her face, like a person in prayer. The father of the baby returned the next evening. He hadn't found a taxi, and he didn't pay Casilda.

Margarita showed me a photo taken at a *curso* Casilda had attended in 1973. The students with Casilda were young women wearing starched white uniforms sitting stiffly in front of a blackboard. A tall, thin young man wearing a white lab coat, probably the doctor who taught the *curso*, stood beside them. I imagined he was a fresh-out-of-school conscript forced to do his duty in the hinterlands, confident but relatively inexperienced. He may not have had much respect for Casilda and the other rustic women who attended the *curso,* most of whom would have been illiterate, even though the midwives had attended hundreds, in many cases thousands, of births.

A few days later I met another midwife in Acatlán, a friend of Casilda, who had attended the same *curso*. She remembered the humiliation she'd felt when the doctor asked the midwives a question they couldn't answer. The question was, "How long does it take for the placenta to come out?" None of the midwives could answer.

"Of course we knew how long it takes, but we didn't know the meaning of the word 'placenta.' We called it *la segunda* [the second part]. He must have thought we were really stupid."

But to Casilda's daughters, attendance at the *curso* had been a source of pride, not humiliation. They were proud of their mother, proud of the picture, and very happy that a stranger had come along—on the first Day of the Dead after Casilda's death—who wanted to hear about her life.

A Pinard Changes Hands: Isabel Rangel Cruz

Isabel.

Isabel lived in Acatlán just a few blocks from my hotel. My visit interrupted her work—she'd been washing clothes—but she didn't seem to mind. After offering me her wrist in place of her wet hand, she invited me into her house. Eighty-four years old, wearing a white satin dress, with long gray hair in a single braid, she looked ancient and tired but still proud and strong. She said washing clothes was her main source of income.

There appeared to be just one room in the house. Spaces for beds, one for her and one for her mother, were partitioned off by curtains hanging from the ceiling. I had a glimpse of her mother through a gap in the curtain, sleeping just a few feet from where we sat. She was 104 years old, Isabel said, and had to be cared for "like a baby."

Isabel was quite deaf, but she worked hard to understand me, and, while I shouted my questions, she answered in a soft, dignified voice.

> One of my aunts was a midwife. One day, when my aunt was away visiting a friend, a woman in labor came to the door. It was an emer-

gency; I had to help her. That was the first time I attended a birth on my own. I was nineteen years old and still single. The baby that was born that day is a grandmother now.

By the time I became pregnant myself, I had already attended several births, so I knew what to expect. One evening I was sitting at my sewing machine when suddenly I felt a gush of water. I gathered the baby's clothes, a pair of scissors, and some string and prepared to wait, but the baby came right away. It probably took about half an hour from the time the bag of waters broke until the baby was born. I didn't feel a single contraction.

I had three more babies, and all my births were easy like that. I was alone for all the births. My husband left me after my fourth baby was born, so I raised my children on my own. I supported myself and my children by sewing, doing laundry, ironing, selling milk, and attending births.

I have one son, who's a teacher, and three daughters. Three different women have wanted to give me their babies, but I always said no. I suffered enough raising my own children.

I moved here to Acatlán a few years ago. My son made me sell my house in the *rancho* and move here because he worried about me when I was living so far away in a place that had no services. I never had any contact with doctors when I lived in the *rancho*, but now that I live in Acatlán I go to meetings they have for midwives at the Center of Salud. There was a *curso* there last year. I went, but I was late on the first day because I had to feed my mother and then I had to walk several kilometers to get there. After that the people at the clinic paid for me to take a taxi and I wasn't late again. The people at the Center of Salud give me alcohol, soap, gloves, and other things I need when I attend births.

I've only had one birth when the baby wasn't coming head first. The woman was my sister-in-law. One of the baby's feet came out, but then there was no more progress. I had to reach in with my hand to find the other foot. Once I got the second foot out the birth was easy.

The only real problem I've had as a midwife was in a birth that took place two months ago. I couldn't get the placenta to come out. The woman told me to pull on the cord, but I wouldn't. I said to the woman, "What if you hemorrhage? I have no injections; I have no IV." I sent someone to get the doctor. He came and took the woman to the hospital.

"Why do you think birth was so easy for you?" I asked. "It seems much harder for women today."

She answered without hesitation. "Because I walked; because I worked. On the day my first baby was born, I got up at 6:00 in the morning, took a bath, milked the cows, and then walked up and down mountain trails all day delivering milk."

I told her that it seemed amazing to me that she could have been a midwife for so long with only that one problem, and she smiled. "The Virgin of Guadalupe helps me," she said. "She is always with me."

Back at my hotel, as I packed my bags in preparation for the bus trip to the city of Puebla, I looked at the pinard I'd bought in Huajuapan. It looked lifeless. An old one that had belonged to a midwife would have been the real treasure. It occurred to me that one of the midwives might have been willing to trade with me: her old pinard for my nice plastic-wrapped new one. I needed to board the bus for Puebla in less than two hours, but Isabel was just a few blocks away. I decided to make a quick visit to see her before I set out for the bus station.

She answered my knock at her door looking pleased to see me. I held up my pinard so she could see what I was talking about and asked her, shouting again, if she knew what it was. She said she did. "Do you have one?" I asked.

"No, I don't," she said, and then she added, happily, "*¡Gracias!*" She took the pinard from my hand and dropped it into the pocket of her apron.

She was too deaf to use it, so I imagine it will sit on her altar—instead of on mine.

We said goodbye one more time, and I raced off to catch the bus to the city of Puebla.

Successful Outcomes in the Traditional Setting

As the bus twisted through the mountains east of Acatlán, I thought about Isabel's long career, calculating that she'd been a midwife for about sixty-five years. And she'd only had one birth she'd considered problematic. Could it be true, I wondered, that all the births the midwives attended had good outcomes?

Yes, I thought, it could be true—if you don't count miscarriages, births of badly deformed babies, or difficult labors that had dragged on so long that the baby was compromised before the midwife arrived. (There were often long delays due to lack of phone service and transportation.) Although such losses do count in national statistics on birth outcomes, the midwives didn't consider them to have tarnished their *personal* records (and I don't suppose doctors do either). And the midwives also discounted the loss of a twin, which was apparently so common that it felt like an act of nature.

I've never found usable statistics on this question. Deaths weren't necessarily reported during the time when the midwives were most active, and now, when Mexico is very concerned about maternal mortality, the focus is on understanding the factors at play in *hospital* births, not home births, which now represent a very small percentage of the births in Mexico. Reporting still isn't reliable—all sources, including public hospitals (see Argüello 2011) underreport fatalities—and reports fail to document key characteristics; for example, they often lump all home births together, whether they were attended by a doctor, a nurse, a midwife, a mother-in-law, or no one. (See Eng 2014 for a better understanding of the difficulty in obtaining meaningful statistics on this matter.)

But I've made my own informal investigation into the matter. I've asked over 1,500 students in my childbirth classes (pregnant women and their husbands, almost all from southern Mexico), as an icebreaker exercise at the beginning of the first session, "How many babies did your mother have? Where were they born (home or hospital)? Was there a midwife present? And did the babies all survive birth?" With all that questioning, which would have covered over 10,000 births, about half of which occurred in the home, I've heard of many cases of babies dying during that critical first year but only three cases in which an apparently healthy, full-term baby died during labor or birth or the first weeks following birth. (One woman had lost two babies born at home *without the help of a midwife*—she'd had only her own husband in attendance—and one loss occurred in a Mexican hospital.) My students did not report any babies dying during a midwife-attended birth. And none of their mothers had died in childbirth.

My questioning didn't constitute a rigorous "study"—I was making conversation, not science—but it left me with the impression that birth in the traditional setting, without medical services, is not as hazardous as people in my world tend to assume. The factors that I thought favored successful outcomes in the work of the midwives were:

- The strong physical condition of their patients. Women of rural Mexico worked hard and walked miles each day. That level of activity must have been what the Creator (or Mother Nature or evolution) had in mind when designing the female body's reproductive process.

- The midwives' skill and experience in optimizing fetal position.
- An atmosphere of trust and patience, a methodology that disturbed the natural process very little, using interventions, for example herbal teas, that were congruent with the daily life experiences of the women giving birth.

It's hard for those who have been molded by a system that honors the "technocratic" model of birth (this is Davis-Floyd's (2004) term for the model that sees birth as fraught with danger and as needing high-tech interventions) to believe that there could have been such a high success rate under the primitive conditions that prevailed during the time when midwives in Mexico were most active. But for those who embrace the opposite view, one that assumes birth is as natural for humans as it is for other mammals, it's hard to imagine how the technocratic model has been so universally accepted. (For an understanding of the discrepancy between these two views, see Davis-Floyd's book, *Birth as an American Rite of Passage*, 2004).

It seemed to me that it was the midwives' vast *experience*—managing fetal position and attending to women in labor—that made their great success understandable. So I had to wonder, *What about when they were just learning? How successful were they when they were first acquiring their experience?*

Many, of course, underwent long apprenticeships. Those women had older, established midwives supporting them while they obtained their experience. But what of the women who said, "I didn't know a thing about birth. The woman begged me to help her. There was no one else available; I had to do it."?

Since birth normally proceeds perfectly well without any intervention at all, most novice midwives would have been able to gain their experience gradually, with birth itself as their teacher. But, if there *was* a bad outcome when an inexperienced woman was trying to help, then that woman would probably not have been asked to help other women in labor. So the potential career of such a woman would have ended before it even began; she would not have come to be known as *una partera* and I would never have met her. Thus a natural selection process meant that I met only midwives who had been successful.

Of course, a system that occasionally left laboring women without any knowledgeable help at all was not ideal. Yet, that very system produced the experienced, wise women who are the midwives of Mexico today.

Fundal Pressure

That afternoon, in an office of the Secretaria de Salud in Puebla, I met a young woman who was involved in overseeing the work of midwives in the state. She spoke fondly of the midwives she worked with. She respected them. She'd gone to a midwife for belly massages herself when she was pregnant.

She told me that her agency had two main goals in its work with midwives. First, they wanted to teach the midwives how to recognize symptoms of risk—in pregnancy, in labor, and in newborns—so they would know when to refer their patients to medical facilities. Second, they wanted to make sure midwives weren't using fundal pressure during the pushing stage of labor.

The "fundal pressure" the woman was talking about (also known as "Kristeller's maneuver") is pressure applied with the hands or maybe the forearm against the top of a woman's belly at the end of labor to help the woman expel the baby. This is not to be confused with the belly massage, which is a caressing, nudging pressure applied all over the belly either to give comfort or, when needed, to optimize the baby's position. The massage may be given many times during pregnancy and labor. Fundal pressure, on the other hand, is applied only at the end of labor. It is a strong pushing down on the top of the belly with the purpose of forcing the baby through the birth canal. The use of fundal pressure is common throughout the world—including in some U.S. hospitals—but is now thought to be inadvisable, except in certain emergency situations, because of the possibility that it might damage the uterus, the pelvic floor, the placenta, or the baby. It is not used, except in rare cases of emergencies, in the hospitals in Oregon where I have worked. But both doctors and midwives in Mexico use the procedure routinely.

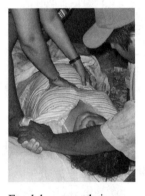

Fundal pressure being applied by a midwife.

There is, of course, significant variation in the amount of force applied. I've heard and read accounts in which patients describe the pressure as being extremely painful, even cruel, and I've seen nightmarish images on the Internet. But some patients, especially women who had given birth with a midwife, found the pressure comforting and helpful.

I mentioned to the woman who worked for the Secretaria de Salud that I'd heard fundal pressure was used by doctors and nurses in Mexico, too, not just by midwives. Women who'd given birth in Mexican hospitals had complained to me that fundal pressure was used while they were pushing and that it hurt. One woman said, "They practically sat on me!"

"Well . . ." the woman from the Secretaria de Salud demurred. It wasn't her job to concern herself with what was done by doctors.

I wanted to defend the midwives. I thought, or hoped, that they, with their vast experience massaging pregnant women's bellies, with their intuition and maternal instincts and the guidance they receive from God and the Virgin, would know how much pressure was safe to apply. I hoped that someday I would have a chance to observe a midwife applying fundal pressure.

Nettles: Eduiges Mendez Jimenez

Eduiges was a modern-looking woman, sixty-five years old, with tightly curled short hair, wearing black slacks and a matching sweater. I'd been given her name by the woman from the Secretaria de Salud.

She and her husband owned a public bathhouse in Puebla, a place where people who didn't have hot water could go for a shower. I found her working when I arrived at the bathhouse, sitting in a little enclosure that looked like the ticket booth of a movie theater, waiting for customers. She got a cleaning lady to take her post in the booth and led me back through the bathhouse, around a huge water tank shaped like a blimp, past a maze of pipes and a row of shower cubicles, to one of three little rooms where she saw patients and attended births. I sat on a chair and she sat on the narrow bed while she told me about her life.

Eduiges.

> I had my first baby at home with a midwife, but then I got health insurance, so I was able to have my second baby in the hospital. I had a bad experience there. They performed vaginal checks roughly and scolded me when I cried out, and the way they pressed down on the top of my belly at the end [they performed fundal pressure] was pain-

ful. After the baby was born they left me lying on a canvas cot on the floor. They had beds, but they didn't let us use them because they were afraid we'd get blood on them.

After that experience, I decided I wanted to become a midwife. I had learned how to bandage wounds and give injections in a first aid course taught by nuns when I was a child, but I didn't know much about childbirth. A friend who was a midwife let me go with her to births, and she showed me what to do. Soon I had clients of my own.

I didn't need a midwife for my own births, not after I became a midwife myself. I never told anyone when I went into labor, not even my mother. I would continue with my normal housework, checking now and then with *el tacto* to see how I was doing, until it seemed it was time for the birth. Then I would tie a cloth around my midriff, lie down on a mattress on the floor, and have my baby. It was always a surprise to my family when they heard the baby cry. My mother used to scold me for not telling her I was in labor.

I used to give women cinnamon or chamomile tea during the hardest part of labor, but now I use an IV instead. I don't start the IV until near the end, because I want women to keep walking as long as possible. In the hospital, women get IVs as soon as they're admitted, and then they have to stay in bed. Women don't like the way they're treated in the hospital. Doctors and nurses yell at them and tell them to shut up. Women come to me because they want to be treated with respect and because they want to be able to move around during labor. But they still want to feel they're getting good medical care. The IV gives them confidence that they are.

Women are afraid they'll have to have a Cesarean if they have their babies in a hospital. Doctors scare women. They say the baby will die if the woman doesn't have a Cesarean. They tell a woman who's just eight months along, "Your baby is formed now. We'll perform a Cesarean next week." Women don't know any better. The doctor tells them it will be safer for the baby if they have a Cesarean. I think it's wrong to take a baby at eight months. It's like cracking open an egg before the chicken is fully developed.

Women come to see me during pregnancy when they're not feeling well or when they have some discomfort. I rock them in the rebozo and massage their bellies, and then they feel great. I learned these things from my friend who was a midwife. Doctors say midwives shouldn't adjust the position of babies, because a baby might get tangled up in the cord, but I've never heard of that happening. I don't know what doctors think we do. We aren't making babies do somersaults in there!

My patients tell me about techniques they've seen other midwives use, like giving the woman hot chocolate with eggs or putting her braid in her mouth or having her stand over hot embers. I don't do those things. My friend didn't teach me those methods, and I've never been convinced they would help. I think the hot chocolate might slow labor down or even stop it.

I tell women, "Your mother-in-law and your grandmother are going to tell you to drink chocolate, or they're going to give you different kinds of teas. Don't drink those things. Let your labor take its natural course."

I don't press on the woman's belly when she's pushing the way doctors and other midwives do either. I just tie a piece of cloth around her midriff above her belly and she pushes against that. If the placenta doesn't come out promptly, I give her some chamomile tea and massage her belly. That always works. It isn't necessary to pull on the cord. After the birth I give the woman a nice massage.

People have lots of different ideas about what might help in labor. One woman rubbed nettle leaves all over her belly and her back. The nettles caused a rash that itched and stung like crazy. Her people believed doing that would make labor less painful and would make the birth faster, but it didn't seem to me to be helping!

I've even helped animals give birth. I never wanted to, but people would come to me with an emergency and beg me to help. Once I had to put my hand into the uterus of a goat to find the baby's feet and pull it out. On another occasion a man convinced me to try to help his pig. He said she'd had one piglet the previous night but the rest of the babies wouldn't come out. When I stuck my hand into her uterus, I found there was nothing in there! Pigs usually have at least six or eight babies—or maybe even fifteen or more—but that pig only had one.

Sometimes women asked me to keep their baby or to help them give it to another woman by putting the other woman's name on the birth documents, but I never did that. I heard once that a midwife had been sent to jail for helping with an adoption in that way. Later, the real mother accused the midwife of stealing the baby.

I used to go to meetings at the government hospital. I liked the meetings; they fed us well and treated us with respect, and we learned things like how to fill out the paperwork necessary to register a birth and how to identify high-risk pregnancies. Also, they gave us a certificate showing we were qualified midwives. But I stopped going because they were pushing the idea of birth control. The church says birth control is wrong.

Faith in God is a basic principle of my work. I always say an Our Father prayer with each woman at the beginning of her labor. I ask

God, "Please bless this woman who is a child of God," and I ask Him to protect the baby and to bless and guide my hands. What more can we ask than the presence of God? After the baby is born, I thank God for His help. I thank Him for the healthy baby.

There was a pinard horn like the one I'd unintentionally given to Isabel on a table next to the bed. I mentioned my interest in pinards, and Eduiges offered me hers. "I have more," she said. "They used to give them out in the *cursos*."

A heavy rain had begun to fall while I was in the bathhouse. Eduiges found a plastic poncho for me and insisted that I take it. We hugged under the awning next to the admission booth and I ran to the bus stop, jumping over puddles and streams in the gutters, clutching the pinard under my plastic poncho.

Home Again

Back home in Oregon, as I placed my new (old) pinard on my mantel I was aware that, although the device has been in use for over a century, it can't really be called "traditional." It was invented by an obstetrician and was handed to Mexican midwives by the medical establishment. I thought of Isabel, who had been left behind when other midwives were learning about modern ideas and receiving pinards in those *cursos*. She'd been so happy when I gave her mine. While to me it represented a step back toward the traditional, to her it represented a step forward toward the world of modern medicine. That's the irony of my interest in traditional ways; while I'm reaching back, so many of the midwives are reaching forward.

A few days after I returned home, while shopping for groceries I ran into Atocha, the woman who'd told me about Jovita. Atocha was with her daughter Remedios, who'd been a friend of my daughter in school. Remedios said she was pregnant and had just been to a doctor's appointment. I said the usual congratulatory things about the pregnancy and asked how the appointment with the doctor had gone.

Both women looked deflated. The doctor had only spent a few minutes with Remedios. "He didn't do anything," Atocha said. I'd heard the same complaint many times, especially from Mexican women. They would come to me after class to ask about some discomfort they were having. When I asked if they'd mentioned the discomfort to the doctor, they would say that they had, but that the doctor had said it was normal.

He didn't do anything. And I'd heard American women complain, too, that their prenatal appointments were perfunctory and brief.

I thought of Jovita back in Atocha's hometown of Chila. If Remedios had been to see Jovita, Jovita would have done something. She'd have given Remedios a tea and a nice belly massage.

Endnotes

1. Other brands of synthetic oxytocin were available to the midwives before Pitocin, and many midwives still used the old names when talking to me, but, for simplicity—and because I couldn't keep the various names straight—I refer to all synthetic oxytocin products as "Pitocin." No prescription is needed for what we would consider "prescription drugs" in the United States. Midwives, along with the general public, can buy Pitocin, antibiotics, and other pharmaceutical products at any pharmacy.
2. A "folk illness" is a combination of physical and psychiatric symptoms that are considered to be a recognizable disease only within a specific society or culture. *Empacho* is digestive distress, especially an obstruction in the digestive system, thought to be caused by eating certain foods or spoiled foods or too much of one food or by swallowing gum. This diagnosis and its various treatments seem to predate the Spanish conquest of Mexico. *Mollera caida* is a condition characterized by digestive and respiratory symptoms and by the fontanel (the "soft spot" on a newborn's head) becoming sunken, creating a depression at the top of the head. The diagnosis and its various treatments are thought to have been brought to Mexico by the Spanish.
3. *Ergotrate* is a plant-derived substance that has been used since the middle ages to control uterine bleeding. Many of the midwives I met said they had used it in the past, but most now use Pitocin instead.
4. A few years later a midwife from the Purépecha indigenous group in Michoacán told me that you can also tell the sex of future babies by looking at the *nudos* in the cord. If a *nudo* is dark in color then the baby it represents will be male; if the *nudo* is white, the baby will be a girl. And Gonzales mentions "reading" the umbilical cord "for signs of future pregnancies" (2012, 137).
5. Doctors also consider the appearance of a hand ("a compound presentation") to be a challenging circumstance, because of the greater dilation required when more than just the head is emerging and because the arm or shoulder may be injured. They try to get the baby to retract her hand by pinching or irritating it or they ease it back inside as Casilda did, but sometimes the birth is allowed to proceed with the hand presenting. These births normally turn out fine, but sometimes a Cesarean is performed to avoid the risks.

Chapter 4

Zihuatanejo

After the trip to Huajuapan, whenever I saw a new moon I thought of Juana, the midwife who said women came to her for belly massages during the new moon. I imagined her patients looking at the same moon as I was and thinking, *time for a belly massage*. I imagined Juana preparing for the patients who would come.

I had yet to see a midwife give a belly massage. Maybe on this trip . . .

Or maybe not. This was to be a family vacation, not a search for midwives, at least that was the plan. I was with my husband, Jim, his daughter Patti, and Patti's seventeen-year-old daughter, Jenna, in Zihuatanejo, a town on the Pacific coast near Ixtapa. I'd chosen Zihuatanejo because it has beautiful beaches, yet the town itself is more typically Mexican than other resorts. I wanted Jenna to see "real" Mexico; I wanted her to practice speaking Spanish. I wanted her to fall in love with Mexico, or at least with the adventure of travel, as I had done when I was her age.

It was July; the temperature was over 90 degrees every day of our stay, and the air was muggy. The only other tourists were Mexicans and there weren't many of those. (Americans come to Zihuatanejo in the winter.) The town seemed quiet and unfrenzied, and we felt lazy. We spent our days at the beach, bouncing in the waves or sitting in the shade of a palm-thatched *palapa* eating guacamole and chips. In the evenings we went to a waterfront plaza in town where families gathered to relax and mingle. Jenna drew admiring glances from young men with romance in their dark eyes, but she pretended not to notice and I pretended not to notice her pretending not to notice.

One night I chatted with a lady who sold popcorn in the plaza and learned that she'd had fourteen children, all born with a midwife. "I had easy births," she said. "You know how a wet bar of soap squirts out of your hand when you squeeze it? That's what my births were like."

She told me about a midwife named Isabel, who lived about a mile from our hotel. Jenna went with me to find her the next day.

Ay, Qué Susto: Isabel Valadez Mulina

Isabel lived in a little house with only one room and a dirt floor in a residential area near the super store where we did our shopping. There was a kitchen area in one corner and a bathing area partitioned off by a curtain in another. The rest of the house was filled with hammocks and beds.

She was a stout little army tank of a woman, just a little over four feet tall, wearing a pink cotton dress and a scowl. Her granddaughter, Sandra, placed chairs for Jenna and me in front of the refrigerator, and we sat down. Isabel sat facing us, looking wary, waiting to see why we had come. I tried to explain, but she didn't seem to understand. Sandra said that Isabel was eighty-two years old and a little *confundida* (confused).

She was also quite deaf. Sandra helped by relaying my questions and remarks, abbreviating them and shouting for me. (I was from AMERICA, and I wanted to know about her *TRABAJO.*)

Isabel seemed prickly and proud and not very friendly, but she also seemed to like having an audience, and there were things she wanted to tell. She didn't feel well, she said. Her back hurt and her shoulders hurt. It hurt to raise her arms. Her hands hurt. "What part of my body doesn't hurt?" she moaned.

She showed me white scars that slashed across the tops of her feet and explained that she'd scraped her feet once, years ago, when she tripped on a curb. She'd put an ointment on the scrapes when she got home, and that had seemed to help, but when she put her shoes back on, her feet suddenly seemed to be on fire. She took the shoes off and ran to put her feet in a bucket of water, but it was too late. There'd been a caustic reaction between the ointment and the plastic of her shoes; the plastic had melted, burning her skin.

She asked if I could get her a *remedio* for the scars. Or could I get a *remedio* for her hearing? She'd heard there was an herb that grew in the mountains that could restore hearing. Did I know what herb that might be?

I wasn't optimistic about being able to find a *remedio* for either problem, but I thought maybe a hearing aid might be useful. "There's an *aparato* that helps with hearing," I told her. Isabel said she didn't want an *aparato*; she wanted a *remedio*, and I told her I'd watch for one.

Isabel drying her hair after bathing.

She said her son had died two years ago, and she hadn't recovered from the loss. Because of that, and because she'd suffered three *sustos* (soul loss caused by a frightening experience) in her life, her brain wasn't working very well.

She said the first *susto* occurred when she was sixteen years old, when her mother tried to kill her. The other two involved snakes. Once a snake fell from a tree onto her shoulders, and once she came upon a huge snake while she was walking on a path in the countryside. "The snake was as big around as a man's arm," she said. *"Ay, qué susto."*

Wait. "Your mother tried to kill you? Why did she do that?"

"Oh, because I was *enojona* [quick to anger] and I always talked back to her." Isabel chuckled, remembering.

I asked Sandra if she thought it was true. Had Isabel's mother really tried to kill her? Sandra said she'd heard the story all her life and she assumed it was true. Supposedly her great grandmother had gone after Isabel with a machete, but an uncle had intervened and saved her. "Grandma's mother was really mean," Sandra said, "and she didn't like Grandma."

"That's true," Isabel added, "She hit me more than she hit my brother. She had a special rope she used and a special way of doubling it to make it hurt more."

When I asked about Isabel's life and her work as a midwife, Sandra went to the other side of the room and stretched out in a hammock next to a small television set, leaving me to do my own shouting with Jenna's help.

> I grew up in a village in the mountains, about six hours from here by foot. I used to have some kind of attacks when I was a little girl; I would suddenly lose consciousness. My mother was a midwife and a *curandera*, but she didn't know how to help me, so she asked the

priest. He had me take a *remedio* for three months, and that cured me. He wasn't supposed to treat illnesses like that, so he did it secretly.

I worked hard as a child. I did all the cooking for the family, and I helped my mother in her work. I was still just a teenager when she said it was time for me to start attending births by myself. I didn't want to, but my mother insisted. One day, after giving a pregnant woman a belly massage, my mother said to the woman, "Your baby will be born tomorrow night, and my daughter will attend the birth." Then, after the woman left, my mother went to visit some relatives in another *rancho*.

Everything happened the way my mother said it would. The woman came back the next day in labor, and I attended the birth. I was scared, but I had to do it!

I had nine children, six boys and three girls. My husband never hit me, although he wanted to sometimes, and once he threatened to shoot me with a pistol. I stopped him by yelling at him. He was a sad man. He was never happy.

I attended births the way my mother did, without medicines or injections, without poking fingers into women. I just used herbs. I never had any problems, except once when a baby was sitting. The woman had come to me many times to have the baby's position adjusted. I would move him into the head-down position, but then he would flip back into the sitting position. When the woman went into labor, he was sitting again and he had his arms crossed.

Everything went well in the beginning, but the baby got stuck at the end, with his bottom partly out. I put my hand in and moved his arms up beside his head, but the woman was so exhausted by then she couldn't push, so I stuck a feather down her throat to make her vomit. Then she was able to get him out. He was dark and nearly lifeless; I blew cigarette smoke on his face to revive him.

He's a tall young man now, still living in my neighborhood. He calls me "Grandmother."

I quit attending births several years ago because of my bad shoulders, but I still give belly massages and perform other cures. One woman who was coming to me for massages kept pleading with me to attend the birth of her baby, but I said, "No, no more births." She came here for a massage on her due date, and she pleaded with me again, but still I said no. When I finished the massage, she had a strong contraction and her water broke. The baby came so fast, there was no time to take her to the hospital, so I had to receive the baby. That was my last birth. I didn't want to attend that first birth when I was a girl, and I didn't want to attend the last one, but they made me do it!

When I told Sandra about my desire to see a belly massage, she said I should come back again, but earlier in the day, and I said I would. Isabel seemed to have warmed to me during the course of our visit. As we said goodbye she squeezed my hand with fingers that were twisted and knobby but surprisingly strong. She told me to be sure to return. Sandra shouted to her that I'd already said I would.

Saved by a Baby Chicken: Bricia Jimenez Hernandez

Jim stayed on the beach while Jenna, Patti, and I boarded a bus a few days later for the one-hour trip to Petatlán, a small town known for its gold market. We shopped for a while among the many stalls selling jewelry, and we bought a few small items; then we found a restaurant where we could escape the heat and drink sodas. The owner of the restaurant, attracted by the young gringa beauty I had with me, made the usual inquiries about where we were from and how we liked Mexico, and I mentioned my interest in midwifery. He said there were no longer any midwives in Petatlán, but a woman sitting at a nearby table interrupted to tell us that she knew of one. Soon we were in a taxi on our way to visit Bricia in a residential area of unpaved streets on the outskirts of town.

Bricia was slender and short, barely reaching my shoulder, barefoot and wearing a thin cotton dress. She was seventy-two years old, she said, but she looked younger, with bright intelligent eyes and jet black hair gathered up at her nape. Her hands and arms were in constant motion, making broad graceful gestures as she talked. She didn't seem to question at all that three gringas should happen along who wanted to hear about her life.

Bricia.

She said she'd been a widow for nineteen years. When I asked about her husband—Had he been a good man? Had he treated her well?—she made a side-to-side tilting motion with her hand, a gesture that means "so-so" in Mexico, and laughed.

I had twelve babies, all with a midwife except for the last one. I managed that birth alone, because the midwife was drunk. Three of my babies died as infants, so that left me nine children: five boys and four girls. I worked hard during pregnancy, cutting wood and loading it onto a donkey, carrying water and washing clothes. I had fast births.

One day I heard my cousin was having a difficult labor, so I went to help her. The baby was born dead, but I learned from the experience. A few months later, when a neighbor asked me to help her in labor, I said I would. That birth turned out well, so other women started coming to me.

I didn't go to school, and I never had any training as a midwife. I just knew what I'd learned by having my own babies. I pray to the Virgin of Montserrat for guidance, and she always helps me. [Other midwives also mentioned the Virgin of Montserrat, who is, they said, "the protector of childbirth."]

I get nine hundred pesos for a birth now, but I used to get very little, maybe just some food or fifty or sixty pesos. Once I was given two baby pigs as payment for a birth. I raised the pigs and sold them, earning enough money to build a house!

There used to be lots of midwives in Petatlán, and we were all busy, but most of them are gone and there's not much business for those of us who remain. I only attend a few births a year now.

I have a neighbor, Alicia, who's also a midwife, but she doesn't speak to me. A woman asked for my help once—she thought her daughter, who was in labor, was going to die—so I went to see what I could do. When I got to the house, I saw that Alicia was already there. I adjusted the position of the baby and helped the woman have a nice, routine birth. That was about fifteen years ago, and Alicia hasn't spoken to me since.

I asked if there had been any particularly challenging births, and she said no, they had all been *bueno*, but then, when I prompted her, she remembered one. The baby had been cross-wise and the cord had been sticking out of the woman's vagina. Bricia said she shook the woman upside down until the cord disappeared back inside and then she massaged the woman's belly to reposition the baby. The birth went well after that, and the baby was fine, but the woman bled a lot. To control the bleeding, Bricia used *bolillos* (boat-shaped bread rolls) cut in half and soaked in alcohol. She put these on the woman's lower belly and on the inside of her elbows to stop the bleeding.

I asked if she'd attended any births of babies born sitting or standing, and she said yes, there had been one baby born standing. She added,

"Thank God both feet came out together; I couldn't have done it if there had been only one foot. The baby was born *privado*, but I was able to revive him. He's ten years old now. I see him occasionally, and he calls me 'Grandmother.'"

"How did you revive him?" I asked.

She explained that she'd put a baby chicken next to the lifeless newborn. The chicken pecked at the baby's bottom, and somehow that revived the baby. He started to cry. "The chicken died, and the baby lived."

"How did you ever think of using a baby chicken?" I asked, wondering if it was a common practice.

"I don't know. It just came to me. The Virgin of Montserrat must have been guiding me."

It was stifling hot in the old bus that took us back to Zihuatanejo, and the windows couldn't be opened more than a crack. The other passengers, even the babies and children, were unusually still. Images from Bricia's story filled my mind. I imagined a pregnant woman being held upside-down, hanging like a trapeze artist with her knees bent over the midwife's shoulders. But it couldn't really have been like that. I wondered how you do get a pregnant woman upside down.

And I pictured alcohol-soaked *bolillos* being held against a woman's flesh. I remembered something I'd heard in a first aid course I took when I was a Girl Scout, something about "cooling the blood" to stop bleeding. Was that what the alcohol was supposed to have done? How would Bricia have known to do that?

The strongest image was that of a young chicken pecking at a baby's bottom, *drawing death* from the baby—that's how it had seemed to me—but maybe it was just startling the baby to make him cry—as doctors used to do when they slapped a baby's bottom.

Jenna sat next to me on the bus, and we talked about the visit. I found myself wanting to defend Bricia's ways—I didn't want Jenna to scorn Bricia for her methods or me for seeming to accept them—but I was afraid my explanation would end up simply cataloging which of Bricia's techniques did and which did not make sense according to the modern medical model.

What seemed important to me was that we'd been granted a glimpse of Bricia's world, a world where the term "natural birth" didn't exist because there was no other kind of birth, where the connection between cause and effect didn't have to be explained by science, where a chicken could save a baby, and where faith and instinct, supplemented by guidance from the Virgin of Montserrat, reigned.

I asked Jenna what she thought about what Bricia had told us.

"Well," she said, "it makes me think that issues of life and health aren't as simple as we think they are."

So, I concluded, *real Mexico* could be allowed to speak for itself.

Busier than Ever: Lorenza Torres Hernandez

Jim and I were in our favorite little thatched-roof restaurant on the beach, eating chips and guacamole, drinking beer. Patti and Jenna had returned to their lives in California.

"I still haven't seen a belly massage," I said.

Jim laughed. "I know what you're itching to do," he said. "Go ahead."

And so we fell into a routine. I disappeared for a few hours each afternoon while he joined other senior gringos under the shade of a *palapa* on the beach. I went first to the town of Palos Blancos, near Petatlán, where I found Lorenza, another midwife I'd heard about from the popcorn lady.

Lorenza, who was taller than other midwives I'd met, almost as tall as I am (5'6"), would have been beautiful as a young woman, I thought; she would have looked like a young Elizabeth Taylor—with the same coloring, the same fine features, the same arched eyebrows, and the same poise. She was lovely still, at the age of sixty-four, and seemed very motherly, or grandmotherly, but I could imagine her being stern when sternness was

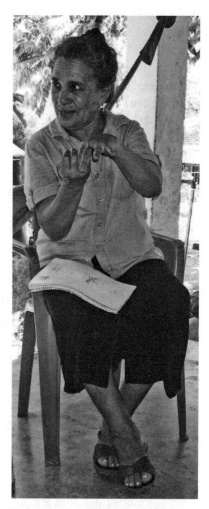

Lorenza using her hands to illustrate a possible complication in the passage of a baby through the pelvis.

called for. She said she hadn't been able to go to school as a child but had attended a school for adults after her children were grown and had completed both her primary and secondary school education. She seemed to relish the opportunity to "talk shop" on all topics related to childbirth.

Her methods were mostly traditional, but she used modern practices when they suited her. She said she gave IV fluids to all laboring women "because it gives them confidence they're getting good care," and she used Pitocin, but she also used herbs, for example lemon leaf or chamomile, to help women relax and a tea made from the leaf of the walnut tree to prevent hemorrhage. She'd rocked women in the rebozo in the past, but had stopped after being told in a *curso* twenty years ago that it was a bad practice. She gave the usual baths, with water steeped in herbs, to both mother and baby after the birth.

Her husband had added a room to their house for her work. She laughed as she remembered, "I used to give women my own bed; I'd have to shoo my husband outside to sleep in a hammock when a woman arrived at night."

She showed me her birthing room, which was made of rustic brick like the rest of the house, with no plaster and no paint. Four narrow beds, each covered with a brightly colored blanket, filled the room, and IV bottles hung from the rafters like old party decorations. A peg by the door held a white lab jacket, probably given to her during one of those *cursos* long ago. A small television set sat on a table in the corner.

We sat in the shade of an awning behind the house while she talked about her life as a midwife. Her husband lay sleeping in a hammock nearby.

> I learned about childbirth by helping my mother-in-law, who was a midwife. One day she became ill while attending a birth, so the woman's family sent for me. I didn't feel qualified to help the woman, but my mother-in-law said, in a stern voice, "I know you can do it," so I had no choice.
>
> I attended a *curso* in Acapulco in 1988. They told us that the old way of sterilizing the cord, by holding a smoldering corn cob against it, was wrong. We were supposed to use iodine instead. But I already knew that; I was already using iodine. We observed an actual birth, and the doctor asked if one of us wanted to check the woman's cervix. The other midwives were too timid, but I said I would. I checked and told the doctor that the woman was fully dilated. He didn't believe me until he checked for himself and saw that it was true. After the baby was born, while the doctor was lecturing us about the delivery of the placenta, I noticed that the woman was still having contrac-

tions. I felt her belly and found there was a second baby yet to be born! The doctor was surprised when I pointed out there was a twin.

If there are complications in a birth, I send the woman to the hospital. There's one near here, in Petatlán, but there's no obstetrician there on weekends, so on Saturdays and Sundays patients have to go an hour and a half away to Zihuatanejo. I'm careful not to wait too long to send them. They beg for more time, but I have to be hardhearted. If I wait too long, it could be too late.

I use massage during labor to help women relax. I treat women with tenderness and love. That's what they really need. If a husband criticizes his wife, I tell him to be kind. I remind him that he's not the one who's suffering. I try to be gentle with the husbands too. It's stressful for them to see their wives in labor.

I have faith in the grand power of God. He always helps me in my work.

Once when I went to attend a birth I found there was something sticking out of the woman's vagina, some skin stretched tight and shiny like nothing I'd ever seen. I thought maybe it was an ear, but I really couldn't tell. When it came out further, I saw it was the testicles. The baby pooped then, an ooze of sticky black goo. He got stuck at his armpits, but I was able to ease him the rest of the way out. His legs remained bent up flat against his chest after the birth, making me wonder if he was ever going to be able to walk. I massaged his hips, pressing on his legs to straighten them, and then weighted them down with a pillow. After a few days of doing that, he was fine.

A nurse in Zihuatanejo has asked me to let her know if I ever meet a woman who wants to give up her baby. Whenever I have a single woman in labor, I remember that nurse and I think, *I should find out if the patient really wants the baby,* but I never ask because I'm afraid it would hurt the woman's feelings.

I teach everyone about birth control and give them their supplies. Men don't want to have vasectomies because they don't want the discomfort and because they're afraid they'll be impotent or their testicles will shrivel up. My husband is against birth control—he thinks that preventing pregnancy is the same as killing babies—but I have to do what I know is right.

A phone rang inside the house, and Lorenza went in to answer. When she came back, she said the call had been from her niece, who was due to have her baby any day. The niece was upset; she'd just been told by a doctor that she'd have to have a Cesarean. The reason, as the niece understood it, was that "her water hadn't broken yet." (This would never be considered a reason for a Cesarean; either the niece hadn't understood correctly or the doctor had manufactured an excuse to operate.) Lorenza had assured the young woman that she could have a normal birth, and they'd made plans for her to have the baby with Lorenza.

Lorenza was reminded of another birth she'd recently attended. The woman had gone to the hospital, in labor with her seventh baby, but when she got there she was told she needed a Cesarean because "her body was all worn out from too many births." She left the hospital and came to Lorenza and had a nice, easy labor.

A young couple arrived by car while we were talking. The husband told Lorenza that his wife, who was seven months pregnant, was having pain in her hip. She couldn't sleep, and it hurt when she walked. A doctor had told her the pain was normal, but the husband's mother had said, "No it isn't normal. You need to go see Doña Lorenza. She'll fix you."

Lorenza led the woman into her birthing room and had her stretch out on one of the beds; then she lifted the woman's blouse, smoothed lotion on the exposed belly, and prepared to give a massage.

A belly massage at last! I watched as Lorenza's hands swept across the round belly with smooth, firm strokes, moving quickly, like a magician's hands, so that I could scarcely tell what I was seeing. She seemed to be centering the "bump" and lifting the baby up away from the pubis. I assumed the baby's head was pressing against a bone or some nerve in the pelvis and that the massage would shift him in a way that would ease the discomfort. If I had been the one giving the massage, I'd have been explaining that to the couple, but Lorenza didn't and no one seemed to expect her to. Lorenza worked quietly and confidently and then had the woman stand up to see how she felt.

After taking a few steps she said the pain was gone. The husband paid Lorenza thirty pesos.

The Belly Massage

As I continued my travels, I saw other midwives adjust babies as Lorenza had done, and I heard countless stories of occasions when midwives had done the same. Twice more I saw women stand up after a massage and say the pain that had brought them to the midwife was gone. I was amazed by how matter-of-fact the midwives were about the process of manipulating fetal position.[1] They would describe a problem, in a pregnancy or a labor, and then say, "so I adjusted the baby" (*acomodé al bebe*)—as casually as I might say I'd moved an infant from the edge of the bed to the center.

The word Lorenza used, the word all the midwives use for their efforts to move babies into an optimal position, was *acomodar*, which, in the context of the belly massage, is normally translated as "to adjust." Other meanings include "to accommodate, to arrange, to settle, to adapt, to fit in or find room for, to make feel at home, to make comfortable." Typically the massage that accommodates and adapts the baby and "finds room for her" aims simply to loosen things up, allowing the baby to settle herself into a position that is more comfortable for her, for the woman, and for an easy labor. The midwife gently lifts the baby up away from the pelvis and eases her from side to side, centering the "bump" as Lorenza had done.

But sometimes the "accommodating" involves deliberate manipulation of a baby from a breech or transverse (cross-wise) position to the head-down position. My world calls this manipulation an "external cephalic version" (ECV). Doctors in the United States used to perform ECV's quite often, until the 1950s, and a few still do—I've seen it done twice in hospitals in Oregon—and many American midwives perform them outside the hospital, but use of the procedure has declined as Cesarean section has become the more popular option for dealing with breech babies. The use of ECV has apparently disappeared completely from the medical scene in Mexico.

Anthropologists who have studied traditional midwifery praise the midwives' ability to *acomodar*. Jordan calls the procedure "a beneficial indigenous technique" (1993, 181), and Goldsmith considers it, along with massage and emotional support, to be "the true contribution of the traditional birth assistant to a tribal mother in a normal birth" (1990, 42). A Medscape article that addresses ECV as performed by modern doctors says that the safety of the procedure "has been well-studied and confirmed" (Ehrenberg-Buchner 2013). Still, modern doctors in Mexico don't practice ECV, and they consider the traditional midwives' use of the technique to be highly dangerous.

But I've never heard criticism of the practice, or even skepticism about it, from members of the general public in Mexico. Everyone I talked to (everyone who had ever heard of midwives' ability to *acomodar* babies) seemed to greatly respect and admire the midwives' skill.

Midwives discount the medical system's criticism of the technique. "They don't know how we do it," they say. "We're *careful*; it's a *baby* in there." And I tend to discount the doctor's criticism of the midwives' practice, too. Giving thousands of belly massages would make them very familiar with the feel of the pregnant belly and with the responses of the baby within. They are experienced, and they are patient. Whereas doctors are normally fitting the procedure into a fixed and relatively brief time slot, traditional midwives always have plenty of time to devote to the process. They said, "It took three hours to get the baby to move," and "I had the woman come back the next day and the next day and the next until finally the baby shifted." I heard more than once, "I adjusted him, but then he moved back into the sitting position, so I adjusted him again."

The Old Scolder: Mariana Oregón Lopez

I had gifts to deliver for Mayra and Erik, a young couple I'd helped in labor in Oregon, so I went to Pantla, a town near Ixtapa, to see Erik's family. They asked if I'd be willing to take gifts back to Erik for them, "just a few things" they promised, and I said I would. They said they'd bring the gifts to me in Zihuatanejo before I left. They told me how to find Erik's great aunt Mariana, a midwife who lived in a village not far away, and I went by bus to see her.

Mariana was just back from a trip to Zihuatanejo where she'd gone to buy the herbs she used in the various soaps, pomades, and medicines she makes. One of the medicines was a *jarabe* (a sweet drink) that cures cancer. It had cured one of her daughters-in-law who'd been diagnosed with stomach cancer. Doctors had told the young woman she had only four months to live, but Mariana's *jarabe* had cured her and now she was working in a hotel in Ixtapa. Mariana named other conditions she treats. Her list included sore throats, various digestive ailments, and a range of "female problems," many of which had to do with the position of the uterus.

We sat in a patio next to the kitchen at the back of the house. Mariana's daughters and daughters-in-law and grandchildren and great grandchildren busied themselves in the open-air kitchen at the other end of the patio, and a baby slept in a hammock beside us. Mariana said she'd been the midwife for the births of all her grandchildren and all her great grandchildren. A two-year-old boy settled into her lap as she told me a story that began like so many stories I'd heard. One day a woman in labor came to the house when Mariana's aunt, who was a midwife, wasn't home, . . .

Mariana had been to *cursos*, starting in the '70s. "They showed us how they attend births in the hospital," she said, "but what good did that do us? We don't have the equipment they have in hospitals." Doctors in those *cursos* had told the midwives they shouldn't rock women in a rebozo, so she'd stopped, or so she said. I asked what she thought about the doctors' ban on rebozos, and she answered, "Well, the same doctors used to tell us that formula was better than breast milk."

I wondered if she really had stopped using the procedure. And had Lorenza? I'd told Lorenza and I told Mariana about the success we'd had using the rebozo in a hospital where I worked back home. Still neither one of them admitted to its use. Maybe they really had abandoned the practice, or maybe decades of being criticized and demeaned for being "backward" had made them cautious about revealing that they still used a practice outlawed by doctors.

Mariana showed me another way of rocking a pregnant belly, one that apparently hadn't been specifically prohibited. She had me lean forward, resting my elbows on the table, and then she stretched a piece of cloth across my lower back and buttocks and started pulling on first one end and then the other, rotating my pelvis in such a way that if I'd had a big pregnant belly, it would have been swinging from side to side like a hammock.

She seemed to have a fairly good relationship with the doctors of the town, who sometimes sent patients to her to have her *acomodar* breech and transverse babies, but she was cynical about doctors in general and enjoyed sharing anecdotes about their incompetence with me. There'd been one case of a breech baby that was wedged too deeply into the pelvis to be *acomodado*. She'd taken the woman to the clinic, but the doctor there had said, "It's not possible to deliver the baby this way. It can't be done." She'd said, "It can too be done. You just catch the baby. I'll do the rest." The doctor had argued, but there were no facilities for surgery in the clinic and there wasn't time to get to Zihuatanejo, so in the end he'd had to do it. Mariana helped the woman push (she provided fundal pressure), and the baby was born fine.

In another case of a breech baby wedged too deeply in the pelvis to be *acomodado*, she took the woman directly to the hospital in Zihuatanejo. She explained the situation to the doctor when they got there, but he didn't believe her. He checked the baby's position himself, using ultrasound, and declared that Mariana was wrong: the baby was head-down.

Mariana repeated for me the rant she'd directed at the doctor, "No it is not, and you'd better hurry up and operate because the baby is suffering." She'd shown him the color of the discharge. She'd stuck it in his face and insisted he smell it. "Can't you see the baby's in trouble?" she demanded.

In the end they'd performed a Cesarean, and they'd found that the baby was breech, as Mariana had said. The doctor asked Mariana afterward, "How did you know the position of the baby? How did you learn that?" But he'd been too busy to listen to her answer.

Chapter Four

She said that in the hospital she was known as *la regañona vieja* (the old scolder).

She mentioned a social worker in the hospital, Sara, who held meetings for midwives. She said I should go to the hospital and meet Sara. I'd seen the hospital she was talking about and was tempted to go, but the memory of being turned away from the hospital in Oaxaca made me reluctant to try.

A young woman, eight months pregnant, arrived at Mariana's house wanting a belly massage. Mariana seemed reluctant to interrupt her chat with me, but when I told her I'd like to watch while she gave the massage she was happy to proceed. Both she and the young woman seemed to think it would be fun to have me observe. They led the way, with me and two of Mariana's daughters trailing behind, to a bedroom inside, and the young woman stretched out on the bed. Mariana exposed the pregnant belly and then took my hand in hers and pressed it into the woman's flesh, moving it over the bumps and bulges of the baby inside. "See . . . here's the knee . . . here's the shoulder . . ." she said. "See?" All three younger women laughed. Apparently it was funny for a gringa to be interested in such things.

"Yes, I see," I said to be polite.

But really what I saw was that it would take a great deal more experience before I would be able to "see."

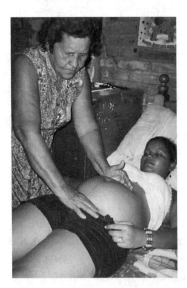

Mariana giving María del Carmen Andrade Rosas a belly massage.

Birth in America: María de Jesús Rosa Ruiz (Chucha Rosa)

Chucha Rosa, another midwife in the same town, also said doctors sent patients to her to have their babies repositioned. She had none of Mariana's cynicism about doctors. One had told her that if she ever had a problem she could call him and he would come to help. She said she used to attend births in women's homes, sometimes walking miles to get there, but one day a doctor told her she shouldn't go to women's homes. He'd said, "Who knows what might happen to you, going out in the middle of the night?" So she started having women come to her house.

Chucha Rosa.

She'd been to the United States once, to stay with her son and his wife when their baby was due. She went with the young couple to the hospital when her daughter-in-law went into labor. "The room was nice," she said, "but they didn't help my daughter-in-law, not the way we do here. [They didn't apply fundal pressure.] I don't see how they can expect women to push their babies out without help. We always tie something around a woman's midriff or have someone wrap their arms around her, and we help her push."

She'd been asked to leave the room when the baby started to crown.

"I'd really wanted to help," she said sadly.

Isabel Gives a Massage

I went again to visit Isabel, the crotchety midwife I'd visited with Jenna, hoping to see her give a belly massage. When no one in need of a belly massage appeared, her granddaughter Sandra went out to the street and found a pregnant neighbor who was willing to participate in a demonstration. Isabel had the young woman lie down on one of the beds and expose her belly; then she slicked her hands with oil and began the massage, pushing into the flesh around the periphery of the pelvis, cupping the baby, centering and lifting him. I had questions, but the shouting that would have been required to ask them seemed intrusive. Isabel was soon done. She said she hadn't needed to make an adjustment. The baby had been well positioned before she started. The young woman said she'd had a belly massage with another midwife just the previous day, so that explained why the baby was already well positioned.

I offered to pay Isabel the few dollars she would have been paid by a regular customer, but she declined. "The baby was fine," she insisted. "I didn't do anything." Her grandson, Sandra's brother, had arrived during the massage, and he insisted that she take the money. "No!" Isabel snapped at him. "The baby was fine!"

An Angel in the Hospital: Sara Castro Mondragón

My trips to and from the towns outside Zihuatanejo took me past the hospital Mariana had talked about. Each time I passed it, I thought of Sara, the social worker who worked there who could, I thought, tell me about the midwives of the region and who might help me observe women in labor in the hospital. Finally, when I had only two days left in Zihuatanejo, I decided I would try to see her.

The hospital waiting room reminded me of shabby bus stations of my childhood, with worn floor coverings, torn plastic upholstery on the chairs, and unused equipment stashed in corners; yet, everyone I talked to seemed diligent and efficient. There were handmade posters promoting breastfeeding on the walls of all the corridors. I later learned that the hospital gave a high priority to breastfeeding and that baby bottles were not allowed in the postpartum unit unless there was a medical need.

I was sent from one friendly clerical person to another—there were no armed guards at all—until finally I found Sara at work in a little alcove that served as her office. The door was open; she offered me a seat facing her over her cluttered desk.

I told her about my visit with Mariana and about my interest in midwives. She said that doctors see midwives as the enemy. They say midwives are backward and stupid, that they do more harm than good. A midwife who brings a patient to the hospital won't be allowed to stay with her. Doctors won't even listen to what the midwife could tell them about the patient's history and about her labor.

Sara said she'd gone to a midwife for belly massages during her own two pregnancies, but both her babies were born by Cesarean anyway, the first because the doctor said the baby was too big and the second because she'd already had a Cesarean.

A stream of patients and their family members and other social workers came into the office while we were talking. Sara would answer a question, help with a form or sign a document, and then turn her attention back to me. One old man told her he'd been waiting all day to see his wife, without success, and he'd had nothing to eat. Sara found a ten-peso coin in her desk drawer and handed it to him, telling him where he could get a snack.

She was interested in my work as a doula. She nodded as I talked about the importance of emotional support during labor. "*Sí sí sí,*" she said. She knew. She said she sometimes went into the obstetrical unit herself to sit with a young girl who was having a hard time. I mentioned my dream of working in a Mexican hospital helping women in labor, and she said she thought she could arrange for me to do it there.

I could scarcely believe her.

She asked how much longer I was going to be in Zihuatanejo, and I told her, "Only two more days."

That wasn't enough time. Did I plan to come again?

I wasn't sure.

She told me to let her know if I planned another trip to Zihuatanejo and to send her copies of any diplomas or certificates I had. She didn't have access to a computer, so I would have to send the information by regular mail.

"I could also teach prenatal classes," I blurted, trying to add more incentive—even though it didn't seem to be needed.

That interested her. She told me to send her an outline of the class I would teach in addition to the certificates and to let her know when I'd be back.

***

I visited Isabel one last time to say goodbye.

She clapped happily when she saw me. We were becoming old friends.

I told her I was leaving but I would be coming back. I hardly dared believe that Sara could arrange for me to work in the hospital, but I had to try.

"Don't forget the *remedio* for my feet," Isabel reminded me. "And a *remedio* for my ears."

I told her again that I doubted I could find the *remedios* she wanted, but I would look for the *aparato* that helps with hearing.

She repeated that she wanted a *remedio*, not an *aparato*.

Erik's parents came with the "few things" I'd promised to take back to Erik, which turned out to be two balls of homemade cheese, each the size and shape of a birthday cake, and two twelve-inch stacks of tortillas.

Two of each?

Yes, Erik had a brother who was also in Oregon. Didn't I know that? No, I didn't. Well, it wouldn't be fair to send cheese and tortillas to Erik and not to his brother, would it?

No, that would not be fair at all.

I told them I wasn't sure I could get food items through customs, but I'd try.

Then Mayra's mother arrived to pick up her gifts and to give me some gifts for Mayra: more cheese, more tortillas, and a package of 18-inch-long slabs of dried meat.

I repeated my disclaimer. I wasn't sure about customs, but I'd try.

The next day, as I went through U.S. customs in Los Angeles, wearing an embroidered blouse and a pink, peeling tan, I must have looked like any other tourist, not like a smuggler of homemade food products at all. I was lucky they didn't have dogs.

When I called Patti from the airport in Los Angeles to tell her we were back in the United States, Jenna answered. I asked her what had been her favorite part of the trip.

She said it was the visits with midwives.

Endnote

1. It seems important to note that, while I admire and respect the midwives' skill at manipulating fetal position, I would never attempt to manipulate a baby in this way myself, and I am not suggesting that any other untrained person do so. See a warning on this subject on the Spinning Babies website under the heading, "A Word on Manual Versions" (Tully n.d.).

Chapter 5

The Hospital in Zihuatanejo

"Oops," I said.

Sara gave me an accusing look.

Six months had passed since my visit to Zihuatanejo with my family. Now I was back, alone this time, ready to start my work in the hospital. I was showing Sara the educational materials I'd brought: videos about childbirth, posters showing the anatomy of pregnancy and birth, a life-size model of a pelvis, and a dilation chart (a plastic model that shows cervical dilation—from one to ten centimeters), all bought with the help of donations from my friends in the Rebozo Club. The dilation chart had slipped from my hand and fallen to the floor.

Sara picked the chart up, looking dismayed as she noticed that a small piece of the corner had chipped away. She found the broken-off piece and began to speculate about the possibility of gluing it back on. I apologized, more than once, and pointed out that the tiny chip wasn't going to affect the usefulness of the chart. She looked offended; she drew the chart to her chest, protecting it from my callousness, demonstrating what it meant to have something new and intact.

She examined the other things I'd brought. The pelvis particularly fascinated her; she rotated it in her hands, studying it as if it were fine art and then looked up to give me a questioning look. I'd already told her I was giving the materials to the hospital, but she looked as if she hardly dared believe it. "It's for you, for the hospital," I said again.

She carefully placed all the materials in a cabinet, which she locked, and then she took me on a tour of the hospital, introducing me to doctors, nurses, and administrators, making me sound rather important and esteemed. I smiled and made small talk, leaving Sara in charge of my professional image.

The next morning she led me to a small classroom on the second floor of the hospital and helped me set up for my first class. Pregnant women started filing into the room, and various administrators joined them, taking seats in the back.

I taught the anatomy of pregnancy, the mechanics of labor, and the factors that contribute to success in labor: relaxation, breathing, movement, and emotional support. I taught exercises the women could do during pregnancy and labor and simple movements they could use when they were confined to the bed. And they would be confined to bed; Sara had told me that. They would labor in bed, and they would labor alone, without the support of family members. I'd expected this; many Mexican women in Oregon had told me about being completely alone when they had a baby in a public hospital in Mexico.

It seemed pointless to elaborate on the value of emotional support if these women weren't going to receive any, but I couldn't hold back my feelings on the subject. When I said that it was wrong to expect women to give birth without emotional support, heads nodded in sober agreement all over the room.

The class was a success. I had lunch with Sara and then taught the same material to another group of pregnant women. And I continued to teach classes on childbirth and breastfeeding nearly every day of my two-week stay. Most were for pregnant women and their families or for pregnant teens, but one was for administrators and one was for social workers. People stopped me in the corridors of the hospital to tell me how much they'd learned.

"Is it really true?" they asked. "Are women in U.S. hospitals allowed to have family members with them when they're in labor?"

"Yes, it's really true. And it's really important."

Tell them, women pleaded. Tell whom? I had no illusions about the extent of my influence.

One day I accompanied Sara when she went to a government office across town to deliver some papers. When she'd finished with her errand, she led me through a room full of clerical workers and then knocked on a closed door at the back. There was someone she wanted me to meet, she explained. We were invited into a small office where two men sat, one behind a desk, the other in a chair facing him. Both men were wearing shirts, ties, shiny cuff links, polished shoes, and an air of elite importance that made me feel like a second-class citizen in my dressed-to-not-impress comfortable clothing (slacks and orthopedic sandals!). Sara introduced the men to me, explaining that they worked for the federal government in an area that dealt with health-care policies, but I didn't catch the name of the agency. I was uneasy—Sara seemed to have an agenda, and the men didn't seem entirely pleased with the interruption—but they were suave and polite and perhaps a little curious. Sara announced, quite abruptly, "Judy says that in her hospital in the United States men are allowed to accompany their wives during labor." And then she turned to me to elaborate.

I was speechless for a moment, totally unprepared for the encounter, but I managed to collect myself and I did my best to introduce the two men to the benefits of giving women support in labor. One of them interrupted to ask bluntly, "Are you a doctor?"

"No," I admitted, feeling I was letting Sara down—I was letting the women of Mexico down—because of what now seemed like a very careless lapse in my education.

"Well, what do you do?" the man asked.

This was hopeless. The men weren't interested in my work or in the idea of allowing women to be accompanied in labor, a change that would add logistical problems to hospital routine without reaping any medical benefit at all (as far as they could see). And they weren't interested in hearing what a gringa who wasn't even a doctor had to say about the subject. In an effort to see if they could relate at all to the idea that giving birth might be more than just a medical event that gets the baby out, I asked about their wives' labors. Both men said their children had been born by Cesarean, and both seemed pleased to have been in a position to make that modern option available to their wives.

I asked about their children and heard about the success the eleven-year-old son of one of them was having on the soccer field. And then we left. Neither Sara nor I ever spoke of the encounter again.

The attitudes and policies that left women alone in labor, without support, were well entrenched in the medical institutions of Mexico, and the obstacles to change were huge. In all my travels and conversations on this subject, I only heard of one public hospital in Mexico that had considered allowing men to be with their wives during labor. They'd tried it once. The man fainted. That was the end of that.

Often during my informal conversations with hospital employees, I talked about the history of childbirth in the United States. I told them that my own mother had been born at home, with my great grandmother serving as midwife. They were surprised to learn that moving birth into the hospital was such a recent event in our history, and they were surprised to learn that we've had to back off from overuse of invasive practices such as the routine use of forceps and strong sedation. They seemed to have assumed that our methods of managing childbirth had evolved in a steady progression from "primitive" to "better" to "better still" to the current "best possible." They thought there was consensus in our country about what constitutes "best possible" care. They didn't know we have factions who differ widely on the appropriate use of various modern interventions. They didn't know there are voices questioning the current global rise in the Cesarean rate.

They didn't know that Mexico has one of the highest Cesarean rates in the world, over 45 percent since 2012 (Suárez et al. 2012), even higher than the U.S. rate, which hovers around 33 percent (Martin 2013), and triple the WHO recommended optimum rate of 15 percent. They seemed to have assumed that the increase in the rate of Cesareans was an inevitable result—and also somehow a benefit—of progress.

In the evening, in my room in an inexpensive hotel in *el centro*, I thought about the changes in birth practices in the two countries during my lifetime. When I was born and when I first visited Mexico in 1964, women in the United States were giving birth without support, heavily drugged, and with routine episiotomies. (An episiotomy is an incision made to enlarge the vaginal opening. It was once used routinely in U.S. hospitals but is now known to carry more risks than possible benefits [Woolley 1995]. Most doctors now use the procedure only in rare emergency cases.) During that same period, women in Mexico were having their babies at home, surrounded by family members and nurtured by caring midwives—the very midwives I'd been meeting. While we who live north of the border were forgetting that birth could be a natural process, Mexico didn't have the resources to make it be anything else. Now it was their turn to forget.

How much technology would they have to have, I wondered, before they would call it too much? Who would fight for reform? The change in the culture of birth in the United States that began in the 1960s and 1970s had been part of a larger movement that championed women's rights in all areas of life. Where would the energy and strength to challenge patriarchal institutions come from in Mexico?

Toco

There were five rooms in the obstetrics department, which was known as "Toco" (short for *Tococirugía*, or "labor-surgery"). The first room, which was for women in labor, contained four narrow beds with curtains between them. (So there was a practical reason why women couldn't have family members with them during labor; there wasn't enough space to allow privacy!) In the middle of the room, facing the beds, stood a desk for the nurse. Behind that was a bed used for triage, where doctors checked to see if a woman had reached the four centimeters of dilation required for admission. Doors in the back of the room led to four smaller rooms: two *salas de expulsión* (delivery rooms) and two *salas de cirugía*, where Cesareans were performed.

A corner of the labor room where people in street clothes could talk to the medical staff was partitioned off by wooden benches lined up end to end. When I wasn't teaching, I sat on one of those benches waiting to help someone in labor. Unfortunately there was a record-breaking slump in the number of births during my visit. (Sara told me I should have come during the full moon; there were always lots of births during the full moon.) Sometimes doctors or other medical personnel joined me on the benches. We sat with our feet aligned according to our status, mine resting on the contaminated side, and theirs, in paper booties, on the sterile side.

There were three female interns also waiting for patients to show up. They were at various stages of the year-long internship that follows the formal study of medicine in Mexico. Each would spend two months in Toco. There were obstetricians on call to supervise the interns and to perform Cesareans, but they weren't much needed while I was there.

I normally avoided the subject of midwives when I was talking to doctors, but one day a hint of my interest slipped out. The doctor I was talking to responded with the curt pronouncement, "It would be better if all midwives were wiped off the face of the earth. Of a hundred of them, maybe one or two have the sensitivity to do some good. The others just do it for money without knowing anything." He then proceeded to tell me a story about a colleague of his, a pediatrician from Acapulco, whose new baby cried all the time. The baby had been given all possible medical tests, but nothing could be found wrong with him. Finally the pediatrician took his son to a midwife, who treated him for *mal de ojo* (evil eye), and he recovered immediately.[1]

I had no idea how I was supposed to reconcile that story with the obstetrician's declaration that all midwives should be banished from the planet.

I did tell a woman from the accounting department, Guadalupe, about my interest in midwives. She said she had a friend who was a midwife, and we made plans to go by bus to visit the friend that weekend. The midwife, Silvina, lived in the countryside north of Ixtapa.

How to Get a Pregnant Woman Upside Down: Silvina Rosas Villegas

When we arrived at Silvina's house, we found her standing on a high platform in her yard, repairing an arbor. She greeted us from above, like a priestess, strong and proud, wearing a flowered cotton dress and sandals; then she climbed down a rustic ladder, rinsed her hands using water from a garden hose, and led us inside.

The house was cool, with tile floors and decorative tiles on the walls. Silvina and I sat in chairs facing each other while Guadalupe sat in a hammock nearby. Silvina was seventy-eight years old, she said. She'd begun her work as a healer when she was just a child.

> I've been massaging bones since I was eight years old. I'd seen my aunt do it, and somehow I trusted that I could do it too. I taught myself, really, and I taught myself to give injections, too.
>
> One day the sister of a friend of mine knocked on my door, out of breath and crying. Her sister was in labor, she explained, and the baby's hand was coming out first. There'd been a midwife with her, but the midwife left when she saw the hand, saying there was nothing she could do. "My sister is going to die," the girl said. "You have to help. Please come. Please hurry."

Silvina.

I went with her, even though I couldn't imagine being able to help. I was only eighteen. I hadn't had any babies of my own yet, and I'd never been present during a birth. All the way there I was trying to think what to do, and then, as we were arriving at her house, it came to me. I had my friend lie down on a blanket. I had her husband hold the end of the blanket where her feet were and her sister hold the other end, and then I had the husband lift his end until my friend was almost upside down. He held her like that while I massaged her belly, pushing the baby back out of the pelvis. The hand disappeared, and they laid her down. I gave her cinnamon tea with chocolate to strengthen the contractions, and then the birth proceeded normally. The baby was born dead, but still people were impressed that I'd been able to save the woman, so other women started coming to me for the births of their babies.

When I got married and became pregnant, I didn't think I needed a midwife, but when I started having contractions my husband and his mother called for one. That midwife didn't know anything. She had me push for two days, yelling at me all the while to push harder, when it obviously wasn't time yet. Finally I got mad and made her leave, and the baby was born two hours later.

I was alone for the rest of my labors. When the contractions began, I'd gather up the scissors, string, diapers, and so on and have them ready, and then I'd do my housework so everything would be clean and neat when the baby was born. When the contractions got really strong, I'd go into the bedroom and lie on the bed, curling up on my side, and push the baby out. I would clean him and then go out and show him to everyone. I never told anyone I was in labor except my husband.

I had fourteen babies. Two of my labors were fast. I remember when I was pregnant with my son Chino, a big contraction woke me up in the middle of the night, and then there was a second contraction right after the first. I woke my husband and told him to get up because the baby was coming. He didn't believe me, but he got up. Chino was born with the third contraction.

The birth of my last baby was almost as fast. My daughter was staying with me to make sure I went to a doctor for the birth. She and her husband thought the birth might be difficult because of my age—I was forty-five years old.

I had my first contraction early in the morning while everyone else was still asleep. Before I got around to telling my daughter I was in labor, someone came to the door to tell us there was a telegram for her, so she went to the telegraph office to get it. The baby was born while she was gone, just three hours after the first contraction. So a telegram saved me from having to have my baby with a doctor.

All my births were beautiful.

The busiest time for me as a midwife was in the 1970s. I lived in Zihuatanejo then; everyone knew me because I gave out free birth control supplies. The government clinic used to give me the supplies to pass along to the people who needed them. I had four beds for my patients and also a delivery table. I was attending twenty to twenty-five births per month sometimes.

Silvina said she'd worked for a government health agency for many years. She was paid almost nothing, but, in her mind, part of the compensation was the special treatment she believed she'd receive if she ever needed medical attention. When one day she did become ill, she was disappointed with the care she was given, so she stopped working for them.

Guadalupe told me as we rode the bus back to Zihuatanejo that "working for" government agencies meant that Silvina and other midwives performed outreach services for the new clinics, receiving only a pittance in compensation. The clinics were in essence "using" the midwives, according to Guadalupe. Women didn't trust doctors. The clinics needed an association with the midwives to help them attract patients.

A Chance, Almost, to Help a Woman in Labor

Finally one day when I went to Toco I found there was a woman in labor there. The nurse told me I'd have to get a doctor's permission to sit with the woman, so I sat down on one of the benches to wait. Soon an intern arrived and granted the necessary permission, but I couldn't cross the benches wearing street clothes; I would have to get a pair of scrubs.

Okay. Where do I get scrubs?

I would have to go to the hospital laundry.

Okay. Where's the laundry? The nurse gave me directions that were too complex to follow but got me started in the right direction.

The hospital was a huge maze. I could barely make it from Sara's alcove to Toco without getting lost; now I had to find the laundry, which was in the most distant corner of the building. It might have seemed hopeless, but at every intersection of corridors I found someone who was pleased to point the way. I went past administration offices and labs and through storage areas. Finally I entered an empty corridor filled with the smell of bleach and detergent.

A pleasant young woman interrupted her work to tell me she couldn't give me scrubs without a request signed by a department head.

Of course. So I went back to Toco. Another nurse, one who'd always been friendly, had taken over for the first one. She slipped me a pair of scrubs that had apparently been there all along!

By the time I'd finally "suited up" with scrubs, paper booties, a hair cover and a mask, it had been decided that the woman, Ana, needed to have a Cesarean because of lack of progress.

No, wait! I didn't have a chance. Ana didn't have a chance.

I sat with Ana, supporting her through contractions, while we waited for the obstetrician to arrive. I hoped for a miracle—for sudden dramatic progress that would make the Cesarean unnecessary—but to effect that kind of change would have required movement, and there would be no support for that. The interns sat across the room, chatting and glancing at me occasionally, making sure, or so I imagined, that I didn't do anything subversive like encouraging Ana to get out of bed. She needed help dealing with contractions and with her disappointment and fear; I focused my attention on that.

The obstetrician arrived. Ana's mother and husband came in and signed two forms, one in which they agreed to the surgery and another in which they promised to donate blood to the hospital. Sara had told me that when a woman has a Cesarean her family members are required to donate blood as part of their payment. The mother and husband would be returning the next day to make their donation; Ana and the baby would not be allowed to leave the hospital until they did.

Another patient arrived. I watched from Ana's bedside as the interns examined the second patient across the room. She looked at me, distress in her eyes. I smiled encouragingly.

Help, her eyes said.

I hoped I'd get a chance to.

She was sent home—not sufficiently dilated—before Ana was wheeled off to the *Sala de Cirugía* (operating room).

A Birth in the Night

The next day was Saturday, so there would be no classes. I went to Toco to see if the second patient had returned, but she hadn't. I found Ana happily nursing her baby and deeply grateful for my help. Her gratitude embarrassed me; I'd wanted to do so much and had done so little.

There were no new labor patients, and I couldn't bear the idea of spending another day sitting on those benches making small talk with the

Lorenza giving a newborn an herbal remedy to prevent colic.

staff, so I went to visit Lorenza, a midwife I'd met on my previous trip, in her village an hour and a half away.

I found her sitting on a bed in her birthing room holding a newborn baby, spooning some kind of herbal concoction into his mouth, "to prevent colic," she said. The new mother was lying on a bed, resting. She looked familiar to me, and the quizzical look she gave me made me think I looked familiar to her too. Then we both remembered. She was the woman I'd seen in the hospital the previous day, the one who'd been sent home because she wasn't sufficiently dilated. We remembered each other from that moment of eye contact.

She was from a nearby village, she said. She explained that by the time she and her family had reached home the previous day, they'd been frantic. They couldn't imagine waiting for labor to become even stronger and then having to make the trip to Zihuatanejo again. So her mother-in-law brought her to Lorenza.

The birth had gone well. The baby was born four hours after they got to Lorenza's house. The young woman was particularly pleased that her husband had been with her for the birth.

A Reluctant Midwife: Alvina Salas Valdorinas

Lorenza told me about a midwife who lived nearby, a woman named Alvina, and I went to see her. It was the heat of the day, siesta time, so I was alone on the streets as I walked to her house. Dogs, resting in the shade of adobe walls, were too listless to even raise their heads as I passed by.

Alvina was seventy-seven years old and married, but with no children. "I never liked being a midwife," she said. "My mother-in-law was the only midwife in our *rancho*, and there were no doctors, so after she died there was no one else to help women; I had to do it."

Alvina knew I'd been talking to Lorenza, so all her remarks about her own former practice (she no longer attended births) were in reference to how Lorenza did things. Alvina didn't give injections. (Lorenza did.) Alvina used to burn the cut end of the cord. (Lorenza used iodine.) Alvina didn't bathe women. (All other midwives did.) Alvina shrugged and scowled to show what a big nuisance she thought *that* would be.

Alvina.

She said she'd never lost a baby. There had been a few babies born dead, but they'd been dead before labor began.

I asked why babies die in the womb.

"It can be because of an eclipse," she explained. "Or maybe something hits the woman's belly." One of her sisters-in-law had lost a baby when a bucket she was carrying on her head fell, striking her belly.

Because of an eclipse . . . I'd heard of the belief, common in many traditional cultures, that an eclipse can jeopardize the well-being of an unborn child. Once, back home, when a lunar eclipse was predicted, a Mexican woman came to my childbirth class wearing a red blouse with safety pins fastened across it above her belly. She said the color red and the pins would protect her baby from the eclipse. She was the oldest woman in the class. The younger women asked her about her precautions and then looked to me to see what I thought.

I said that "we" (Americans of the sort one finds working in hospitals) don't believe that eclipses damage unborn babies but I knew it was a common belief in Mexico. I suggested that if anyone was worried, it certainly wouldn't hurt to wear safety pins and the color red for a few days.

I mentioned red blouses and safety pins to Alvina, hoping to impress her with my knowledge of eclipse-related precautions. She harrumphed and sputtered and said she'd never heard such ideas. She scowled, dismissing me and my strange American ways.

Un Aparato for Isabel

"*¡Qué milagro!*" (What a miracle!) Isabel said when she saw me at the door. She was speechless with surprise and pleasure.

Isabel wearing her new hearing aid.

She was alone. There were no grandchildren to help me explain the workings of the hearing aid I'd brought. It was a simple device that would hang from a cord around her neck, with little buds to be placed in her ears and controls she could theoretically manage herself. It used batteries she could find in Zihuatanejo, but I'd brought some spares to get her started. She looked at the strange device and then at me, an expression on her face that suggested I might be preparing to install a pacemaker in her chest. I managed to get the earbuds in place, in spite of her doubts, and it seemed clear to me that she could hear better once it was all set up, but she didn't seem convinced. Still, she left the device on.

I'd brought some lotion too.

"Is this the medicine that will cure my scars?" she asked.

"Well, it's not exactly scar-curing medicine, but it's good for your skin. It's supposed to make it softer."

"Good!" she replied.

She was still wearing the hearing aid and clutching the bottle of lotion as I said goodbye. *Would she give the hearing aid a chance?* I wondered. Would her family encourage her and help her get used to it? Probably not. Her grandson might need the batteries for his own electronic gadgets. I imagined the hearing aid being placed next to candles and figurines on a shelf somewhere, a memento of the visit from the strange gringa who liked to talk about birth.

Birth on a Rock: Mariana Gomez Sanchez

The next day, in the village of Coacoyul, south of Zihuatanejo, I met another very old, very deaf midwife and wished I had another hearing aid to dispense. Mariana was so deaf it was almost impossible to get her to elaborate when I had questions.

I shouted, "How many births have you attended?"

"Ay señora, muchos, muchos."

She'd had twelve children of her own, she said. Once she went into labor while she was at a river washing clothes. She sat down on a rock, hoping there would be a break in the contractions so she could make her way home, but there was no break. The baby was born right there on the rock.

"How did you get home?" I asked.

Someone had gone to tell her family, and they had come to get her. They carried her home in a hammock, and then she cut the cord herself.

Mariana.

Loved and Missed: María de Jesús Vandolinos León (Doña Chucha)

The hotel owner's sister told me about another midwife, one who lived right in Zihuatanejo, not far from *el centro*: Doña Chucha. I found Doña Chucha sitting in a wheelchair in a shaded veranda next to her daughter's large, modern home. She was eighty-four years old, shrunken and stooped, wearing a thin cotton nightgown, frail, weak, and almost as deaf as Mariana, but still dignified and with a sharp mind. She worked hard to understand my questions and answered thoughtfully.

Doña Chucha.

She said that her father had blamed the midwife when his first baby died at birth, so he took special care in selecting a midwife for the birth of his second baby. The one he found was a *tío*. Doña Chucha's father watched how the *tío* managed the birth, and then he attended all the rest of his wife's births himself. After her father died, when Doña Chucha was ten, her mother started attending births. Neither parent had gone to any *cursos*.

She told me about births of twins, explaining that the thing to do when there are twins is to adjust the second baby's position right away, as soon as the first baby is out. "That always works," she said. And she told me about her most harrowing experience.

The woman's husband was desperate for help—it sounded like the woman was dying—but he couldn't explain what the problem was. I went with him, even though I suspected the woman would be dead before we got there. It was a long, hard trip, on horseback at night, with only a small lantern to light the way. I kept thinking, "What can I do for this woman? This is useless."

When I got there I saw that the woman's uterus had come out with the baby. [The medical world calls this condition "prolapsed uterus."] I washed it and pushed it back into position. After that I massaged her belly to get everything back in order. I heard later that she'd recovered completely.

"There were no doctors," she said. "I had to do everything." She'd removed bullets, once from a man's head, once from a three-year-old girl's shoulder. "The little girl's wound was really bad; there was a lot of pus. My daughter fainted when she saw it." And she had treated abscesses when breastfeeding women got infections from clogged ducts, cutting them open and draining them. She used regular sewing thread to stitch the wounds and strips of fabric to cover them.

Doña Chucha seemed to love telling her stories, and she chuckled when she saw how they affected me, but she soon became tired and I prepared to leave. Her daughter, who had stayed in the house but must have heard all the shouting (my half of the conversation), came out when she heard me saying goodbye. She wanted me to know that people of the village still came to visit Doña Chucha and still cried when they talked about how much they loved her and how much they missed her.

Cesarean or Vaginal?

I taught an early class the next morning and then stopped by Toco to see if there were any labors in progress. There were none. One of the interns said there'd been a vaginal birth during the night. The baby had come fast.

I asked the three interns what kind of births they hoped to have when the time came for them to have their own babies. Would they want Cesareans or vaginal births? Two of them said they would want Cesareans. They grimaced, showing distaste for the struggle, pain, and messiness of the kind of birth they'd seen the previous night.

The third one said she would like to try for a vaginal birth. I presumed she meant she'd hope for a vaginal birth within the system as it exists, not that she would fight for change to the policies that are making

Cesarean sections ever more routine in Mexico today. Still . . . I imagined she would offer support to women who, like her, "would like to try."

Mother and Daughter: Antonia Alonso Vargas (Tonia) and Norma Hilda Jaime Alonso

With no more classes to teach that day and little hope that there would be a labor in Toco, I decided to visit another midwife I'd heard about from the hotel owner's sister. The midwife, Tonia, lived high on one of the hills that surround Zihuatanejo. A taxi driver took me as close as he could to her house, but the final stretch was too steep. He left me at the base of a block-long stairway of stone steps. The houses on either side of the stairs were simple structures made of the usual rustic brick and rusted metal, jammed together almost on top of each other, humble but with a stunning view of the city and the bay. I'd been hearing that a cruise ship was expected. The shopkeepers in town were eagerly awaiting the business it would bring. Now, looking out over the bay, I saw that it had arrived; it was so big it made the bay look small.

Tonia with two of her grandchildren.

To get away from the noise of her busy household, which at the moment included two of her teenaged children and several grandchildren, Tonia led me to the small room where she saw patients. Her daughter Norma, who helped her in her work, joined us.

Tonia said she'd learned to be a midwife from her two grandmothers and an aunt. She used to be busy, but business had declined in recent years. Still, she and Norma had attended four births the previous week. She said, "Women still come to me because they're afraid if they have their babies in the hospital they'll have to have Cesareans."

Many of their clients were from the area around Acapulco. Norma said that women from that area weren't used to going to doctors. "They have different customs than we have. They don't like it when we make them take a shower the day after the birth; they think they should wait a

Chapter Five

Norma with two of Tonia's grandchildren.

week. And they expect to be given herbs during labor. We don't do that."

Norma said she'd always wanted to be a midwife like her mother.

When I was a little girl, I used to pretend I was a midwife. I'd catch a chicken and stick my finger into its birth canal. If I could reach the egg easily, I would say to the chicken, "Well, Mrs. Chicken, your baby is going to be born soon," but if the egg was way back inside the chicken, I would say, "Your baby is going to be born tomorrow."

Norma seemed to see herself more as an assistant to her mother than as a midwife herself, but she'd attended a few births on her own when her mother wasn't available. Her stories were like others I'd heard: "I told the woman I couldn't, but she begged me . . ." and "My mother had *promised* to attend the birth, so when she wasn't available I had to do it."

Norma wondered about her future. Would there be any business at all for midwives in years to come? I told her I thought she might be busier than ever when the older midwives were gone.

The Birth of Saira's Baby

After teaching a class the next morning and finding there were still no patients in Toco, I headed back to the hotel. I wasn't sure what to do with the rest of the day. I didn't have the energy for my usual quest.

As I walked past the reception area in the hotel, I saw the desk clerk on the phone, looking confused. She said to me, "Maybe this call is for you. Did you give this number to anyone?"

Yes. I'd given it to Tonia, the midwife who lived on a hill overlooking the bay. The desk clerk handed me the receiver.

Tonia was calling from her granddaughter's cell phone to tell me she had a labor in progress. Would I like to join them?

Suddenly I wasn't so tired after all.

The patient, Saira, was having her first baby. She'd come to Tonia's house the previous evening in early labor, and she and her husband had spent the night in Tonia's little birthing room. When I arrived, after being introduced, I asked Tonia how far along she thought Saira was, and she said she was just about to perform *el tacto*. She suggested that maybe I should be the one to do it. I wanted to—I'd always been curious to know how it felt—but I said no: *No puedo* (I can't) and *no me dejan* (they don't let me). Vaginal checks are not within a doula's scope of practice. So Tonia performed the check (without a glove) and then spread her fingers about six centimeters apart to show me how dilated the cervix was. Or was it that the baby's head was six centimeters back from the opening of the vagina? Either way, Saira was doing well!

Once she knew that I couldn't perform vaginal checks, it became important to Tonia that I do so. She seemed to think the *real* reason I'd never done it was that I was afraid; she was sure I just needed a little encouragement.

I rationalized that the "scope of practice" rule might not apply, since I hadn't identified myself as a doula (no one there had ever heard of a doula), but I still felt it would be wrong to subject Saira to an unneeded vaginal check, a procedure my neighbor Leonora's aunt had traveled from Oregon to Oaxaca to avoid. I declined again, but then Saira joined in the coaxing, apparently eager to play a role in the furthering of my education. So it seemed it would be rude *not* to. I allowed myself to be persuaded.

Apparently Tonia knew enough about modern ways to assume I would want a glove. Norma found one for me: a rubber glove like the ones I use in the kitchen at home, not new but apparently clean. I donned it, Tonia put a few drops of oil on it, and I proceeded with my assignment, introducing just one finger only until it touched the baby's head. I didn't perform what would be called a "vaginal check"—I didn't touch the cervix—but I felt the hard mass that was descending through the softness of the birth canal. Amazing. And enough. I ended my invasion. Excuse me, Saira. Forgive me, enforcers of doula ethics.

It was time for Saira to bathe, and a pot of water that had been heating over a wood fire in front of the house was deemed ready. One of Tonia's grandsons carried the steaming water in a bucket to a barrel behind a plastic curtain in the courtyard. It was to be what my family used to call a "splash bath." Norma gave Saira clothes—an old T-shirt and a full cotton skirt—to put on after the bath and a cup to use for dipping. Tonia and Norma changed clothes too. They put on shorts and T-shirts that were apparently their "uniforms" for attending births.

After the bath, Saira walked for a while longer, but then she suddenly stopped, frozen, her eyes huge and round. She didn't say a word, but her expression said something like *caramba*, or maybe something even stron-

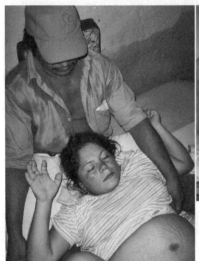
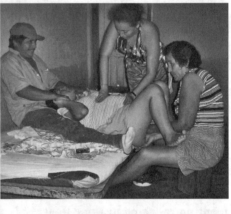
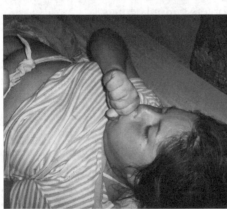
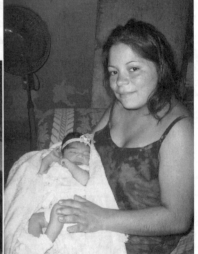

ger, and Tonia suggested she start pushing. She sat in the bed, leaning against the wall, and Norma tied a rag around her midriff, above her belly (for her to "push against"). No one explained how to push—they didn't coach her at all—but Saira knew what to do, or her body did. When her efforts started to look serious, Tonia performed *el tacto* and told Saira she should keep pushing. She had Saira's husband sit cross-wise on the small bed, leaning against the wall, and positioned Saira between his legs, leaning back against him. Tonia sat on a stool in front of them with Saira's feet resting on her knees.

Norma bent over Saira, applying pressure on her belly to help her push (applying fundal pressure). How forcefully did Norma push? Would a critic have seen her efforts as being potentially harmful? I couldn't say. Norma seemed confident and experienced and careful in the placement of her hands, which appeared to be cupping the baby's bottom through the layers of flesh and muscle. Saira didn't appear to mind having help, but it would have been hard to tell. She was at an intense stage of labor; she was working hard and straining.

Saira's husband never stopped grinning.

At one point, when Saira looked distressed, Norma offered to give her a shot of Pitocin to speed things up. After two more contractions, Saira asked for the shot and Norma gave it. The baby was born a few contractions later. It was a girl. Tonia had Saira blow into her fist (to put a little pressure on her diaphragm) and the placenta soon came sliding out.

Saira's husband was sent to town to get supplies. Tonia told him to get diapers, a *faja* (a flannel wrap to compress the baby's belly button), two shirts for the baby, pain pills for Saira, and tacos and soft drinks for Saira and himself. He barely got to see the baby before setting out, still beaming, on his errands. Norma massaged Saira's uterus until it was firm. (Doctors also do this; the purpose is to be sure the uterus has contracted so there won't be excessive bleeding.)

Saira's husband returned with all the needed supplies except the pain medicine. He hadn't been able to find the brand Tonia had asked for—or he hadn't been able to afford it. Saira was in pain; she wanted the medicine. So I went to town myself, found a *farmacia*, and bought it. I also got a fluffy pink blanket and a pretty headband for the baby.

Back at Tonia's house, I found Saira calmly feeding her baby, examining tiny fingers and toes, and stroking the little girl's cheek. I presented my gifts and then I joined Tonia's family for a festive meal prepared by Tonia's husband.

Last Class and Goodbye

I returned to the hotel. I packed. I slept. The next morning I returned to the hospital, stashed my suitcase behind Sara's desk, and prepared to teach my last class. I would be talking about "How to Support Women in Labor"—to nurses who were training to work in obstetrics! My dream of encouraging better support for laboring women in a Mexican hospital was being realized in a way I hadn't imagined.

I told the nurses what my teacher Penny Simkin told the class when I was training to become a doula, what Penny has told the world: that women are changed by their birthing experiences, that they remember those experiences for a lifetime, and that how we give birth matters—to women, to babies, and to families. I talked about the importance of emotional support during labor and the importance of movement. When I said that in my opinion lack of emotional support and lack of movement during labor were two of the main reasons why Mexico has such a high Cesarean rate, the nurses looked at each other and at me. Again there was surprise. *Is our Cesarean rate high? Is that bad?* They knew they personally had wanted vaginal births, but they hadn't thought about the issue from a broader perspective.

They nodded solemn acceptance when I pointed out that providing support and encouraging movement would be *their* job when they began working with women in labor.

When the class was over, I hugged my angel Sara and then dragged my suitcase to the street and hailed a taxi for the airport.

Three months later I asked a neighbor who was going to be vacationing in Zihuatanejo to deliver a few things for me. I sent Tonia two sets of photos of the birth, one for her and one for Saira, and I sent the nurse—the one who gave me a set of scrubs when I needed them—a video we'd talked about that shows the stages of labor.

I sent Sara a brand new dilation chart to replace the one I'd dropped and chipped.

Endnote

1. "Evil eye" is a folk illness that results when someone looks at the victim with envy or malevolence. The concept was brought to Mexico from Spain.

Chapter 6
Chiapas and Tabasco

Quadruplets: Emiliana Ruiz Mazariegos

*E*miliana was a bosomy, matronly woman wearing a purple dress and pink apron. Her hair, white with streaks of faded dye, was cut in a pageboy. I watched as she changed the dressing on a newborn's umbilical cord and then as she examined a woman who had what sounded like a urinary tract infection. She massaged the woman's belly and told her to buy a medicine I'd never heard of, which I hoped was an antibiotic.

When the patients were gone, we sat on a couch, facing her altar, beneath a wall of framed pictures and certificates from old *cursos*.

Emiliana.

> My mother died when I was nine years old. As the oldest child in the family, I took over for her, caring for my brothers and sisters, cleaning the house, shopping for food, and cooking. I spent time with a neighbor, a midwife who'd been letting me help her since I was a little girl, but she died too, a few years later.
>
> When I was fourteen, one of my cousins told me he was worried because his wife was pregnant but he didn't have money to pay for a midwife. I told him I could help her.
>
> He said, "What do you mean? What can you do?"
>
> I said, "Didn't you know? I used to help the midwife."

So I was with my cousin's wife for the birth of her baby. I did everything. I even injected Pitocin when the baby was crowning. I didn't have string, so I used a piece of cloth to tie the cord. My cousin bathed the baby while I bathed his wife, and then I hurried home. My father had been at work while I was gone. I never told him about attending that birth.

A friend of my cousin's wife asked me to help her in labor too, and I did, and then a few days later another woman needed my help. That family sent me a big basket of food after the birth. When my father asked where the food came from, I just made some excuse. I didn't tell him what I was doing, but of course it wasn't long before he found out. One day he overheard when someone came to the door asking for my help.

"No," he said, "you can't go."

I told him I had to, because there was no one else to help the poor woman. My father was so surprised he didn't know what to say. I left and helped the woman.

When I came home after the birth, my father said, "You mustn't get involved in these things. It's dangerous. If something goes wrong, people will blame you."

But he couldn't stop me. He couldn't control what I did when he was out working. He began to see that people depended on me. Women would be desperate for help. How could I say no? How could he make me say no?

People called me *la partera chica* [the little midwife].

I used to attend ten or twelve births a month when I was really busy, but now I only attend one or two a month.

I went to a *curso* when the local clinic first started offering them, but I had a lot of experience by then and I'd learned all I needed to know from the midwife who taught me when I was a child. There was an exam at the end of the *curso*. Those of us who couldn't read had to take it orally, standing in front of a group of officials. I was really nervous, so I drank some *posh* [an alcoholic drink made from sugar cane and maize] to give me courage. When they announced that I'd passed, I was so happy I sang a song. They gave us each a case full of supplies.

Eighteen years ago I had a patient who was so big I was sure she was going to have twins. After the first baby was born, I checked her belly and found that there was another baby, just as I'd expected. After that one came out, the woman complained that she was still having pains, so I started to massage her belly, but then I saw that a third baby was crowning. And then there was one more after that! It was very exciting. The placenta was so big that when I first saw it I thought it was a fifth baby. I said to the father, "Look, here comes another one," and he fainted.

I sent for more midwives until we had one midwife for each baby. All the babies were born healthy. The first one was normal sized. The second one weighed 2.3 kilos [about 5 pounds], the third one weighed 2 kilos [4.4 pounds], and the last one, the only girl, weighed one kilo [2.2 pounds]. The girl was tiny but well formed and she was breathing well.

The woman had three-year-old twins already, and now she had four more babies. I told her next time she'd probably have seven. She had her tubes tied. News of the birth of quadruplets was in the newspapers. The governor of Chiapas paid my fee and gave the family some money to help with the expense of raising four babies.

I asked Emiliana to show me the supplies she'd been given when she passed that first exam. She found the black case behind a pile of boxes in the bedroom. We sat together and admired the contents, which included a pinard horn, clamps, and some kind of metal beaker, all still sealed in plastic wrappers, never opened, never used. When we were done, she put everything carefully back into the case—a souvenir of her triumph.

El Congreso

I was in San Cristóbal de las Casas, in the state of Chiapas, for a *congreso* being held by Luna Maya, a birth center that offers midwifery services and also various outreach programs for women in their childbearing years and for local midwives. I'd arrived a few days early to give myself time to explore the town and look for midwives.

The morning of the first day of the *congreso* was cold and crisp, but I dressed lightly, knowing it would soon be hot. I set out for the *congreso* on foot, intending to buy bottled water somewhere along the way, but all the stores I passed were closed. The sidewalks and streets were oddly empty too. When I finally did find a store that was open, I asked the man working there where everyone was.

"*Es el partido,*" he said.

"*¿Cómo?*"

He pointed to the corner of the shop where a small television was showing a soccer game. It was an important game, he said. A victory would help cinch Mexico's chances of qualifying for the World Cup.

Normal commerce would resume when the game was over.

The name of the *congreso* was *Nacer . . . Renacer . . . Congreso Internacional de Partería y Parto Humanizado* (To Be Born . . . To Be Reborn . . . International Conference of Midwifery and Humanized Birth). It was held in a compound designed for special events, a place popular for weddings, I imagined, with neatly trimmed lawns surrounding a pond and with a room large enough to seat a few hundred people.

Although the movement to "humanize" birth, (to offer woman-centered care, to give emotional support to women in labor and to respect their dignity and autonomy, to empower women to participate in decisions related to the management of their labors, to avoid unnecessary interventions, and to preserve traditional knowledge about birth) is a global one, it isn't a matter of wide concern in Mexico. I doubt that anyone I'd met in Oaxaca and Guerrero—not the doctors, not the general public, not even the midwives—had heard of the term "humanized birth" or of *congresos* like this one. Still, there are strong, passionate women in Mexico, and a few men too, who have taken up the cause, and many of them were present at the *congreso. These,* I thought as I looked at a group of young Mexican women on that first day of the *congreso, are the women who will fight for change in the childbirth scene in Mexico.* I would see, in the days that followed, that there were bright, articulate young women, many of them midwives, with great passion and conviction. And they were better prepared in some ways than the women of my youth who fought for changes in the birthing culture of my country; they had strong, wise older midwives supporting them, and they had social networking tools that helped them connect with each other and with like-minded women in other countries.

There were about two or three hundred attendees at the *congreso*, about half from Mexico and the rest from all over the world: from Europe, Central and South America, Canada, and the United States. There were modern midwives, doctors, childbirth educators, the anthropologist, Robbie Davis-Floyd, and at least one other doula. An American woman who was writing a historical novel set in the ancient Mayan world was there to learn about traditional Mayan practices relating to birth.

Twenty midwives had come by bus from Morelos, traveling nonstop, sleeping in the bus along the way. Another group came in a van from Tulum, near Cancún, and yet another from Guatemala. Local indigenous midwives came from the *comunidades* (small settlements, sometimes just a cluster of a few homes) around San Cristóbal. There were students from CASA, a private midwifery school in Morelos that teaches both traditional and modern medical knowledge. It's a small school, graduating only a handful of students each year, but it has an excellent reputation, and it was at that time the only midwifery school in Mexico that had received government recognition.

Christina Alonso, the founder of Luna Maya, set a reverent tone in her opening remarks.

> This encounter brings together many people whom I admire for their courage and their capacity to love—people who are changing the world, day by day: artists, warriors, alchemists, and above all, people of wisdom who believe deeply in the ability to be born, that to be born is to come home and that this arrival deserves all the respect and love that can be given. We [midwives] need support; we need to tell our stories; we need to be heard and valued. This is the space for that. I know that you will . . . feel sheltered by this network of wise women who love each other, value each other, respect each other, and need each other.

The midwives I'd met had been so eager to share their stories. I wished they could have all been there, sharing in the camaraderie with the other traditional midwives and basking in the respect that those of us who came from other countries felt for them.

Why Are There So Many Cesareans in Mexico?

In one of the sessions, Robbie Davis-Floyd, speaking in her precise Spanish, talked about the alarming increase in the Cesarean rate around the world, especially in Latin America. She said that the rate had topped 45 percent in Mexico and noted that in private hospitals in large cities in the northern part of the country (Guadalajara, Monterey) it was as high as 90 percent.[1]

After hearing Robbie Davis-Floyd's remarks, I had lunch with a group of midwives from San Cristóbal. I asked them, "Why is the Cesarean rate so high in Mexico?"

They said:

"Because doctors don't want to take the time for normal birth."

"Because doctors make more money with Cesareans."

"Because doctors don't know the position of the baby!"

I had asked many people in Mexico that same question: *Why are there so many Cesareans?* Midwives were the only ones who blamed the medical system. Other women of my generation blamed young women of today. They said:

"Today's young women are lazy. They aren't willing to struggle."

"Young women are weak. They don't work like we used to."

"Women have horrible diets. We used to drink milk and *atole* (a drink made of cornmeal mixed with water or milk). Now women drink soda pop. We used to eat fresh things we raised or gathered ourselves. Now people eat processed foods and foods poisoned by chemicals."

Young people, on the other hand, seemed to think the higher Cesarean rate was an inherent result of modernization. They were surprised when I told them that Mexico's Cesarean rate is higher than that of the United States. They were surprised to learn that the increasing use of Cesareans is a matter of concern to someone from the more technologically advanced country north of the border.

Some people, young and old (but not midwives), thought that modern Mexican women *preferred* Cesareans, and apparently such a preference *is* a factor—but only among women of higher economic groups, especially in big cities of northern Mexico. Gonzalez-Perez and his colleagues state that "for many women from certain social sectors—those with greater educated and higher socioeconomic position—Cesarean sections are culturally accepted, seen as the optimum form of delivery and, therefore, are requested" (2001, 66). And an obstetrician in Monterey illustrates this attitude: "My maid has natural births," he said, "but Mrs. X of the upper class doesn't" (Zarembo 2001).

The point of view that sees Cesarean section as the *preferred* option had seeped into southern Mexico. I'd seen it in Zihuatanejo—those two interns had wanted Cesareans, and the wives of the two government VIPs probably did too—but I never heard any *midwives* mention the possibility that some women might prefer Cesareans. The women the midwives dealt with *did not* want them, and the women I met (from rural southern Mexico) in my classes and in hospitals in Oregon didn't either.

Many people I spoke to thought doctors made more money when they performed Cesareans, but that is true only in private clinics and hospitals. Doctors in public hospitals are salaried. There are, however, other factors at play in those public institutions—policies and attitudes that the midwives and I could only vaguely sense. I heard and read more about them in years to come when the subject had moved more into the arena of public debate.

One factor is that no form of pain relief is offered to women in labor in the public hospitals of Mexico. A Cesarean is the only alternative for women who find unmedicated vaginal birth (with no mobility and no emotional support—but with Pitocin) to be unbearable.

Another institutional factor was mentioned by Dr. Karina Ledesma, an obstetrician from Michoacán I met at a *congreso* in Morelia in 2013. She explained that interns and residents in public hospitals *need to observe Cesareans and practice performing them.* The women of Mexico serve as laboratory subjects for these *practicantes.* I later saw confirmation of this shocking assertion in an article addressing the subject of "obstetrical violence," in a Mexican federal government publication (Almaguer González et al. 2010, 8; translated by me). The authors acknowledge, "Now we know that a significant proportion of Cesareans that take place in health institutions are performed in order to facilitate the practice of interns and residents. This is a taboo element that no one talks about."

Gonzalez-Perez and colleagues name other institutional attitudes that seem likely to play a part: "the deep-rooted belief among the medical profession [in Mexico] that the caesarean section is very safe and implies few risks, the speed of the procedure compared to vaginal delivery, the obstetrics teaching practice in hospitals, and [the fact that] a caesarean in the first delivery . . . means that subsequent deliveries [will be] performed in the same way" (2001, 66).

After the San Cristóbal midwives shared their thoughts regarding the high Cesarean rate, I brought up something they hadn't mentioned: the fact that laboring women in Mexican hospitals receive little emotional support.

"Yes!" they all agreed. "That too!"

I asked them if they thought our sedentary lifestyle has made birth more difficult.

Absolutely!

They talked about how hard life had been in the "olden days" and about their own labors. Ana María, a woman in her fifties wearing a contemporary short hairdo and a knit pantsuit, told about the birth of her second baby.

Birth by the River: Ana María Moren Hernandez

My husband was a teacher in a small village about twelve hours from here by horseback. We had a house in the village, but we stayed here in San Cristóbal with our families in the summer. One year I was pregnant with my second child and nearing my due date when it was time to return to the village. On the day of the trip, as my husband was getting ready to leave, I told him I thought I was in labor. That made

Ana María.

him mad. He said I was just looking for an excuse to stay in San Cristóbal.

So I went with him. He rode one horse with our little boy, and I rode another. We had traveled about three hours when I began to feel the urge to push. I told my husband I had to stop, but he kept going. I got down from the horse and had my baby beside a river. I tied the cord with hair from the horse's tail, and then I stretched it out on a big rock and hit it with a smaller rock until it tore apart. I tore my rebozo lengthwise into two pieces, one to wrap around the baby's belly and one to wrap around my own belly.

A man came along on horseback, and I explained to him what had happened. He rode off and found my husband and brought him back. I put some of my older boy's clothes on the new baby, and then I got back on my horse and rode nine more hours to the village.

I was outraged. The other women at the table, all of whom had heard Ana María's story before, laughed, enjoying my indignation.

"What's your relationship with your husband like now?" I asked Ana María.

She smiled. "I left him years ago."

Do Storks Deliver Babies?: Francisca Orduño Armenta

Francisca, a tall, slender woman from Morelos who had the coloring and bearing of a Spanish aristocrat, talked to me during a break between sessions.

> My grandmother was a midwife, but she used to chase us kids out of the house when she was with a patient, so I never learned a thing about her work. When I asked her how babies came into the world, she said that an airplane brought them. A doctor who lived next door said that a stork vomits up a baby and then carries it to the woman's house.
>
> Neither of those stories made any sense to me. Babies were being born at our house and at the doctor's house, but I never saw any airplanes and I never saw any storks.
>
> I used to spend a lot of time at the doctor's house, playing with his children. One day I hid behind a curtain and watched while a

woman had a baby. When I returned home and told my grandmother what I'd seen, I protested, "There was no stork. There was no airplane." She grabbed me by the ear and slapped me.

After that I looked for more chances to watch births from behind the curtain. I must have seen about twenty or thirty births before I was ten years old. One day a woman came to the doctor's house clutching her crotch with a baby about to be born. The doctor wasn't home, so his wife helped the woman get up on the examining table. Then she just stood there, not knowing what to do. I put on a pair of gloves and prepared to

Francisca.

help the woman. I was so little the gloves came up to my elbows. The doctor's wife said, "You can't do this," but the baby was coming, so someone had to help the woman. After the baby was born, I said, to impress the doctor's wife, "Now we have to wait for the *bola de sangre* [lump of blood]." She said, "That's not the right word. You're supposed to call it the 'placenta.'" I clamped and cut the cord and the doctor's wife bathed the baby.

After that birth the doctor let me help him. My grandmother told me not to do it. She said, "People will blame you if something bad happens," but the doctor said that it would be his fault, not mine, if anything went wrong. I helped him for about four years, until he moved away. After he left, women started asking me to attend them in birth. I was only fourteen years old, but I knew what to do. One of my aunts had shown me how to massage women's bellies and adjust the baby's position, and the doctor had shown me the rest.

Born, Not Made: Francisca Catalina García

Another Francisca from Morelos, an eager, cheery woman with curly gray hair, said her mother had been a midwife, but her mother "hadn't taught her anything."

> As I prepared for the birth of my own first baby, when I was sixteen, I decided I didn't want anyone with me. I'd heard my mother talk about the fact that the womb had to be completely open before a baby could be born and about using *el tacto*, so I took one of her gloves and

hid it in preparation for the birth. My husband was at work and I was alone when my labor began. It was a quick, easy labor. I didn't even need the glove.

I'd had one more baby on my own when a woman in labor came to the door one day and I had to help her because my mother was away. It turned out she was having twins! The second baby was sitting, so I had to adjust his position, and then he was born normally.

My mother always said, "*Una partera se nace, no se hace.*" [A midwife is born, not made.] Once, when I asked her what to do if I ever had a case in which the placenta refused to come out, she said, "You need to ask God that question, not me. *Una partera se nace, no se hace.*" She said that a woman who is *born* a midwife is more loving to her patients than a woman who is *made* a midwife.

I had nine babies. All my labors were fast, about half an hour each, and painless. Birth takes longer now because women aren't as active as we were in the past. I used to work like a man, with a hoe and a hatchet, and I walked miles each day.

I didn't keep track of the births I attended before I went to the *cursos*, but it must have been about 2,000. Now I document the births I attend; there have been 1,510 since that first *curso*.

Faith in God is everything to me. When I'm attending a birth, I pray, "God, let love rain on this woman and on this birth." God always guides me in my work.

Tenejapa Midwives

I talked to midwives from Tenejapa, near San Cristóbal, during breaks between sessions, with one of the younger ones translating for those who didn't speak Spanish. (They spoke the indigenous language Tzeltal.) They mentioned the changes they've seen during their lifetimes. For example, topics related to reproduction are discussed more openly now than in the past, although the distribution of condoms is still not accepted. No one told *them* about sex or about menstruation, but they told their own daughters. When I asked if their daughters were interested in carrying on their work, they all replied sadly that they were not.

The novelist, Marsha, who did not speak Spanish, asked me to find out if there was a traditional method of producing the effect modern men get by using Viagra. Apparently some twist in her plot depended on there being an herb or procedure that performed such a function. The Tenejapa midwives said there was a tea made from the leaves or roots of a local tree (the name of the tree sounded like "varoom" in Tzeltal) that strengthens the male libido. No one knew the name of the tree in Spanish.

Later a midwife from Morelos, Mirna Amaya, gave us other options for "stimulating desire." One involved eating cooked bull testicles. Marsha liked that method for her story. Apparently her character wasn't supposed to know his libido was being boosted. So a little testicle meat added to his stew would serve quite nicely.

One of the speakers listed the challenges that make it difficult for indigenous women to access modern health services. They included: the women's sense of modesty, their fear of modern medicine, lack of transportation, the language barrier, and lack of respect from medical providers (prejudice against them because they were women, they were poor, and they were of an indigenous group). One of the Tenejapa midwives told about an experience she had when she took a laboring woman to a maternity clinic in San Cristóbal.

> The woman was nervous about being in the clinic, yet she had to go into the labor room alone to be examined by a male doctor who didn't speak her language. They said it wasn't time. They told her to go outside and walk.
>
> There was no private place where she could do that, so we went along the sidewalk and into a parking lot, hiding behind cars when she had a contraction. She was embarrassed to be laboring in public. We went back to the clinic, and I begged them to let her stay, but that just irritated them. They said she had to keep walking. When I was sure the birth was near, we returned to the clinic, and they took her back to the delivery room. Soon a nurse came out to the waiting room and told the husband to go buy diapers and sanitary pads, because the baby had been born.
>
> I felt sad that the woman had to labor like that, hiding behind cars in a parking lot, and that she had to give birth alone with people who didn't speak her language—without the support of her husband and her midwife.

Other Tenejapa midwives talked about their experiences when they took women to the same clinic. One said "My patient was bleeding heavily, but they made her wait for an hour. I begged them to see her." Another said, "The doctor laughed at me. He said, 'So . . . you bring your patient here because you don't know how to take care of her in your community.'"

One day I asked a group of Tenejapa midwives to tell me about how they had begun their work as midwives. They formed a circle around me and listened solemnly to each other's stories, taking turns as if it had all been prearranged. They were all soft-spoken and reserved but seemed determined to be heard. Their stories were brief, bare of details, and always about responding to a need. "A woman came . . . I had to do it."

The last one who talked to me, Rosa, said she wasn't sure of her age because no records had been kept, but she thought she was close to eighty years old. She was a tiny woman, but she stood proudly straight and spoke with dignity.

> I had a sad life. My parents forced me to get married when I was only thirteen years old to a mean man who often beat me. I had a baby every year during the first years of my marriage. I was alone the first time I went into labor. No one helped me. The baby was sitting, and he died at birth.
>
> I never had any help in labor, but I was better prepared after that first one, and the rest of my babies came head first. I would have a knife and string ready before I went into labor. I knew what to do.

Tears welled in her eyes and in my eyes too. "I had a sad life," she said again.

The other Tenejapa midwives all watched me as Rosa talked. It seemed my attention to her story mattered to all of them. I took Rosa's hand. I told her I was sorry she'd had such a hard life.

"It's not fair," I said.

Sometimes I felt guilty for having had so much security, freedom, and opportunity in my life, but I never felt that any of the midwives begrudged me my fortune.

Adoption

When the *congreso* was over, one of the midwives I'd met there invited me to her granddaughter's birthday party. While the midwife and I sat with other adults watching children in party clothes circle a table piled high with gifts, she pointed out the people whose births she had attended. "See that man?" she asked, indicating a young man who was talking to her husband. "His mother abandoned him with me the day after he was born. I knew nothing about the woman, not even where she was from, so I had no way of finding her. After waiting about a week, I took the baby to my sister to give to her son whose wife couldn't have children. I never told a soul that I'd done it. I didn't even tell my husband. No one knows."

Except me.

Other midwives had whispered similar stories, and three different midwives told me they had adopted abandoned babies themselves. They all said it was a secret. No one knew. Most importantly, the child didn't know and never would. Two of the midwives who had adopted babies themselves had been well past their childbearing years when they got the baby. "Didn't people suspect?" I asked. "Didn't people question the fact that a baby suddenly appeared when there'd been no mention and no evidence of a pregnancy?" I know people didn't talk about "those things" (like pregnancy) in the past, and a lot could be hidden under a rebozo, but still . . .

When I asked the midwives these questions, they looked at me as if I were oddly untrusting and cynical.

I asked one of the midwives who'd adopted an abandoned baby if she was afraid someday someone who suspected the truth would tell her son.

"Why would anyone do that?" she asked. "That would hurt the child."

The midwife at the birthday party said she put the names of her nephew and his wife on the birth documents indicating that they were the natural parents of the baby so they could easily register him as theirs. Although a few midwives claimed never to have done that, most said they had done the same.

It didn't seem that they were bypassing the standard adoption process: it seemed that their method *was* the standard process. I asked many people what the "official" procedure for adoption would have been, but no one knew. Some thought the local priest or maybe the president of the village would be involved. Others named various government agencies as possibilities.

Since there was no official policy on how to legalize an adoption, or if there was one, no one knew what it was, it made sense that the job of finding loving arms for unwanted babies was left in the hands of trusted midwives who handled the matter with their usual wisdom and pragmatism.

In the days that followed, I visited other midwives I'd met at the *congreso* who lived in San Cristóbal.

A Proper Courtship: María de Jesús Pérez Torrez

María de Jesús had just returned from the market with a huge basket full of fresh flowers when I arrived at her house. She showed me her consulting room, which contained a narrow bed, shelves full of medical supplies, and a large enameled baby scale that must have been a gift from a

Chapter Six

María de Jesús.

government agency. She started arranging the flowers, studying each one carefully before placing it in an ornate vase, talking to me as she worked.

My husband brought mariachis to serenade me and gave me flowers and candy when he was courting me. We weren't allowed to be alone together until after we were married.

Men no longer court women with music and flowers and candy. They just get a girl pregnant and then they disappear.

We didn't have "sex education" when I was young. No one talked about such things. I didn't know what was going to happen after I got married: I learned from my husband. No one told me about menstruation either. I was at a dance when I started bleeding for the first time. I didn't even know it was happening until my friends told me my skirt was stained. I was upset because I had to leave the dance to go home and change my skirt. Later I told my mother about the blood. She told me it's a normal thing that happens to women every month.

So . . . we learned about menstruation by menstruating;[2] we learned about sex by getting married; and we learned about childbirth by having babies.

After I'd had a few children of my own, a woman asked me to help her in labor, and so I began my work as a midwife. My husband didn't like my being away from home. Sometimes he tried to stop me—I would be getting dressed to leave, and he would be trying to take my clothes away from me—but I always managed to go. When I started helping my own daughters and daughters-in-law with their labors he saw the value of my work and stopped complaining.

I attended my first *curso* about twenty years ago. The main emphasis was on getting us to send women to the clinic when there were signs of high risk. They also taught us how to cut episiotomies and how to perform *el tacto*, but those procedures aren't necessary. Women don't want to be touched *down there*. They don't want to be cut. I can tell how a labor is progressing by watching the woman's lower belly, and I can help ease a baby into the world without using scissors.

I've only sent one woman to the clinic. She was really scared—I couldn't calm her down—and her labor wasn't progressing. Her husband thought the problem was that she'd been with another man. He said that if that was the case, then she wouldn't be able to have the baby. Maybe she had been with another man; maybe that was why she was so scared. I don't know. I took her to the clinic. The doctor would have let me stay with her for the birth, but I had to hurry home for another woman in labor. Before I left the clinic, I made sure the doctor acknowledged that both the woman and the baby were fine. I didn't want to read in the paper the next day that I was being blamed for something that had gone wrong. I told the doctor to keep the husband away from the woman until after the birth.

I haven't attended a birth in over two years. Women still come to me for belly massages, but they go to doctors for the birth.

Doctors used to send women to me when the baby was poorly positioned. Twice they sent women who were in labor with a baby's foot sticking out. In a case like that, with the vagina and cervix squeezing the leg and cutting off circulation, the foot gets so dark the baby may appear to be dead. I would tickle the foot to see if the baby was alive. I would have to find the other foot with my hand so the baby could be born.

Doctors no longer send women to me to adjust the position of the baby. Now they just perform Cesareans.

María de Jesús said she'd heard of the practice of predicting the number and spacing, and even the sex of future babies by looking at the lumps in the umbilical cord.

"*Es una mentira*" (It's a lie), she said, setting herself above the more rustic midwives who believed such things. She'd also heard various beliefs about how events in the natural world affect unborn babies. "People say that if a pregnant woman goes outside during an eclipse the baby will be born with a cleft palate," she said. "And they say that if there's an earthquake during a woman's pregnancy the baby will have the cord around his neck. They believe that if a woman looks at a dead body when she's pregnant, the baby will be born with a veil [with the amniotic sac over his face]. None of these beliefs are true; all are *mentiras!*"

I told her what Avila (1999) says about the origin of such beliefs, that some of them may have been proposed originally by healers or respected elders who were trying to help women cope with their grief after a pregnancy ended in tragedy. A woman who has lost a baby might torture herself with thoughts such as, *I should have slept more (or less)* or *I shouldn't have taken so many cold showers,* or *I should have visited my grandmother when she was dying.* A healer might try to ease the pain by providing a less personal explanation, one related to the natural world of eclipses and earthquakes and corpses.

María de Jesús wasn't interested in speculating about the origin of such *mentiras*. She scowled and harrumphed and pointed out that women *shouldn't* take too many cold showers during pregnancy, and they *should* visit their grandmothers, *especially* when they're dying.

Not Very Friendly, Luisa

Tami, a chipper young woman who worked in the hostel where I was staying, offered to take me to her village in the mountains not far from San Cristóbal. There were midwives there, she said, and with her as my escort I would be assured a welcome.

I'd been warned about traveling outside San Cristobal alone, and one of my guidebooks said that "towns in Chiapas beyond the most visited ones tend to be very suspicious of strangers," so I appreciated Tami's offer, but we could never find a time when we were both available. Either I was busy at the *congreso* or she was on duty at the hostel. So I decided to go by myself. Tami had decided I'd be all right on my own; she told me how to find the *colectivo* (a taxi that runs a fixed route like a bus) that would take me to the village and advised me, "Just tell everyone you know me." I didn't think to ask her last name, since "Tami" is an unusual name in Mexico and the village was small, so I set out with just the name "Tami," or, if needed, "Tami-who-works-at-a-hostel-in-San-Cristobal" as my supposed ticket to acceptance in the village.

After about an hour of travel on a narrow highway through forested mountains wet with fog, the *colectivo* stopped. The village was "up there," the driver said, pointing to a gravel road that led uphill into the forest, and so I began the climb. It was eerie to be walking through a forest; I was used to open vistas in Mexico. I reached the outskirts of the village, but I saw no people. It seemed like a ghost town. I wondered if everyone had seen me coming and was hiding from the dreaded *stranger*. (But a more likely explanation was that they knew what changes were about to take place in the weather and had already taken cover.) There was a wall of mountains just past the village, green and soggy with fog, not tall but very steep. Black clouds, the blackest I'd ever seen, curled over the tops of the mountains looking poised to spill over onto our side.

I found a few people when I got to the little plaza in the center of the village. None had ever heard of Tami, but a woman selling tamales said there was a midwife living behind the church. She called to a group of girls who were walking by and told one of them, "Take this woman to your grandma's house."

I followed the girls and waited while they went in to fetch the grandmother. Soon she came out, a short, stout woman, probably in her sixties, wearing a pinafore apron over a plain cotton dress. She stood before me with her arms folded in a defiant pose, her mouth pursed tightly shut. I mentioned my friend Tami and my interest in midwifery.

All the midwives I'd met thus far had been eager to talk to me, but this one was suspicious and reserved—and she didn't know Tami. I elaborated on my interest in midwives.

"Okay," she said finally, "I'll listen."

"No, I'm not here to try to tell you something or sell you something. I was hoping we could just talk."

She stood with her arms still folded, not saying a word, but she didn't disappear back into the house, and there was a little spark of interest in her eyes. When I asked for her name, she pursed her lips even tighter and jerked her head back in a Mexican gesture that means "no way." She wouldn't tell me her age either, but she couldn't resist answering my questions about her work as a midwife. Her mother had been a midwife, she said. After her own children were born, she began attending births herself.

Had she ever had any particularly challenging births? No. Did she ever send a patient to the doctor? No. Had she attended any *cursos*? No. Did she give injections? No. Perform *el tacto*? No. Give belly massages? Yes. Make adjustments to the fetal position? Yes. Did she use herbs? Sometimes, but she didn't seem inclined to tell me which ones. Birth always took place in the home of the patient. Some people paid a little, but most did not. "We are poor," she said simply.

There's a Mayan ritual commonly used in the San Cristóbal area that involves holding a live chicken over the laboring woman's belly. She said she didn't believe in the ritual herself, but she was willing to do it if the patient wanted her to.

She was interested in hearing about the birth customs in other parts of Mexico. The way the rebozo is used in the area around Oaxaca intrigued her, but the idea of having a woman drink urine sounded as gross to her as it did to me. She had never heard of giving women hot chocolate with raw egg.

"Does the egg get cooked by the hot chocolate?" she asked.

I told her I'd wondered the same thing but had never thought to ask. We speculated together and decided that yes the eggs would be cooked by the hot chocolate.

When I mentioned a practice a midwife in Guerrero had told me about that involved holding a piece of fresh placenta against someone's face to dry up pimples, she considered the idea for a while, looking doubtful, and then said seriously, "We don't do that. We bury the placenta."

I asked what she did if the people didn't want the placenta. Did she bury it herself? I was thinking of Margarita in Huajuapan whose husband buried abandoned placentas in his own courtyard. She gave me a blank look, and it occurred to me that disposing of the placenta wouldn't be a concern of the midwife if women have their babies in their own homes. "Oh, right," I said, "I guess you don't go around carrying placentas home from your work."

She thought that was funny. She chuckled and I did too.

I gave her one last chance to tell me her name as I prepared to leave, but again she refused. Still, she wished me well, *que le vaya bien*, and clasped my hand for a moment. She was still smiling about the placenta joke.

When I saw the tamale woman again, in the plaza, she asked me, "Did you find Luisa?" So I learned the midwife's name after all.

When I got back to the hostel, Tami asked me about my day in her village. "No one has ever heard of you!" I told her.

"Oh," she said. "My real name is Patricia. I just use the name 'Tami' when I'm here in the hostel."

Recent Widow: Lucía Jiménez Mendes

I scanned the small shops and adobe homes that lined the street, looking for something that looked like a clinic, thinking surely we should have reached it by now. I was on my way to visit a *doctora* I'd met at the *congreso*. She'd told me the name of the *colectivo* I should take and had said I should stay on the *colectivo* until it reached the end of its route. Then I could ask anyone I met how to find *la clínica de la doctora García*. The clinic was only half a block from the *colectivo* stop, and everyone in the neighborhood knew her. It had sounded easy.

But when the *colectivo* reached open countryside and began climbing into pine-studded mountains, I had to accept that I'd somehow made a mistake. I was on the wrong *colectivo*, and I had no idea where I was going. We circled around one foothill and then the next as wisps of fog drifted along the slopes and settled in the gorges. There didn't seem to be anything I could do except wait until we came to a town; I wasn't going to ask the driver to drop me off beside the road in the middle of nowhere.

There were three other passengers, two in back with me and one in front, all old men wearing baggy pants, loose shirts, and big sombreros. The man sitting next to me had a few whiskers, white and coarse like fishing line, scattered across his chin and cheeks. I tried not to press against him when the *colectivo* swerved around the mountain curves, and he seemed to be trying, too, but we were occasionally thrown together in spite of our efforts. Following usual *colectivo* protocol, we both pretended not to notice. This pretense entailed much gazing out the window and discouraged conversation. He probably didn't speak Spanish anyway. I'd heard him speaking one of the local indigenous languages when we were boarding the *colectivo*.

The other passengers must have been wondering who I was and why I was going to wherever it was we were going, but they didn't ask. I could have asked the driver to tell me our destination—I'd heard him speak Spanish—but as we got further and further from San Cristóbal, I felt embarrassed to suddenly ask, "Oh by the way, where are we headed?"

My main concern was that the trip would take so long I wouldn't be able to find a *colectivo* returning to San Cristóbal that same day. Finally I asked the driver how much longer the trip was going to be, and he told me we were "almost there." I relaxed a little, still straining to keep a few millimeters of space between me and the old man with the whiskers.

Then suddenly, as we rounded yet another curve, I saw a town stretched out across the valley floor below us. It looked like a mythical lost city, so unexpected, so unlikely, surrounded by steep hills frosted with mist. The streets were laid out in a grid of rectangles, and there was a large park in the center next to a massive stone church. The *colectivo* twisted down into the town and stopped in front of the church.

I walked over to a government building at one end of the square and read the lettering above the door: "Municipio de Tenejapa." I was in Tenejapa. I had thought of trying to visit Tenejapa, but its remoteness had seemed daunting. And now suddenly I was there, without having made any effort at all. I thought of the midwives I'd met at the *congreso* who were from Tenejapa; I would have loved to see one of them again, but they weren't from the town itself. They lived in *comunidades* somewhere in the region. So I would find a midwife in the town. I entered the government building and asked a thin young man sitting behind a desk, "Are there any *parteras* in Tenejapa?"

"¿*Parteras?*"

"Yes, *parteras*. You know . . . the women who used to help women have babies before there were clinics and doctors."

"¿*Cómo?*"

"You know... the women who massage the bellies of pregnant women?"

"Oh. ¡*Parteras!*" He took me to the home of the midwife Lucía.

Lucía was a solid woman, about four and a half feet tall, probably in her sixties. Her home was a cluster of one-room buildings made of adobe, rough wood, and cinder block, with dirt floors glazed hard by years of sweeping. Her first language was Tzeltal, but she also spoke Spanish.

"My husband died five months ago," she said, explaining the black dress she was wearing. She showed me an old, faded, black-and-white picture of her late husband, a handsome man, about forty when the picture was taken, sporting a trim moustache and a white sombrero. He was holding a plastic cup to his lips. She told me later that he'd been a heavy drinker.

We sat in the living/eating/sleeping room next to the kitchen where a pot of beans bubbled over an open fire. Three of Lucía's grandchildren peeked at us from just outside the door, ducking out of sight whenever I glanced their way.

> I lived in a *comunidad* in the mountains when I was young. My mother died when I was four, and my father found a second wife. My stepmother was mean to me and to my brothers and sisters and to her own children, too. She hit us. She didn't feed us. We were always hungry.
>
> About a year after my stepmother came to live with us, my father found work in another *comunidad* and left, taking his new wife and all the other children with him, leaving me with my sister-in-law. She treated me well, but one day, when I was about five years old, a man came and started *macheteando* everyone . . .

I interrupted her to ask about the word *machetear*.

Judy and Lucía with two of Lucía's grandchildren.

She swung her arm, slicing it through the air, to demonstrate the meaning, and then, when I still didn't understand, she took my hand in hers and guided it to the back of her head. When she pressed my hand into her hair, I felt ridges in her scalp, one just above her hairline, one from ear to ear above that, and a third above that. They were deep, thick scars. Of course. *Machetear* means "to slash with a machete."

"Why did the man do it?" I asked. "What possible reason could he have for wanting to hurt a child?"

> I don't know why the man attacked us. He went after children and adults alike. Four children died, and my sister-in-law died too. I was near death myself and there was no one to take care of me, so someone brought me here to Tenejapa and left me with the midwife Celia. She nursed me back to health and then let me stay with her. She raised me with her own two children.
>
> The man went to jail, but he wasn't there for long. I used to see him in the village when I was growing up. Everyone was mad at him, so eventually he moved away, and he died a few years later.
>
> I have eleven children, all born with Celia as my midwife. The first one was born when I was fourteen years old. Celia was a good midwife. She treated women with kindness and love.
>
> I didn't attend births myself until years after Celia died. When I was about forty I attended a *curso* here in Tenejapa. They taught us how to give injections, but I've never seen a need for that. Celia didn't use injections. Later I went to a one-week *curso* in San Cristóbal, and then I went to one for three days in the secondary school here. The *cursos* emphasized the importance of cleanliness. They told us to cut our fingernails short and to wash our hands carefully when we were attending a birth. And if we found a woman's house was dirty, we were supposed to clean it. Also they told us to be sure pregnant women took iron pills.
>
> After I'd been to the *cursos*, women started asking me to help them in labor. They never paid me, except maybe with a chicken or something like that, but I didn't expect them to. I did it because there was a need. I used to attend three or four births a month, but now I only attend three or four a year.
>
> I don't have to touch a woman's private parts to see how she's progressing. I can tell by touching her lower belly. It gets warm when she's in active labor, and hot when the birth is near. Celia used to have women kneel when they were pushing, but that makes more work for the midwife. I have women lie on their backs.
>
> Some midwives put warm leaves on a woman's lower belly to hurry labor, but I do as Celia did; I give women a tea made with cin-

namon leaf and the herb *mixto* [a kind of sage]. If the woman is in real labor, the tea makes the contractions stronger, but if she's not in real labor, the tea will stop the contractions and make her sleep.

I've attended many births of babies that were coming feet first, and a few of babies that were sitting, without any problems, but once when I went to help a woman I found that the baby was half born with his legs sticking out. His arms were crossed in such a way that he couldn't come out any further. I could tell he'd been like that for a long time, because his feet were cold. I said to the people, "Why didn't you call me sooner? We're neighbors. I would have come right away. Now it's too late to shift the baby." I told them to take the woman to San Cristóbal and they did. I don't know what happened, but I know the baby lived. I watched him grow up in my neighborhood.

I had a similar problem once with twins. The first baby came out easily, but the second one, a big baby coming feet first, got stuck halfway out. I found someone with a car to take the woman to San Cristóbal, but the baby died on the way. Since then I tell women having twins to go to a doctor for the birth.

We have a maternity clinic in Tenejapa now, but many women still prefer a midwife. They like that we massage their bellies and encourage them with gentle words. They like having their babies at home.

I have a good relationship with the doctors here. If I have to take a woman to the maternity clinic, they let me stay with her. The doctors in San Cristóbal never let me do that. I remember one woman became exhausted during labor and refused to push. I went to the clinic and got the doctor to come back to the house with me. He spoke to the woman, telling her in a stern voice, "You have to push," and then she did.

Three years ago a fourteen-year-old girl came to me saying she was pregnant but she didn't want the baby. She had an older woman with her who wanted to adopt it. They asked me if I would attend the birth and then say that the baby had been born to the older woman. I said, "I don't give babies away! This girl has breasts full of milk to give *chichi* [slang for breast]. She needs to take care of her baby herself."

Somehow the girl had managed to hide the pregnancy from her family. I went with her and made her tell her mother. She kept the baby, and her mother is helping her raise him.

My husband used to hit me. In the *cursos* they taught us that men shouldn't hit women and parents shouldn't hit children. They told us about a place in San Cristóbal where we could report child abuse, but I wouldn't do that because I don't believe in getting involved in other people's business. They said that if a man hits his wife she can report it to the police. I told my husband that I would do that, and he never hit me again.

"How long ago was that?" I asked.

It had been twenty years. She'd had almost twenty years of relative peace.

In the *colectivo* on the way back to San Cristóbal, I scrolled through the pictures I'd taken of Lucía. She'd seemed so weary and sad when I first arrived, but she was smiling happily in the pictures. I thought again of what Cristina Alonso had said at the *congreso*: "We [midwives] need support; we need to tell our stories; we need to be heard and valued."

Lucía hadn't attended the *congreso*, but I had listened; I valued her work.

Rattlesnakes in the Kitchen: Laura Aguilar Landero

I went with Marsha, the novelist I'd met at the *congreso*, to visit Palenque, an archeological site in northern Chiapas. The characters in her book were real historical figures who had lived, loved, fought for political power, and perhaps eaten testicle stew, in Palenque during the fifth century AD. Marsha had visited the site several times before, always finding that her characters whispered their secrets to her as she wandered among the ruins.

But other voices were calling to me. After a few hours at the site, I left Marsha there communing with her dead Mayans and went to find a *colectivo* that would take me through the lush, fertile lowlands of northern Chiapas to the state of Tabasco. There, in the town of Emiliano Zapata on the banks of the mile-wide Usumacinta River, I found the midwife Laura.

Laura was a plump, cheerful woman, fifty-four years old, with short, curly hair and glasses. Dead snakes, curled up like garden hoses, hung from the rafters in her kitchen. They were rattlesnakes, she said. She used them in a medicine she made that cures cancer. She'd started making the medicine when her mother was diagnosed with cancer of the stomach about two and a half years earlier. The original recipe had come from a healer in the Philippines, but the idea of adding dried rattlesnake meat was her own inspiration. Her treatment had been successful. Her mother, whose case had been supposedly hopeless, was ninety-eight and in good health.

Laura.

She had treated other victims of cancer since then, with similar success. People gave her dead rattlesnakes or sold them to her inexpensively because they knew she used them for a good cause.

Her story of how she became a midwife began with the birth of her own first baby. She'd been alone when she went into labor.

> The pain was terrible; I thought I was going to die. At the end I felt I had to pee and poop and I thought I was going to burst from the pressure. I was squatting when the baby was born. It was a boy. I just left him there on the dirt floor until after the placenta came out. I thought the placenta was my own guts. I put it and the baby on the bed, but then I had no idea what to do.
>
> My husband came home about half an hour later. He didn't know what to do either, so he left and went on foot to get his mother, leaving me alone for three hours. I must have been in shock. I didn't even think to clean the baby or cover him. When my husband's mother arrived, she cut the cord and took care of the baby, but he died six days later, probably because of the neglect when he was born. We should have looked for someone who lived nearby to help instead of having my husband go for his mother.
>
> I had six more babies; another boy and five girls. I was alone for all their births too, but I knew what to do and they all lived.
>
> My husband left me when my children were young. He hasn't helped me at all since he left, but I don't complain. I want my children to have a good relationship with him. He's their father. I had to get a job after he left, but I had only attended one year of school, and I had no skills. I found a job working in a private clinic as a cleaning lady. The doctor would occasionally ask me to help him in simple ways, and eventually he taught me how to sterilize tools and how to give injections and put in IV needles. I even helped when he operated.
>
> One day, when I'd worked in the clinic for about three years, the doctor told me I could stay and receive patients in the evenings after he went home, but first I had to attend a birth with him watching to be sure I did everything correctly.
>
> I was nervous when I attended that first birth. My hands were trembling as I reached to cut the cord, but everything turned out well. I began to work by myself in the evenings. I would call the doctor for complicated cases, but I could do routine things like bandage wounds, give injections, and attend births by myself.
>
> After a few years, another doctor offered me more money, so I went to work for him doing the same thing, and then later I worked for a third clinic. I worked long hours in the clinics. That was hard

when my children were young, so eventually I quit and started attending births on my own as a midwife. Women wanted to have their babies in their own homes, but I told them, "I need to be with my own children. If you want me to come to your house, I'll do it—I'll cut the cord and bathe you and the baby and stay with you for a little while—but then I'll have to leave. However, if you're willing to come to my house for the birth, I'll watch you all night and bathe you the next day." Women wanted the extra care, so I ended up doing most of my work at home.

I learned how to adjust the position of babies from the first doctor I worked for. I know doctors don't know how to do that anymore, but the first two doctors I worked for did.

I went to a *curso* about thirty years ago, and I still go to monthly meetings for midwives at the hospital, but really I learned all I need to know from the doctors I worked for. I send women to a lab to have ultrasounds and blood tests before the birth, and I give them IV fluids during labor, with Pitocin at the end. I give them a shot of *ergotrate* after the birth, so they won't bleed too much, and have them take an antibiotic to prevent infection.

I went a long way from not knowing anything when my own first baby was born to being able to help so many other women in labor. I don't attend many births now, maybe only two or three a year, but I still give massages and perform other cures. My children support me now.

***

A few days later, back in San Cristóbal, I said goodbye to Tami/Patricia and hailed a taxi to take me to the station where I would catch the bus to the airport. When the driver asked about my stay in San Cristóbal, I told him about the *congreso* and about my interest in Mexican midwives, and I asked him about the births of his own children. He said that all three were born by Cesarean. I commiserated, not that he seemed to think it was a tragedy, and said something about how it's getting harder and harder to have a vaginal birth in Mexico.

He asked me the question I'd asked so many times, "Why is that? Why are there so many Cesareans?" and I turned the question back to him. What did he think?

He pondered for a moment and then made a guess: "Is it because women are getting smaller?"

Endnotes

1. I don't comment on policies in private hospitals in Mexico, which account for about 20 percent of the births in the country (Suárez et al. 2012, 107), because my travels didn't bring me into much contact with women who can afford private medical care, but as Davis-Floyd suggested, the Cesarean rate is even higher in private hospitals—77 percent nationally according to a report in the *Christian Science Monitor* (Villagran 2013).
2. Other midwives said the same; no one had told them about menstruation. Many said they thought they were dying when they got their first period. And the prohibition against talking about such things meant that they were afraid to ask. One woman said, "My mother never said anything, but she had a kind of knowing look when she saw me washing out the rags, so I figured it must be normal." They used rags to catch the flow. Those who lived in the most rustic circumstances—in those *ranchos* in the mountains—didn't even have underwear. They held the rags in place with their thighs.

Chapter 7
Yucatán Peninsula

Mayan Mother and Daughter: Antonia Echeveria and Elena Uk Kupul

*A*hhh . . .

I was in Tulum, with Antonia, a midwife I'd met at the *congreso* in Chiapas, in her bedroom, on her bed. She was massaging my belly, probing, finding organs (bladder, uterus, ovaries) and nudging them into a better position, kneading, smoothing, pulling inward from the circle of my pelvis. It seemed that my innards had been frozen and sore, needing just *this* pressure. She pressed her fingers into my bellybutton and the flesh beyond, which she called the *cirro,* becoming still, as if she were listening.[1] I could feel my own pulse pounding against her fingers. She pressed that pulsing point from the sides, centering it, *acomodándolo.*

I felt a lump of sadness rise in my throat as Antonia did her work. It seemed that she was touching more than just organs. She didn't interpret the experience for me afterward, nor did she claim to have "fixed" anything. She simply touched me deeply, and what I felt afterward was *deeply touched.*

A teenager, five months pregnant, had arrived, also wanting a belly massage. I moved to the corner of the bed, back by the wall, and the girl took my place. The girl's mother was with her; she talked to me while Antonia kneaded her daughter's belly, *acomodando* the baby within. The mother told me that the baby would be her first grandchild. The girl had been seeing a doctor, and she would go to the Center of Salud for the birth, but the mother needed Antonia's assurance that all was well and she thought the massage would help ensure an easy labor. The girl sighed

Antonia with her granddaughter and her mother Elena. Elena is sitting in a hammock.

with pleasure as Antonia's hands slid across her flesh. I remembered Francisca telling me her prenatal massages had felt *muy rico*.

After the mother and daughter left, Antonia knelt briefly in front of her altar, giving thanks for the payment she'd received, and then she took me to see her mother, Elena, who lived in a room separate from the rest of the house.

Elena was a thin, frail woman, bedridden (actually, hammock-ridden), sixty-nine years old, with dark circles under her eyes. Antonia wore shorts and a T-shirt, but her mother was wearing the traditional Mayan dress, a long white shift with a broad band of embroidery at the neckline and hem. She spoke only Mayan, so Antonia translated.

> One day, when I was fifteen years old, my father told me he had planned a marriage for me. The matter had already been settled. He threatened to strike me with a machete if I didn't cooperate. So I married the man, but I wouldn't have relations with him, not even when he got mad and beat me. Finally, after about a year, I relented, but still he beat me. I would have to hang onto the pole in the middle of our hut while he struck me with his hands or with a strap or a stick.
>
> I had fourteen children, all born at home, except one. The last one was born in the hospital. I knew the doctor would cut me [he would cut an episiotomy] when the baby was coming out, so I tried not to let anyone see how my labor was progressing. I kept my face calm, even at the end, and I didn't make a sound. I had a sheet over me, so no one saw the birth. Afterward I said to the nurse, "Look, here's the baby."
>
> I've dreamed I was attending births since I was a child. Even before I started working as a midwife, I would dream I was giving women massages and that I could see inside their bellies. In that way, by seeing, I would know what to do. I didn't want to become a midwife—I don't like blood—but there came a time when I could no longer ignore my dreams. I was about fifty years old when I began attending births.
>
> Some people hit a woman if she starts to panic in labor. They think that helps, but I think it's better to be gentle. I always encourage women, saying things like, "You need to be calm, *mi amor*. You can do it. We all go through this. God will help you."
>
> I think it's better to learn from dreams than from books and *cursos*, because dreams tell you exactly what to do.

When Elena began to look tired, Antonia and I returned to the main house, and Antonia talked about her own life.

I got married at the age of sixteen and became pregnant right away. The only midwife we had at that time was a *tío*, so I went to him, but I didn't like the way he treated me when I was in labor. He yelled at me. He told me to start pushing when I didn't feel any urge. Pushing didn't feel right to me, and I know now that I should have waited, but I felt I had to do what he said, so I ended up pushing for three days and I tore. Of course no one thought of stitching up a tear in those days. I was in pain for about two months, but eventually the wound did heal.

What a horrible experience that birth was. I didn't want another labor like that, so when I became pregnant again I decided to have the baby by myself, without a midwife. I didn't trust the *tío*; I didn't think a man could know what was natural for a woman.

I wanted to learn all I could, so I convinced the *tío* to let me go with him to a birth. Once again he told the woman to start pushing in early labor. I said, "No, it's too soon."

He said, "Who's the midwife here, you or me?"

The baby came feet first and got stuck halfway out. The woman was so exhausted by the time she actually needed to push that she could hardly do it. The baby was eventually born, but he was dead.

In the years since then I've attended many births of babies that were feet first like that, always successfully. My brother-in-law's sister had six babies born feet first. I attended all the births, and they all went well.

I went to another birth with the *tío*, and once again he started telling the woman to push when I thought it was too soon, but it was the woman's second baby—the first one had been born with a different midwife—so she knew what to do. She just ignored him.

Even though I didn't want him with me for the birth, I still went to the *tío* for my belly massages during pregnancy. One day while he was massaging me, his hand strayed under my waistband where it shouldn't have gone. When that happened, I sat up quickly and said, "Okay, that's enough. I feel fine now." After that my husband gave me my belly massages.

Doctors say you can kill a baby by massaging the woman's belly, but they just say that because they don't like midwives and because they don't know how we give massages. We do it gently and carefully.

I wanted to experience birth with no interference, no midwife telling me what to do, no teas, and no one pushing on my belly. God would be with me, and my baby would be with me; I didn't want anyone else. The idea of having that kind of birth was like a vision for me.

When my labor began, I told my sister-in-law, but I didn't tell anyone else, not even my husband. My sister-in-law wanted to help me, but I asked her to leave. I kept doing my chores, sweeping the floor and cleaning the kitchen, even after my husband went to bed. When I felt that it was time to push, I checked with my fingers to be sure. Then I lay down on my hammock and had my baby. He was born with only two pushes, without even breaking the amniotic sac. We say such babies are *embolsado* [in the bag]. People say that if a baby is born *embolsado* it's because the mother has eaten the stomach of a cow.[2]

The entire labor lasted from two o'clock in the afternoon until two o'clock in the morning. After he was born, I broke the amniotic sac and cleaned him, and then I woke my husband and asked him, "Do you want to see your new son?" It was a lovely experience for me. Labor was painful, yes, but it was beautiful too, because I had faith in God and because I knew my baby would soon be in my arms.

I continued to have my babies by myself, without any help. I bled a lot after the birth of my fourth baby, and then, a week after the birth, when I was lifting a heavy basket, I felt something come down into my vagina. It was my uterus. I had my husband hang me upside down and massage my belly, but it didn't help. I was like that for a year. It was painful to go to the bathroom, so I tried not to eat or drink very much, and I became quite thin. I didn't go to a doctor; I just waited, and finally my uterus shifted back up into its normal position.

I had a miscarriage after that and then a baby born a month early. The baby born at eight months was fine, but all those problems made me nervous, so I went to the doctor when I became pregnant again. The doctor told me to terminate the pregnancy. He said I could die if I had another baby. But I had faith in God. I knew my baby and I would be safe. I went weeks past the due date, and the doctor wanted to induce labor, but still I trusted God. I waited.

Some people say that to get labor started you have to hit yourself nine times on the thighs with a bridle and then let the bridle fall to the floor. The reason that's supposed to work has something to do with the fact that horses have pregnancies that last nearly a year and humans are supposed to have nine-month pregnancies. I'm not sure I really believe in that, but I tried it. The next day I felt that the baby was crosswise, so I adjusted her position. She was born quickly after that. She weighed 4.7 kilograms [over ten pounds]. The day after the birth I went to the Center of Salud to show her to the doctor. He said, "Who delivered the baby?" I told him I did it myself.

Women started asking me to help them in labor when I was only nineteen years old. They trusted me because they knew I'd had my own babies without any help. Women started calling me *comadre* (in this context, "midwife"), and children called me *madrina* (godmother). I was embarrassed to be treated with such respect when I was so young. I thought people would say, "What is she doing, attending births at her age?" But women needed my help. They were glad to have a female midwife instead of the old *tío* with his wandering hands.

Sometimes I dream that I'm with one of my pregnant clients in the hospital. I take such a dream as a warning that there might be complications in the birth, so I'm especially watchful. If I have to transfer a woman to the Center of Salud during labor, I go with her. They usually make me wait outside, but sometimes they let me stay; it just depends on which doctor is there at the time. I remember once they let me stay, but I wasn't supposed to watch what was happening. I was allowed to stand beside the bed and hold the woman's hand, but I had to look away so as not to see what they were doing. I couldn't help peeking every now and then. They would threaten me, saying, "If you look again, we're going to kick you out," but they let me stay.

My daughter had one of her babies at the Center of Salud because she had preeclampsia [a potentially dangerous condition of pregnancy, characterized by high blood pressure]. We purposely stayed home until she was eight centimeters dilated, thinking she would have a better chance of having a natural birth if she didn't go too soon, but still they cut her [cut an episiotomy]. I saw them do it. I was watching through a window that looked into the room, through a little gap in the curtains. I know they always cut women like that, but still it upset me to see it. My other daughter had two babies at home without being cut and without tearing.

One day I took a woman with a baby that was coming feet first to the Center of Salud, because doctors were telling us we couldn't attend those births. When we got there, the doctor said, "You're the midwife. You deliver the baby." He made it sound like I had to prove something, but I think he just didn't want the responsibility. I didn't mind. I attended the birth, with the doctor watching, without any problem.

When I was young we used only herbs, but when doctors came to Tulum they told us we should give Pitocin at the end of labor. One doctor brought the midwives together and taught us how to give injections, having us practice on oranges. There's an herb that speeds labor, which I liked better than Pitocin, but it didn't seem right to ignore the doctors' advice, so I gave the injection. Women started asking for it. They believed the injection helped them. They would buy the Pitocin ahead of time and have it ready when they went into labor.

Once a woman came to get me to help her neighbor who was in labor. Apparently the neighbor's sister-in-law had been attending the birth, but when an odd-looking body part started to come out she got scared and left. The woman was alone after that until the neighbor heard her screaming. I didn't want to go, but I felt I had to. I told the neighbor that it wouldn't be my fault if something went wrong since the sister-in-law had been attending the birth before I got there.

The strange body part turned out to be a foot. I pushed on it gently, with a bouncing motion, until it disappeared back up into the uterus. Then I massaged the woman's belly to get the other leg straightened out, and soon both feet appeared together. The birth was easy after that and the baby was alive, but he was badly deformed. His head was soft, and he had no upper lip. We set out as quickly as we could to take him to the Center of Salud, but he died on the way.

When we got to the Center of Salud, I explained to the doctor that someone else had been attending the birth, that I had only been involved at the end, and he told me not to worry. He knew it wasn't my fault that the baby died. He knew me. He knew I was a good midwife.

I stopped working as a midwife after that, for ten years, until a Swiss woman, Sabrina, asked me to teach her how to attend births. She said that ever since she'd had her first baby with a midwife in Switzerland she'd wanted to become a midwife herself. She was married to a Mexican and living in Tulum.

I said, "No, I can't teach you. I don't do that work anymore." But she insisted. I told her I didn't think women would want a foreigner to attend their births. She said, "Don't you worry about that. If I find the clients, will you come with me to the births?" Finally I agreed. I really didn't think she would ever find any clients, but she did! I started attending births with her, and soon I was attending them on my own again too. So Sabrina got me back into working as a midwife.

Sabrina has formed an organization of the midwives in our area, the Asociación de Parteras Tradicionales de Tulum. We have meetings and help each other at births. Sabrina got a local politician to finance our travel to the *congreso* in Chiapas and also to one in Morelos. At the *congresos* we met midwives and doctors from other countries who said not to use Pitocin in every birth. Sabrina had been saying the same thing, but it was hard to believe. Everyone—doctors, other midwives, and even patients—thought it was important to give Pitocin at the end of labor. I use it less now: only if a labor is stalled or if the woman is bleeding heavily afterward. Sometimes women insist on having it. I tell them, "Your baby can be born just fine without an injection."

Many people think that having a baby naturally is old-fashioned, that the modern way, with injections and episiotomies and Cesareans, is better. What I liked about going to the *congresos* was that I got to meet other midwives, and doctors too, from all over the world who respect God's way.

Blond Mayan Midwife: Sabrina Speich

The original purpose of my trip to Tulum had been to attend a *congreso* being held by Sabrina's *asociación*, but an epidemic of swine flu was sweeping the globe and all fingers were pointing at Mexico as the supposed source, so the *congreso* had been canceled. I'd decided to make the trip anyway.

Sabrina.

I went to visit Sabrina, who was now living in her husband's village about an hour from Tulum, and found her exhausted from the effort of preparing for and then canceling an international *congreso*. We sat in a thatched-roof building in the compound that was home to her husband's extended family, surrounded by children, Sabrina's own seven plus her many nieces and nephews. I distributed my usual gifts, Matchbox cars for the boys and fingernail polish for the girls, and then tried to ignore the children's noisy activity while Sabrina and I talked. We spoke in Spanish, but I later learned that she speaks English perfectly well also. Tall and robust, with lush curly blond hair, Sabrina might have looked out of place in a traditional Mayan village, but she didn't. She looked at home. She was wearing a Mayan dress, and she was seven months pregnant.

She laughed when I asked about finding those early clients.

"Antonia didn't think anyone would come to me, but they did. I think my being a foreigner actually helped. People assumed I'd had training, when in fact I didn't know anything! I just knew that Antonia would be with me, ready to help if I had a question or a problem."

In many ways talking to Sabrina was like talking to any Mexican midwife—she practiced in the Mayan way, assisting Mayan women, massaging their bellies and offering herbs instead of drugs—but she'd had other influences too. She'd given birth with a Swiss midwife, she'd studied on her own, she'd attended many *congresos*, and she knew birth professionals from all over the world. She advises her Mayan sister-midwives to be judicious about adopting the practices of modern medicine. She tells them not to use Pitocin indiscriminately, not to use fundal pressure, not to be so quick to move birth from the hammock to the bed.

I'd been thinking about the vaginal tear Antonia told me about, the one that was never stitched. I wondered how often tears like that occurred and went unnoticed in a traditional world that "doesn't look," and I thought Sabrina (who does look) might know. She said she thought vaginal tears were quite rare in the midwives' practice, but when they did occur they were often left to heal on their own.[3] She said once one of her own patients had torn.

> I wanted to take the woman to the Center of Salud for stitches, but no one else thought we should go. Other midwives who were with me at the birth said, "Just leave it." The woman's relatives were worried that if we went to the clinic I might get in trouble with the doctors. I said, "Never mind what the doctors might think—I'm taking her." So we went. Fortunately the doctor on duty was one I had a good relationship with. I had to listen to the usual speech about how supposedly the woman wouldn't have torn if she'd had an episiotomy, but other than that he didn't give me a hard time.

That was the only vaginal tear Sabrina had seen. Given what Michel Odent says, "The best way to protect the perineum, to avoid a serious tear, and to eliminate the reasons for episiotomy is to deviate as little as possible from the physiological model of birth" (2003, 9), one would expect there to be fewer tears in the traditional setting than in a high-tech one.

Sabrina gave me the name of another midwife, Filiberta, who lived in Tulum near my hotel, and promised to let me know when the *congreso* was rescheduled.

A Breech Great Granddaughter: Filiberta Quijano Tun

Filiberta was like a bird, always in motion, graceful and slender, wearing the traditional Mayan dress. Her house was quiet when I visited, except for a large parrot that sat in a cage beside us, jabbering and screeching. Filiberta moved him to the courtyard behind the house so we could talk more easily. Like other midwives I met on the Yucatán Peninsula, she spoke both Mayan and Spanish and she wore the traditional dress.

> My grandfather was a *tío*. He was like a doctor really. He could receive babies and stitch wounds, and he knew all about herbs. There

Filiberta standing next to a cabinet that holds birthing supplies.

was one herb he used, called in Mayan *x-kakaltun* [a kind of basil], that's great for healing cuts and abrasions. You mash the herb and apply it directly to the wound. I use it myself.

My mother was a midwife too. She and my grandfather were both greatly respected and loved.

My mother had five children with her first husband and then five more with my father. When I was seventeen years old, the husband of one of my older half-sisters started trying to mess around with me. When I told my mother about it, she said, "Don't tell your father." She was afraid my father would kill my brother-in-law if he found out. She said the only solution was for me to get married.

There was a man interested in marrying me. I'd seen him at dances, but I didn't really know him and I didn't particularly like him. He talked to my father, and my father agreed to the marriage. My mother went along with it because she wanted to get me away from my brother-in-law. So suddenly I was married.

Life was hard for me, living with a man I didn't love and having nine children with him *a la fuerza* (by force). My husband died twelve years ago, but life continues to be a struggle. I have to support myself and my two grandchildren who live with me. I have problems with my back, but I have to keep working. One day, when I came home staggering from fatigue after a birth, one of my sons told me that I shouldn't work so hard. I said, "Who's going to support me? You?"

I became a midwife by helping my mother and grandfather. I used to be busy, sometimes attending two or three births a day. Doctors and midwives got along well in those days. We helped each other. I remember one wonderful doctor who used to say, "If you ever have a problem with a birth, just call me and I'll come."

There are still a few doctors who value the skills of midwives. Every now and then a woman will come to me pregnant with a baby that's crosswise or sitting or standing and whisper that a doctor has said she should see me to have it repositioned. But most doctors want women to stay away from midwives. They tell women all kinds of things to scare them. They say that if a baby is born with a midwife it might die or the woman will be in trouble with the authorities. They say the child won't qualify for government services later in life.

Women still come to me in spite of those warnings. Many women come after they've been told by a doctor that they'll have to have a Cesarean. I ask the woman what reason she was given. If she tells me she has diabetes or high blood pressure or some medical condition like that, I try to help her understand that she needs to do what the doctor says, but if she says it's because supposedly she's too tight or too thin or too young or too old or she's had too many children or the baby is too big, I'll check her myself. If I don't find any problems, I tell her, "You can have a normal birth. I'll help you."

Later, if the doctor finds out the woman had her baby with me, he scolds her, saying, "I told you to go to the hospital for a Cesarean. You could have died having your baby with a midwife. Aren't you afraid of dying?"

So I'm still busy. Women come to me because they don't want Cesareans or they don't want episiotomies or they're afraid of being alone with medical people—or even because they're afraid their babies might get switched in the hospital. They trust midwives because we're well-known by everyone in the community and we treat women in a caring way. We encourage them lovingly. We tell them, "You can do it," and we reassure them, saying, "Everything's going to be okay."

Like Antonia and Sabrina and all the midwives I later met on the Yucatán Peninsula, Filiberta described a typical birth as taking place in a hammock. To show me how that works, she had me sit crosswise in one of the hammocks that stretched across her living room; then she sat in front of me and put my feet on her knees. My husband or some other helper would be in a chair behind me, she explained, with his arms around my midriff, giving me "something to push against." Or the woman can stretch out lengthwise in the hammock grasping and pulling on the strings above her head. The woman stays in the hammock after the birth, she said. The midwife can massage her uterus and bathe her right there.

None of the midwives of the Yucatán Peninsula used a rebozo in birth. Antonia, Filiberta, and Sabrina had heard about the technique at *congresos*, and they thought it sounded like a good idea, but they hadn't tried it. They accomplished all the necessary manipulations of the baby's position by massaging the belly.

Filiberta talked about various methods that help *despegar* (unstick) a stubborn placenta. There was an old technique, one her mother and grandfather used, that entailed having the woman squat over a bucket of steaming herbal water, but that seemed to Filiberta to be asking a lot of a woman who's just given birth. She found that massaging the uterus and having the woman breastfeed were usually sufficient. When more drastic measures were required, she might place heated orange leaves or rags on the woman's belly or smear the cord with mashed garlic or give the woman something disagreeable to drink, for example mashed garlic in water, to make her vomit. A method she thought was effective, though not always convenient, was to wrap the umbilical cord with nettle leaves. (Antonia had mentioned this technique also.) The stinging of the cord by the nettles makes the placenta come free from the uterus. Filiberta warned me, in case I should ever try this myself, to be careful to protect my own hands and the woman's skin.

If nothing works, she clamps and cuts the cord, ties it to the woman's leg so it won't go back up into the uterus, and sends the woman to the Center of Salud. She loses the clamp when she does that. She's gone to the Center of Salud later, hoping to get her clamp back, but they can never find it.

I made a mental note to bring Filiberta some clamps if the *congreso* was rescheduled and I managed to attend.

Both Antonia and Filiberta said they waited to cut the cord until after the placenta came out. They said that in the past, before they had contact with doctors and *cursos*, they sterilized the cord by burning it with a candle (made of tallow), and they mentioned the precautions that were needed to protect the baby's skin from being burned. They said they put fabric or cardboard against the baby's skin at the base of the cord, or maybe a nopal leaf. To prepare the nopal leaf (which is good insulation because of its fleshy thickness), they first removed the needles, and then they punched a hole in it. They put the leaf against the baby's belly, with the cord stub sticking out through the hole, and then they could safely apply the flame.

When I visited Filiberta again before I left Tulum, her granddaughter Lidia was with her. The young woman was six and a half months pregnant with a baby that was in the sitting position according to both Filiberta and the doctor at the Center of Salud.

"The doctor says that if the baby stays in this position I'll have to have a Cesarean, but I'm going to have Grandma adjust him," Lidia told me.

When I told her I would love to see her grandmother do that, Lidia took it on as a personal cause to provide me with a demonstration. Filiberta wanted to wait until closer to the due date, but she succumbed to Lidia's pleading. Lidia stretched out on a cot in the corner of the living room and exposed her belly. Filiberta slicked her hands with oil and began the massage, talking to me as she worked.

> You have to go slowly. You try one direction; if the baby doesn't budge, you try the other direction. Some babies don't want to move. You nudge them, and they move a little, but then as soon as you release the pressure they go right back to the way they were before. When that happens, I tell the woman, "*Ni modo* [no way]; you'll have to go to the hospital for the birth."
>
> Sometimes, when a woman comes to see me after I've successfully repositioned her baby, I'll find that he's moved back to the sitting position again. I'll try two or three times. If the baby is still sitting after that, I tell the woman she has to go to the hospital. I explain, "The baby doesn't want to be in the normal position."

Lidia's baby didn't seem inclined to budge, and Filiberta quickly abandoned her attempt. But the baby would eventually be moved into the correct position; both Filiberta and Lidia seemed confident about that.

Filiberta said she'd attended many births of feet-first and bottom-first babies before the Center of Salud came to town. She picked up a Barbie doll that sat naked among candles and saints on her altar and used it to illustrate. Babies in the sitting position are harder to birth than feet-first babies, she said, doubling Barbie at the hips to demonstrate, but one-foot babies are the most difficult of all. (She stretched one of Barbie's legs back down.) You have to push the baby back up higher in the pelvis until the foot disappears, and then, hopefully, when the baby starts to emerge again there will be two feet coming together. "You take both feet with one hand, just like when you're grabbing onto a live chicken." That leaves one hand free to press on the top of the woman's belly.

She had also received babies that were coming forehead first and face first. She laughed remembering that once when she was performing *el tacto*, her finger went into the baby's mouth! She said that babies born that way are funny looking, with their faces oddly swollen, but after a few days they're fine.

She said she used the Barbie doll often to illustrate various fetal positions for her patients. I added "miniature pelvis and matching baby" to my mental list of things to bring if I returned to Tulum.

Paciencia: Francisca Montantez Aldana (Panchita)

Eager to see more of the Yucatán Peninsula, I boarded a bus for Ticul, a town of about 20,000 inhabitants in the highlands of the state of Yucatán. I was hungry when I arrived. It was late—stores and restaurants were closed—but there were still a few vendors in the *zócalo*. I bought homemade candy from one of them, an older woman, and talked to her while she packed up her wares. She told me about her own labors and offered her theories about why there are so many Cesareans in Mexico. (Because young women today don't work like women did in the past or because people think Cesareans are safer or because of the sprays and fertilizers that are used on crops these days.) She told me about a midwife who lived on the outskirts of town, whom I visited the next day.

Panchita looked more modern than other midwives I'd met—she was wearing shorts and a tank top—but her manner and practice were traditional. She said she'd learned midwifery from the woman who helped her when she was having her own babies.

Panchita stands in front of her new birthing hut.

My midwife's name was Maximina. She had no children, no daughters who could carry on after she was gone, so she taught me. She died after my fourth baby was born, leaving me to handle the births of my last three babies by myself. I knew what to do; I'd learned from my beloved Maximina.

Maximina taught me how to tell a baby's position. She used to guide my hands across women's bellies, explaining what we were feeling within. "Here are the baby's feet," she would say. "Here's his head . . . and here's his little bottom." You can tell the position more easily if the baby is awake and moving. We would sit together, Maximina and I, with our hands on a woman's belly, waiting for the baby to shift or kick.

I can adjust a crosswise baby, but I don't try with babies that are sitting or standing. I send those cases to the Center of Salud, and I also send women if they're having premature contractions.

When I go to the Center of Salud with a patient, they let me stay with her for the birth, so I've seen how they do things. It seems that all their practices have the goal of speeding things up. They break the amniotic sac; they press on the top of the woman's belly to help her push the baby out; they cut the vaginal opening; they cut the cord as soon as the baby is born; they pull on the cord to get the placenta out; and then they clean out the inside of the uterus with their hands after the birth.[4] Everything is hurry, hurry, hurry. I don't do any of those things. Maximina taught me that it's important to be patient. While I'm waiting for the placenta to come, I start cleaning the baby and I make him cry. The baby's crying helps loosen the placenta from the uterus.

Birth is natural, and nature has its own timetable for how things should happen. I can still hear Maximina saying, "*Paciencia, paciencia, paciencia.*"

Many women have their babies with me because they know if they go to the hospital the doctor will cut them [will cut episiotomies]. I don't do that. Another reason why women come to me instead of going to the hospital is that nurses and doctors and student nurses and student doctors do *el tacto* so often.[5] I only do it every few hours, just to make sure the woman is making progress. If I check four times without finding any change, I send the woman to the hospital.

Doctors are even in a hurry to abandon a baby. They say that if a baby doesn't start breathing in the first two or three minutes after the birth, you should stop trying to revive him because he'll be damaged. I know of a baby that didn't breathe for fifteen minutes, and he was fine. He's eighteen years old now. He lives in my neighborhood, and he's a good, hard-working boy. So I wouldn't give up easily if a baby was slow to start breathing. I would keep trying to revive him.

Could that be true? I wondered. *Could a baby have survived that long without breathing?* Maybe it just seemed that long. They wouldn't have had watches, and panic might have distorted their sense of time.

And maybe the practice of leaving the cord intact, still pumping oxygenated blood to the baby, made a life-saving difference.

Construction was almost complete on a new birthing hut, which was being built next to Panchita's house. It was a small, square building with a pointed, thatched roof and a dirt floor. A thin partition divided it into two rooms: a waiting area and a workroom. There was a straw mat on the floor of the workroom, with blankets spread over it to make a bed for patients. Panchita was using the hut already, even though the walls still needed to be plastered with mud and straw.

I spent an afternoon with her in the new hut, watching her give belly massages. One patient, about five months pregnant, was getting her first prenatal massage, and one was having her organs put in order because she was hoping to become pregnant. There was a male patient, a skinny old man who'd been told by a doctor that he had gastritis. Panchita had me feel how hard his belly was before she started the massage and how much softer it was when she was finished. (Actually, he was so thin, his muscles were so taut, and my touch was so tentative, I couldn't really tell the difference.) While she worked on him, he told us about his family, his poor departed wife, his son (who was involved with unspecified "vices") and the daughter who lived with him and prepared his meals.

Panchita massaging an old man's belly.

The women told me about the births of their babies, some in the hospital and some with midwives, and about the births of the babies of their friends and relatives. People in the waiting area joined in the conversation through the partition as one patient told me of a woman they all knew who had given birth to twenty-six babies. The woman had kept the first twenty-five, but when the last one was born she gave him to someone who couldn't have children.

Panchita listened and occasionally added a remark, but she remained focused on her work, using talcum powder instead of the usual oil to help her hands slide across the skin. She massaged each belly in its turn, pressing strong hands into flesh, prodding the organs inside. She paused now and then to probe the area beneath the bellybutton, as Antonia had done, also referring to this point as the *cirro*. Sometimes, with the patients who weren't pregnant, she worked to *acomodar* it.

Panchita told me about another midwife, Feliciana, who lived in the next *colonia*. I went to visit her that evening.

Indentured by Her *Don:* Feliciana Cocom

It was dark when I got to Feliciana's house. Her yard was small and cluttered with old cars, car parts, plastic buckets, and potted plants. I could dimly see some men standing beside one of the cars smoking, but they ignored me. An older man who appeared to be drunk approached to see what I wanted. When I asked for Feliciana, he pointed vaguely to the door of the house, indicating she was inside.

The house was small and dimly lit, with a thatched roof. It felt like a tent inside, with clothes, hammocks, and blankets hanging from pegs and ropes everywhere. Feliciana was a large woman with a jowly face like a bulldog and a Buddha belly filling out her ample Mayan dress. I sat on a plastic chair while she sat in a hammock facing me, gesturing with fleshy arms outspread as she talked.

Feliciana.

> I had ten children, five boys and five girls. A midwife attended the births of most of them, but sometimes she didn't get there in time. After I'd had a few babies by myself, a woman asked me to help her daughter-in-law in labor. I said I couldn't; I didn't want the responsibility. I told the woman that if something went wrong, everyone would blame me.

A few months later my own daughter-in-law went into labor, and I helped her. I had to; there was no one else around who could. After that, when I was asked again to help a woman in labor, I agreed to do it. That was the beginning for me. Women just kept coming. I don't know how to read, I don't even know what month it is, and I never went to any *cursos*, but I know everything I need to know about attending births. I learned by myself. God taught me.

After I'd attended several births, I learned from a dream that being a midwife was my *don*, my gift from God. A virgin, like the Virgin Mary, wearing blue robes and a black rebozo over her head, said to me in the dream, "The peace of God arrives in this house." She picked up a baby boy and gave him to me. She said, "The holy spirit has given you the *don* to receive babies. Wherever you go, the mouth of Christ is with you. This *don* is for you. Don't ever deny it."

I wondered, "Why did I dream that?"

A few days later I had the same dream again, but this time the baby I was given was a girl. As she gave me the baby, the virgin said, "This is your *don*. Take care of it. Don't ever deny it."

Because both dreams emphasized that I was never to deny my *don*, I no longer felt I could refuse when someone asked for my help. People came to me for the most difficult births. When I got to a home, I might find that there was already a midwife there—sometimes there were two or three—and they didn't know what to do. Sometimes the people would tell me that another midwife had left when she saw the birth was complicated. I would think, *Well, I don't want the responsibility either*, but I couldn't leave. I had to stay and help because I couldn't deny my *don*.

One man who came to get me said there were three midwives with his wife already, but they didn't know what to do. The labor was advanced—the baby was beginning to appear—but what they could see didn't look like a head or like any other body part they could recognize. It was just a glob. They thought the baby was dead.

My husband didn't want me to get involved, but I told him, "The sin is on me if I don't go."

When I got there, I saw right away that the "glob" was the amniotic sac that hadn't broken yet. Those inexperienced midwives had never seen that. So I just broke the sac with my finger, and out came a perfectly formed baby. He was *privado*, so I put him in warm water, cleaned the phlegm out of his mouth with my finger, and breathed into his mouth. Then he was fine.

Once after walking seven kilometers to get to a woman's home, I found that one of the baby's feet was sticking out. The woman had been like that, with the baby's foot out, since before the husband set out to get me. I put my hand into the uterus to try to find the other foot, and found that the cord was around the baby's neck, pinning the second leg up against his chest. I had to untangle all that to get the second foot down so the baby could be born.

When a baby came bottom first or feet first like that, when the head was the only thing left to be born, I would put one hand on the back of his head and the other over his chin, with my fingers in his mouth. That's how I gripped the baby's head if the woman needed help to get him out. It's better to manipulate the baby into a good position before labor begins, of course, but not all women come for prenatal visits. They don't think they need a midwife. They don't look for help until there's a problem.

I don't attend births any more, but women still come to me when they learn that their baby is crosswise or sitting or standing. Some say their doctor advised them to see me. I have no idea how those doctors found out about me.

Other women hear about me from their friends. When a woman is told she'll have to have a Cesarean because the baby is poorly positioned, a friend will say to her, "Go see Feliciana. She'll adjust the baby." I don't know what the doctors think when a woman goes back to the Center of Salud after I've adjusted the baby. I don't care what they think.

I don't use injections; injections can kill people! I don't use herbs either. I tell women, "God put the baby in there. He'll decide when it's time for it to come out." I don't have women start pushing until I can see a little of the baby's head. Other midwives have women start pushing too early. Women get tired; they can't push at the end when they really need to.

I charged very little for my work, just a few pesos in the beginning and only five hundred pesos at the end, because it was my *don*. It was my gift from God, and I had to share it with anyone who needed it.

Campeche: Feliciana Cocom May

I met another Feliciana a few days later, in Bolonchén in the state of Campeche. This Feliciana was a slender, soft-spoken woman with delicate features, seventy-three years old, wearing the traditional Mayan dress. Her house was a bungalow with plastered walls and tile floors. Her many certificates from *cursos* she'd attended hung from the walls along with formal portraits of her family. She pointed out that some of the cer-

162 Chapter Seven

Feliciana.

tificates had her name wrong because her mother had never registered her birth. She'd been called by various names over the years: Elisa, Felecita, and Feliciana. After her mother died, she arranged the paperwork to register her existence and make her name official.

> My family was poor. We didn't even have shoes. I hated walking barefoot when it rained and the land was muddy, so I used to slip corn husks onto my feet. One day my sister made me a pair of shoes out of wood. She traced my feet on a board to get the shape of the soles; then she cut them out and nailed pieces of fabric onto them. The shoes were very pretty; my sister had even embroidered flowers on the fabric. Everyone asked me where I got them, and I said, "My sister made them for me."
>
> We were often hungry. There were times when we had nothing to eat but plants we found growing in the wild. My father found work when he could, usually field work for which he was paid in corn. I remember waiting for him to come home, looking forward to the tortillas we would have when he brought corn. One day he didn't come home. He'd been so hungry he drank some pozole that had gone bad, and it killed him. I remember waiting for him—being hungry and waiting and being told finally that he would never come home again. I was eight years old.
>
> My mother was a midwife. When I was about nine or ten, she had me start massaging children, and I started massaging adults a few years later.
>
> One day, when I was fifteen, a woman came to the door looking for my mother to help her daughter in labor. My mother wasn't home—she'd gone to give someone a massage—so the woman sat down to wait. After a while she became impatient. She decided I

should go with her. I told her I'd never received a baby, but she insisted. She said, "*Muchachita,* you know how to massage. You can do it."

So I grabbed some string and went with the woman. It was string I'd made myself by twisting strands of thread together. When I got to the woman's home, I washed my hands with soap and then was careful not to touch anything, not even my own clothes. I prayed for God's blessing on the birth. I said, "God, let this baby I'm about to receive be born okay." When the baby's head came out, I wiped his eyes and mouth with a clean rag. I waited for the placenta to come out and then cut the cord with a razor blade, using my fingers to measure the correct length. According to my mother, the cord was supposed to be left three finger-widths long. Finally, I washed the woman's breasts and told her to feed the baby.

I told the family to take him to the doctor to have him weighed and measured. We had one doctor at that time. I don't know if he was really a doctor, with diplomas like doctors have today, but we called him the doctor. He was a doctor and a midwife and an herbalist. The baby seemed fine, but I was glad the doctor would be checking him to be sure.

I was married soon after that, at the age of fifteen. I was anxious to leave home because my mother had a new husband who was mean to me. He wouldn't buy me clothes or shoes. My husband had a stepmother who treated him badly, so we were a good match. He didn't have a mother, and I didn't have a father.

I had ten children, all with my mother as my midwife. She missed a few of my births—I had fast labors—but she always cut the cord. My babies came out after only three or four contractions. Birth is more difficult now than it was then because of the way people live. We used to work hard, fetching water from a well and carrying it, washing clothes, ironing, and making tortillas. Women don't work as hard now, and they drink coke. We didn't have coke. We just had *atole* and coffee.

I can tell if a woman is pregnant or not after about two months. Once I told a woman she was six weeks pregnant and the baby was a boy. I took her to the doctor because she was feeling weak, but he said she wasn't pregnant. I said, "Yes, she is. Wait and you'll see." After a few months he saw I was right. I was right about it being a boy, too.

I haven't received a baby for almost a year now. Women go to the Center of Salud—or to the hospital in the next town if they need a Cesarean. Actually the doctor we have in the Center of Salud this year [a young doctor doing his year of *servicio*] is afraid to attend births, so everyone has to go to the hospital, but other doctors we've had here in the past have handled normal births.

I was the midwife for the births of all my grandchildren—I don't know how many I have—and for the births of all eighteen of my great grandchildren. I took one of my daughters to the Center of Salud for a birth once because the baby was coming bottom first. The *doctora* on duty said my daughter would have to go to the hospital for a Cesarean. I don't know why I even took my daughter to the *doctora*. I knew what she would say. I was just confused because I'd heard doctors insisting that it was a medical emergency if a baby was sitting or standing. I didn't want my daughter to have a Cesarean, and she didn't want one, so I massaged her belly, moving the baby into the head-down position, and received him myself.

The next day we went to the Center of Salud to show the baby to the *doctora*. It was obvious my daughter hadn't had a Cesarean. "Who delivered the baby?" the *doctora* asked. I told her I did. I told her how I'd adjusted the position of the baby. The *doctora* said, "You'll have to teach me how to do that." But she never brought the subject up again.

Touched by a *Don:* Leonisa Trujeque Fuentes

Back in Ticul, while trying to find the Center of Salud, I was misdirected to a small second-floor office occupied by government health-care administrators. There I met Vicente, a Mayan man fluent in Spanish who was interested in traditional medicine. He took me to a small village, Yotholín, to meet the midwife Leonisa.

Leonisa was a tiny woman, only about four and a half feet tall, her slender body lost in a loose Mayan dress. Her home, at the edge of the village, was a cluster of thatched-roof shelters and animal pens situated in a yard that seemed like a jungle, filled with tropical plants and littered with feed bags and plastic containers. Leonisa's husband, a thin, sinewy man who sat bare-chested on a stool nearby, smiled pleasantly but didn't speak. Leonisa spoke mostly Mayan with a few words of Spanish mixed in and an occasional explosive little "hah!" that must have had some other meaning in Mayan but which seemed to me to say, "So imagine that!"

Vicente translated from Mayan to Spanish for me.

> People say that being a midwife is a *don*. My parents knew I would have a *don* even before I was born, because twice while I was still in my mother's belly they heard me cry. Hah! If a baby cries while still in

the womb, that's a sign that he or she will have a *don*. I was born *embolsada* [still inside the amniotic sac], which is another sign,[6] and when I was a young girl a spiritualist told my parents that I had a *don*. So there were many signs, but my parents never told me. They didn't tell anyone. They were afraid someone might say bad things about me or do something bad to me if they knew. People can be jealous and superstitious.

After my parents died, my uncle told me about all those signs, but by then I already knew about my *don*. I'd had a dream in which a beautiful woman dressed in white robes gave me a big round crystal. The crystal was my *don*. It was my gift from God, my ability to be guided by Him to help women in labor and to help people who are sick or injured. God does everything. He guides my hands when I work. That dream helped me understand why it was that I'd always been the one people turned to when they needed help.

Leonisa.

I got married when I was twenty-six years old and became pregnant right away. I didn't know anything about birth. I'd never seen a baby being born—that would be strictly forbidden—and of course in those days no one ever talked about such things. Children weren't even allowed to listen to their parents' conversations. If children tried to listen when adults were talking, they would be swatted.

I wanted to be alone for the birth of my baby. I didn't know what was going to happen, but I'd seen my sisters-in-law getting ready for their labors, so I knew what I would need. I bought alcohol and string, and I washed some rags. When the time came for the birth, I knew what to do. I can't explain how I knew. God told me. It was my *don*.

I had five babies, and I was alone for all their births. I never had a doctor or a midwife. Hah!

Before my first baby was born, when a neighbor asked me to help her in labor, I said I didn't know how, but after I'd had a baby myself I felt confident, so when women asked after that, I said yes. God was always there for me. He always guided my hands. Sometimes he told me in dreams what to do.

My second baby got bronchitis when he was about a year old. I took him to a doctor several times, but he wasn't getting any better. Then one day I was told in a dream that I should cure him myself. The dream showed me which herb to use and how to prepare it. I did as I was told, and within a few days my baby was well.

I went to a *curso* in a nearby town about forty years ago. It was taught in Spanish and the midwives all spoke Mayan, so we didn't understand much of what the doctor said, but we followed along as best we could. Every now and then I would say to myself, "That's not right," but I didn't say it out loud. I don't read or write—I don't know a single letter of the alphabet—but I know everything I need to know about birth. What were they going to teach me? Hah! I know by looking at the woman if she's in true labor or not. I can tell by examining her belly and watching her face if she's going to be able to have the baby with me or if there's going to be a problem. If the birth is going to be difficult, I tell her to go to the doctor.

Being a midwife is hard work. Sometimes I attended four births in a week, and I did the woman's laundry too and cooked for the family for eight days after the birth. People didn't have any money in those days. Sometimes they only paid twenty *centavos*. I remember once I was paid twenty pesos, and I thought that was a lot of money.

I've had a lot of good fortune in my life. My husband is a lucky man to live with me and receive the benefit of all my good fortune. People say I'm lucky, but it's not really luck; it's my guardian angel watching out for me. It's God. Hah!

Leonisa said she'd known I was going to visit her. She'd had a dream in which a tall stranger came to see her and hugged her. So when it came time for us to leave, I prepared to participate in a hug that had been prophesied in a dream. Leonisa was so tiny—if she'd been a child, I would have gone down on my knees to hug her or I would have picked her up, but instead I bent over her and put my hands on her back. She reached up and started to stroke me, pressing and sliding her hands down my cheeks and then down my face, over my eyes. She stroked my shoulders, my chest, my arms, and then my face again, spreading a goose-bumpy, shimmering feeling with her hands. I knew I was being touched by someone with a *don*.

The *Congreso*

I returned to Tulum six months later for the *congreso*, which had been rescheduled. Before it began, I visited Filiberta to give her clamps and a miniature pelvis set. I asked her about the birth of Lidia's baby, the one that was breech when I visited before, and she said she'd successfully adjusted him into the head down position and had attended the birth without any problems.

Antonia had become president of the *asociación*, so she had many responsibilities related to the organization of the *congreso*. She showed me a list of presenters, which included activists for humanized birth from around the world: obstetricians Dr. Marcos Leite from Brazil and Miguel Solis from Ecuador, midwives Suely Carvalho from Brazil and Debbie Díaz from Puerto Rico, Dr. Mercedes Juarez of the World Health Organization in Geneva, and anthropologist Robbie Davis-Floyd. I don't suppose they came for the compensation, which couldn't have been much, so I imagine they were there because they wanted to meet with each other, because they wanted to support those who are trying to improve the situation for birthing women in Mexico, and because Tulum is a paradise—with magnificent white-sand beaches, an intense blue sky, and clear air still charged with the magic of the ancient Mayan world.

A group of midwives from Morelos, many of whom I'd met at the *congreso* in Chiapas, came by bus, traveling twenty-four hours nonstop. They stayed for free in a new hotel on the beach that wasn't really ready for occupancy; there was no electricity and almost no furniture. Some slept in chairs, some on the floor. They cooked their own meals over a gas stove in the hotel kitchen using beans, rice, and eggs supplied by Sabrina.

There were also dozens of Mayan midwives from south of Cancún, all in their beautiful embroidered gowns. There were volunteers translating all the necessary combinations of the three languages, English, Spanish, and Mayan. They sat in makeshift booths at the back of the room, transmitting to any of the attendees who chose to wear a headset. It was like the U.N. (well . . . like the U.N. if all the representatives wore embroidered shirts and dresses and loved and respected each other).

Sabrina wanted the attendees to create a proclamation of rights for birthing women, which we would all sign and she would then present to officials of the local medical establishment. The officials would have to take the proclamation seriously because of the eminence of the people involved in creating it. At the end of each long day of impassioned speeches there was a forum during which attendees worked on the wording of the proclamation.

There were a few local doctors in attendance too. I wondered why they had come and what they expected. The stature of the presenters would have made the event nearly irresistible, but still . . . it had been organized by midwives! Were the doctors listening? Did they understand that while

Mexican medicine has been whizzing ahead on the road to making birth an ever more high-tech endeavor, many health-care providers in the rest of the world were rethinking the wisdom of such a course and doubling back?

Sabrina was busy dealing with her many *congreso*-related responsibilities. I didn't have a chance to exchange more than a few words with her until the last day, when we found ourselves on the beach, a few feet from the soft waves of the Caribbean, waiting for a bus to take us back to town. I asked her about the birth of her baby a few months earlier. She said she'd wanted to have the baby by herself, but she'd been a little nervous.

> My midwife brain, which knows all the things that can go wrong, made me think I might need help, but my instincts told me I could manage on my own. When my labor began, I still hadn't decided if I wanted other midwives with me or not. When my contractions got really strong, I called one of my midwife friends and asked her to get Antonia and come. Then I prayed. I prayed for my baby to come quickly, before my friends got there—unless there was a problem. If there was a problem, I wanted him to wait so I would have their help.
> I was already nursing him when my friends arrived.

So, like her mentor Antonia, Sabrina had achieved her dream of giving birth on her own.

The bus arrived and took us back to the conference hall where we lined up to sign the proclamation. We returned to the beach a few hours later, at

Midwives return to *el centro* after a day at the *congreso*, which was held in a hotel on the beach.

dusk, for one last ceremony during which elder midwives of Morelos and elder midwives of Tulum were given special clay lamps. A flame was passed, and the lamps were lit. One of the Morelos midwives explained that the flame represented the unity of the midwives of Mexico: their shared vision and their shared struggle to maintain dignity, sacredness, and respect in childbirth. The midwives promised to keep the flames burning for a year.

Elder Mayan midwives after lighting oil lamps that represent the unity of Mexican midwives. They promise to keep the lamps burning for one year. (Antonia is the third in the line; Filiberta is the fourth.)

When I had a chance to talk to Sabrina a few years later, I asked if her proclamation had had any impact on medical practices in Tulum.

She laughed. "No, none at all."

Endnotes

1. "*El cirro*" is another name for the *tipté,* which Jordan calls "the most important organ in Maya ethno-anatomy" (1993, 185). Gonzales says that the belly button "is the seat and regulator of the spirit," and that "the *tipté,* which exists below the belly button, regulates the organs and is part of 'energetic anatomy' as a moderator of well-being." She explains that work such as the massage Antonia gave me is "pulse work that harmonizes energetic pulses" (2012, 144). I learned all this about the *cirro* (the *tipté*) by reading about it when I was back home, not by asking midwives. Antonia (and other Mayan midwives) gave only vague answers to my questions about the subject. It seemed that the *cirro* was an organ—or entity or essence—outside my frame of reference that I could not be expected to understand.
2. I heard other beliefs about what being born *embolsada* or "with a veil" (with part of the sac covering the face) meant. Some said the baby would be especially intelligent; others said he would be friendly. The Mayans see it as a sign that the baby, if it is a girl, will be a midwife. One midwife said it meant the baby would suffer a serious illness during the first year of life. She said that in such a case it was necessary to dry the placenta and part of the cord and save it for use later in a treatment that would cure the illness.
3. Although the worst tears do require stitches, evidence-based practice in modern medicine recognizes that minor and moderate tears will heal nicely without stitches and this is often the preferred option. A seasoned obstetrical nurse once told me, talking about how readily tears in the perineum (the area between the vagina and anus, the most common site of tears) heal, "If you put two perineal cells in the same room, they will find each other and join together." And a Cochrane review agrees that many vaginal tears can be allowed to heal on their own (Elharmeel et al. 2011).
4. The insertion of hands into the uterus that Panchita mentioned is called "manual revision." Its purpose is to ensure that no remnants of the placenta remain inside. This is an extremely painful procedure that increases the risk of infection. The preferred method is to carefully examine the placenta once it is out; if it is found to be intact, then all is well.
5. Many women who had given birth in Mexican hospitals complained about the many vaginal checks that were performed. This problem is apparently another example of how the public hospital system provides interns and residents with opportunities to "practice." One woman writing about her feelings when a stream of *practicantes* took turns inserting their fingers into her vagina while she was in the prep room *waiting to have a Cesarean* said it was like "sanctioned rape" (Figuera 2013).
6. Barbara Rogoff (2011) found that Mayans in nearby Guatemala also considered being born with the amniotic sac over the head to be a "birth sign." She was told that when a girl was born with this sign, it meant she was destined to follow the sacred path of midwife.

Chapter 8

Vera Cruz, Puebla, and Morelos

"I have seventeen grandchildren now," Delia said proudly. I asked if she'd been involved in their births, and she said no, they'd all been born by Cesarean.

All? I expected outrage, but either she'd accepted that the surgeries were necessary or she didn't want to talk about the fact that her children trusted the new medical system more than they trusted her.

I was in Mexico for another *congreso* at Luna Maya in San Cristóbal (I was to lead one of the sessions this time) but was taking some time before it started to visit midwives I'd met at the *congreso* in Oaxaca seven years before. Delia was the one I'd ridden on the bus with after the *congreso*, the one whose story had begun, "I fell in love with my mother-in-law when I was a little girl."

She hadn't bought the delivery table she'd been hoping for, so she hadn't been able to revive her practice, but her friend Socorro was still working as a midwife. I'd met Socorro. She was one of the midwives who'd been traveling with Delia. Back in my hotel room after my visit with Delia, I called Socorro to see if I could visit her. She said she didn't have time. She was busy getting ready for a birth. Could I come the following day?

She was busy getting ready for a birth. "Can I come now?" I asked. "Can I be there for the birth?"

She said yes. Her usual assistant was out of town, so she could use my help. I wasn't sure how much help I'd be, but I didn't mention my reservations. I hurried to get ready and went out to the street to find a taxi.

172 Chapter Eight

The Birth of Rosa's Baby: Socorro Espinosa Sanchez

The person who came to the door when I knocked at Socorro's house was Rosa, the young woman in labor. She and her husband Alfredo, both sixteen, and various members of Alfredo's family were passing the time in a little vestibule at the front of Socorro's house, waiting for the contractions to become stronger.

I introduced myself and made sure it was okay with Rosa for me to help with the birth. She was having back labor, so I applied pressure to her lower back with the heel of my hand during each contraction, and she said it really helped.

When Socorro came to check on her patient and found that I had arrived, she asked me to join her in the birthing room at the back of the house. The doula in me felt a little uncomfortable about abandoning the patient, but neither Socorro nor Rosa had asked me to be a doula; I was

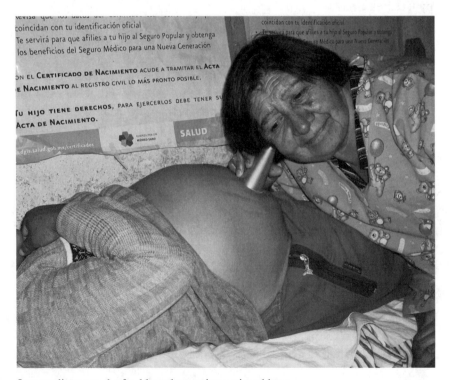

Socorro listens to the fetal heartbeat using a pinard horn.

there to be Socorro's helper. I followed Socorro to the room where the birth would take place.

She said she'd checked Rosa just after I called and found her to be seven centimeters dilated. I was surprised. Rosa had seemed relaxed and composed. Seven centimeters; it wouldn't be long.

There was a delivery table at one end of the room, an uncomfortable-looking thing made of metal with a thin pad covered by stiff plastic and with leg rests that could be raised into place when needed. Shelves around the periphery of the room were crammed with medical supplies, religious objects, and knick knacks.

We talked while Socorro prepared for the birth, laying out tools and supplies on a sterile cloth over a tall table. She said she had always wanted to be a midwife. She'd studied nursing when she was young and had worked for a doctor, but she hadn't liked working for him. He drank a lot. Another doctor told her she could attend births on her own, so she began her work as a midwife. She used to attend twelve to fifteen births a month, she said, but that number had dwindled since the Seguro Popular was put into effect.

I asked if she used the rebozo to rock women. "No," she said. "That's not our custom. Adjusting babies with my hands is my *don*."

Rosa's mother-in-law came to tell Socorro that Rosa's contractions were getting stronger, and Socorro had the woman send Rosa back to the birthing room. Socorro checked Rosa (performed *el tacto*) and said it was "almost time." She had her put on a gown and started an IV with Pitocin. Once the IV was in place, she had Rosa stand beside the table and encouraged her to walk around as much as the IV tubing would allow. Rosa was happy to have me resume the pressure on her lower back. I mentioned the rebozo, hoping Socorro would want to try using it, but she said again that it was "not her custom."

We heard a commotion from the waiting relatives, and Socorro went to see what was happening. When she came back, she told us that Rosa's mother had arrived and was angry that Alfredo's family had brought Rosa to a midwife instead of a doctor. I continued to support Rosa, using my doula skills, while Socorro went back and forth between the two rooms, applying her diplomatic skills in one and keeping tabs on her patient in the other.

Socorro quizzed Rosa. Did she trust Socorro? Did she want to stay? Was she sure? When Rosa didn't waver in her certainty that she was happy where she was, Socorro went to tell the mother that this was what Rosa wanted. Soon she returned and told Rosa, "Your mother wants to take you to a doctor *ahorita* [right now]. You have to tell her yourself that you want to be here with me."

Rosa seemed reluctant to talk to her mother. "I don't want to make her mad," she said.

The mother joined us; I watched as she took in the scene. I thought she would be reassured when she saw the delivery table, the shelves full of supplies, and the IV pole with its bag of liquids dripping into her daughter's vein, and maybe the gringa helper would add to her confidence too, but she was not ready to be mollified. She hissed at Rosa, "Why did you let them bring you here?" Rosa didn't respond. She was having a contraction.

I introduced myself and asked the questions I usually ask grandmas-to-be. How many children did she have? How were her labors? Did she have other grandchildren? She relaxed a little. She must have realized, at some point, the impracticality of trying to move Rosa at such a late stage in labor.

There was a knock at the door of the birthing room. Socorro went out and learned that now Alfredo's family was upset because Rosa's mother had been allowed to come back to the birthing room and they had not. Finally, after more negotiations, Alfredo joined us. He seemed about to explode—whether from anger or concern for his wife, I could not tell. The mother left. Alfredo stood at Rosa's side, clenching his fists and his face, fighting to contain his young emotions. I told him he could take Rosa's hand, and he did. Then suddenly he collapsed into her arms, sobbing. They clung to each other for a few moments; then, when he had composed himself, he returned to the waiting area.

Rosa said she had *ganas de hacer dos* (urge to "go number two"), and she began to push spontaneously during contractions, so Socorro had her get up onto the table. After checking her, she encouraged Rosa to continue pushing. I supported Rosa's head and a leg and suggested all the position changes I could think of that seemed possible within the constraints of the table, and she gamely followed my suggestions. Socorro sat in a chair on the far end of the room and watched, not giving any sign that she was impressed by my efforts but not objecting either, projecting calm and *paciencia*.

Rosa cried out *"No aguanto."* She wanted an episiotomy. She said she wanted a Cesarean. She asked for Alfredo, and Socorro had him come back into the birthing room. He managed to remain composed; he held Rosa's hand.

Socorro had me tie a cloth around Rosa's midriff and asked Alfredo to put his hand on top of Rosa's belly. She told him he could press down "a little." It was apparently time for someone to help Rosa push, but Socorro must have known from her interactions with Americans at the *congresos* that I couldn't be expected to be the one to do it. This was, I imagine, one of the jobs the real helper would have performed. Alfredo didn't seem to understand what was being asked of him, and Socorro let the subject drop. I imagine she felt uncomfortable asking for fundal pressure in my presence. I didn't know what to say. I thought Rosa was perfectly capable of pushing her baby out herself, and doctors, midwives, and teachers I respect all say that the use of fundal pressure, except in emergency situations, adds unnecessary risk; yet I'd been influenced by the many Mexican women I'd heard ask, "How can a woman be expected to push out her baby *without any help at all?*" I said nothing, but I wished later that I'd at least expressed my confidence in Socorro and my respect for her ways.

Rosa pushed her baby out all by herself about forty-five minutes after getting back up onto the table.

Socorro was busy after the birth and Alfredo was once again in a state of near collapse, this time from relief and joy, so I was the one designated to take the news to the family. "It's a boy," I said, though they'd already known it was going to be. The two new grandmothers locked eyes for a moment, both beaming (hostilities temporarily forgotten) and then joined the general murmuring of happy speculations that filled the room. I returned to the birthing room. Socorro cleaned both mother and baby and settled them in a twin bed in the next room. The family visited briefly, and then everyone, including Alfredo, left.

As in the birth I'd seen in Zihuatanejo and the times I was at Delfina's house shortly after a birth had taken place, the goal seemed to be to get the mother and baby cleaned and wrapped up together as quickly as possible and then to *leave them alone.*

After Socorro straightened up the room (another job that no doubt would have fallen to me had I been a true helper), she and I went to a neighborhood restaurant to celebrate. Although I may have helped Rosa a little, I really hadn't helped Socorro at all; still she thanked me and treated me as a colleague. She seemed to have enjoyed the camaraderie of our shared experience as much as I had.

When I visited the next day, I found Rosa and Alfredo sitting up together in the bed, with their new son in Alfredo's arms. Both were smiling—at the baby, at each other, at me, at the world. Rosa's face was so swollen from her ferocious pushing that her eyes squinted shut when she smiled. I praised her efforts and admired the baby and then left them to their reverie.

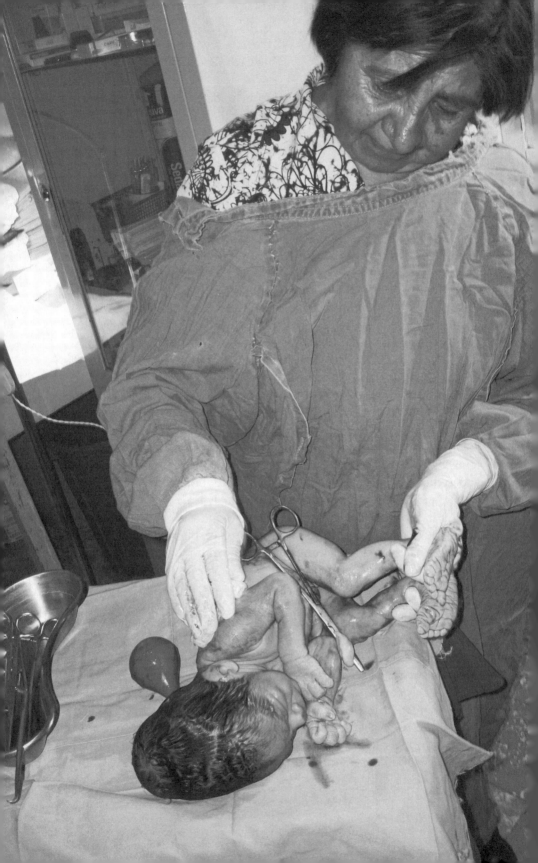

Delia, the midwife I'd originally come to see, was there, having come to say goodbye to me. Socorro told her about the previous night's birth, mentioning my wonderful "massage technique" (pressure on the lower back)—making me feel like a schoolgirl being praised by a favorite teacher. I showed them how to do it. They urged me to stay longer, but the *congreso* was starting in a few days and I'd planned to go to Morelos before heading south to Chiapas. So I said goodbye and went back to the hotel to pack.

The Birth of Lucita's Baby: Angelina Martinez Miranda

The midwife I went to see in Morelos, Angelina, had been one of the presenters at the *congreso* in Oaxaca seven years before. She was outspoken and confident and accustomed to dealing with people of other cultures. She had learned midwifery from her grandmother, she said, and she continued to use the traditional ways, but she had also learned from doctors and from midwives of other countries. She served as a mentor to students of the nearby midwifery school CASA, allowing them to spend three weeks with her, watching, helping, and learning.

Angelina.

Shortly after I arrived at Angelina's house a labor patient, Lucita, arrived, and we went to Angelina's birth center, a separate building beside her house, for the birth. Angelina checked the fetal heartbeat a few times with a hand-held Doppler (an ultrasound device), but other than that, she left Lucita alone. Lucita paced around the room, not talking much, pausing when she had a contraction. Her young husband sat on a chair in the corner, watching Angelina for cues. Angelina's quiet confidence told him, *Everything is fine; there's nothing we need to do.*

There was no IV, and no drugs were used. I saw modern equipment, an oxygen tank and a device that can be used to suction mucus from the baby's lungs, and also a rebozo, but none of these were needed. Words of

[Opposite page] Socorro examines Rosa's baby.

affection flowed from Angelina like a drug from an IV. *¡Ay, mi amor, mi reina, mi dulce! ¡Sí, mi hija, mi ciel, tu niñito tan hermoso va a nacer! Eres fuerte, cariña. Dios te ayuda.* (Aye, my love, my queen, my sweet one! Yes, my daughter, my heaven, your beautiful little baby is going to be born! You are strong, dear. God is helping you.)

When it was time for Lucita to start pushing, Angelina had her sit on a small stool in front of me, leaning back against me with her arms draped over my thighs. She spread a sterile cloth under Lucita and then waited patiently, checking the fetal heartbeat now and then, but not touching Lucita. *¡Sí, mi hija, mi reina, mi ciel! Ya viene tu bebe!* (Yes, my daughter, my queen, my heaven! Your baby is coming!) Lucita had a sweet, natural birth surrounded by her husband and women who respected her process.

I spent what was left of the night in one of the two spare bedrooms Angelina kept available for her many visitors. Although I slept late the next morning, Angelina did not. By the time I got up she was busy with a patient who had come for a prenatal checkup. Other patients sat on folding chairs in her courtyard, waiting their turns.

I said goodbye to Lucita, who was happily nursing her baby, and *hasta luego* to Angelina—I would be seeing her again in a few days at the *congreso*—and set out for the bus station.

Musing on the Bus

As I relaxed in yet another comfortable first-class bus, now on my way to Chiapas, I thought about the births I'd seen in Mexico. I remembered all the times I'd tried to get a midwife to talk about the specifics of a birth, but she could only tell me about the social context in which the birth had taken place, and I could see why that would be so. What would Socorro remember about the birth of Rosa's baby? Not details related to dilation or how long a particular phase took. The birth had been routine and unremarkable. What Socorro would remember would be the drama with the family. What would Angelina remember about the birth of Lucita's baby? Possibly my presence, but maybe not even that: she had a lot of visitors.

In the births I'd seen, the midwives had waited longer than we do before getting involved. They let the patient and her family deal with labor on their own until it was very active, and then they worked and waited quietly, without much explaining, coaching or encouraging.

(Angelina's litany of endearments was unique to her own personal style.) Faith in the patient's ability to give birth felt innate, like our faith that there will be air for our next breath, that our children will be able to grow teeth and that they will learn to walk. *Of course Saira and Rosa and Lucita could do it.*

I thought of the many layers of influence I'd seen reflected in the various midwives' practices. They had learned, in varying degrees, from the experience of giving birth, from their grandmothers and mothers, from other midwives, from women giving birth, from doctors in *cursos*, and from people like me who didn't agree with everything those doctors told them. As long as there have been mothers and grandmothers and healers of any kind, there have been ideas about how to help make birth easier or faster or safer. It seems to be human nature, when faced with the challenge of birth, to want to *do something*. And so we do things. And babies keep surviving, even thriving, sometimes thanks to, and sometimes in spite of, the things we do.

We give a woman herbal teas or hot chocolate and raw eggs or Jell-o and juice—or maybe a narcotic like Nubain or Stadol or Demerol. Or we give her Pitocin or human pee! Sometimes we break the amniotic sac; sometimes we rock her in a rebozo. We have her walk or we don't let her walk, or we numb her body so that walking is no longer an option.

We wipe her brow and praise her and tell her *she can do it*, or we threaten and scold her. Some caregivers pray with her. We put a braid in her mouth or apply fundal pressure or tie a cloth around her midriff. Or we urge her to hold her breath and push harder, harder, harder while we count to ten.

We have her get on her knees or on a birthing ball, or on her side, or on a special chair, or in a squat, or in a hammock or on a delivery table with leg supports.

Some rub her body with antibiotic soaps, others rub her with nettles.

Some surgically enlarge the vaginal opening or create an alternative to the vaginal opening by making an incision in her belly.

And always (except for a few rare cases of the sort that "don't count"), the baby is born and is, as far as we can tell, just fine. In that triumphant moment when we hear the baby's first cry, when we place the baby in the mother's arms and share in her relief and joy, we experience the great satisfaction of knowing that what we did must have been *exactly the right thing to do.*

Congreso in San Cristóbal

A few days later I stood in front of a group of traditional midwives and spoke on the topic, "Traditional Midwives as Teachers in Their Communities." I asked, "Why are there so many Cesareans in Mexico today?" The midwives gave me the answers I expected, answers that blamed the medical system. Then I asked, "How do you think your countrymen, those who have not been involved in childbirth as a profession, would answer that question?"

They had no idea.

I told them what I'd learned from all the people who had shared their speculations with me: "Old women blame the lifestyle and laziness of today's young women, young people blame 'progress,' and, most sadly, the women who are leaving the hospitals with fresh scars slashed across their bellies blame themselves."

I said that they, the midwives, needed to tell their countrymen that it's the medical system that is failing, not today's women. I urged them to remind people what they, better than anyone else, knew to be true: that women, given support, *can still do it*.

Chapter 9
Oaxaca and Home

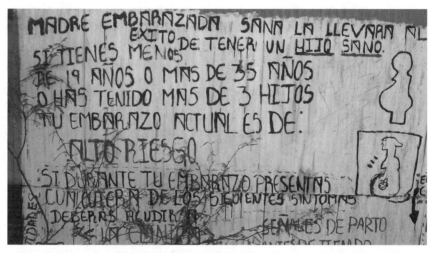

A sign seen in a small town in Oaxaca tells pregnant women, "Being healthy will lead you to the success of having a healthy child. If you are less than 19 years old or more than 35 or if you have had more than three children, your current pregnancy is HIGH RISK."

The sign goes on to say that women who suffer from one of these "risk factors" (too old, too young, too many previous pregnancies) should seek medical attention (i.e., they should not have their babies with midwives).

An obstetrician in the city of Oaxaca told me that when women with high risk pregnancies, as defined by that sign, arrived at the public hospitals, they would be told that Cesarean section was their only option, and obstetrician Karina Ledesma said that the same age guidelines were followed in the public hospital where she worked in Michoacán. She said an eighteen year old who was eight centimeters dilated when she arrived at the hospital was sent directly to the operating room for a Cesarean—simply because of her age.

Both obstetricians confirmed what I had heard before, that the need to provide instruction and practice for interns and residents was a significant factor explaining the high Cesarean rate in public hospitals in Mexico. They said doctors now see so few normal labors that they no longer understand or trust the natural process. A labor has to be extremely fast to be allowed to proceed normally.

And they both said that unnecessary vaginal checks, shaving of pubic hair, use of enemas, cutting of episiotomies, forcing women to labor on their backs with their legs elevated and restrained, attempting to stretch the cervix manually (ouch: I hadn't heard of that before), fundal pressure, and manual revision of the uterus, were routine in hospitals where they had worked.

The Mexican government is addressing these abuses, trying to move the medical establishment toward practices that are more humane and more in line with scientific evidence. For example, a 2014 official "guide for clinical practice" (Centro Nacional de Excelencia Tecnológica en Salud) says that none of the procedures listed above should be used routinely, and it recommends delayed cord clamping, immediate skin-to-skin contact between mother and baby, prompt breastfeeding, and continuous emotional support for women in labor. Unfortunately, the new guidelines are not being taught in medical schools in Mexico, and there is great resistance to change, especially among obstetricians. As Davis-Floyd points out, "All efforts that go against the technocultural grain will be opposed and, always, will face the penultimate challenge of co-option—that is, of apparent but not real change" (Davis-Floyd 2007, 64). Just as the midwives gave only token agreement years ago when they were told in those *cursos* that supine positions were better than vertical positions, modern obstetricians nod their heads when told the opposite and then continue to practice as they always have.

The term "obstetrical violence" or *violencia obstétrica*, was being used more and more often in discussions that acknowledged there was a crisis in obstetrical care in the world and particularly in Latin America. There was a new awareness, worldwide, of how vulnerable women are to abuse at the hands of authority figures who might put personal and institutional agendas ahead of the goal of providing nurturing care (and ahead of scientific evidence regarding what constitutes good care). It was clear that this was an international issue, not a Mexican issue, and that there was much work to be done.

That was the world of modern obstetrics that was displacing my beloved (Mexico's beloved) midwives. The rate of midwife-attended births in Mexico, which was close to 50 percent when I first went to Mexico in 1964 and was still 15 percent in 2003 when I went to that first *congreso*, had dipped to 2.1 percent (Suárez et al. 2012, 84).

I was in Oaxaca to revisit midwives I'd met at the first *congreso* nine years before, but my first stop had been to deliver photos of a new grandchild to a family in Santa Ana Agache, near Ocotlán. I was on the back of a little scooter taxi, leaving town, when I saw the sign about risk factors in pregnancy. I had the driver stop. I looked at the sign for a long time, my heart heavy, as if I were standing before a shrine to the demise of midwifery. I thought of the midwives I'd met whispering *you can do it* to women in labor—and all the midwives who came before them whispering the same words: *You can do it.*

The sign was proclaiming in bold letters that today's women *cannot do it*. I remembered Nachita telling me how she'd said to the doctors, "With you it's always *puro cuchillo, puro cuchillo*" (just knives, just knives). I hadn't known when I met her how true her assessment was.

I'd heard from my friend Francisca, before I left for Oaxaca, that her husband's grandmother Julia, the midwife who'd had a "special chair," had died. Now I wondered how many more of the midwives I'd met were gone. I had no way of knowing; I had contact information for only a few. Would I find Lena still alive? And Paulita?

A Family of Doctors

I found Marta, the woman who had begun working as a midwife after her doctor husband died, still living in the same house in Ocotlán, looking much older, but, she said, still attending births. Her daughter had finished medical school and was now in a village a few hours away performing her year of *servicio*. Marta's son, Salvador, who had completed a residency in obstetrics and was living with his mother, joined us while we talked. He'd worked as an intern in the hospital where I confronted the man with the rifle and as a resident in another large hospital in Oaxaca. He confirmed what I'd heard about the policies in these hospitals and added that any woman who arrives at the hospital having been with a midwife for part of the labor will also deliver by Cesarean, regardless of the circumstances. Receiving attention from a midwife had "complicated" the birth, making a surgical delivery necessary. As an intern and resident he had not challenged those policies.

Salvador said he and his sister and his brother, an anesthesiologist now, wanted to open a birth center in Ocotlán. They would offer natural birth and vaginal birth with an epidural. And, he assured me, they would provide the kind of support their mother had always given women in labor.

I remembered Marta saying that she used to take her children with her when she attended births. So they'd been in the presence of normal birth all their lives. They'd heard the sounds women make when they're fighting pain and making fierce effort. They'd heard their mother's words of encouragement—*you can do it*—and they'd breathed in the atmosphere of elation when the pain and effort were over and a new baby is placed in his mother's arms. Hopefully their mother's trust in the natural process had survived their training by a system that believes that women, for the most part, can't do it and that the triumph of bringing new life into the world belongs to medical practitioners, not to women.

I wondered if the new clinic would be affordable to the poor women Marta had always served, but I didn't ask. I knew that clinics like the one they proposed to open tended to cater to women of means, women who could afford the luxury of birthing in an environment of respect.

Silvia Hears Her Story

Silvia, the midwife whose baby had been born on the dirt floor just as she was coming home with her Day of the Dead purchases, seemed confused for a moment when she found me standing at her gate, but then she remembered, and she embraced me like a sister. She was a little thinner now and had a few strands of gray hair in her braids.

She said there was no longer much business for midwives now that women could have their babies for free in the public hospital in the city of Oaxaca. When a woman came to have a baby with her now, it was because labor was progressing so fast she didn't have time to get to the hospital or it was because the woman was so poor she couldn't afford transportation to the city. So the income Silvia derived from attending births was negligible. She supported herself by giving belly massages, making miniature black pottery figurines, and selling *chiles rellenos*.

She'd been to two *cursos* since my last visit. She said a doctor in the most recent one said midwives *shouldn't* give Pitocin at the end of labor.

She didn't know what to think; she'd been told the opposite for so many years. "The doctor who said that was very young," she said.

We sat together in the main room of her house, next to her altar, and I read what I'd written about my previous visit with her, translating as I went along. She was very still, listening. She looked with wonder at the typed pages in my lap. She seemed astonished that they contained *her* words telling about *her* life. I interrupted my reading sometimes to ask her, "Is that right? Did I get that right?" and she would nod and then look at the pages impatiently, eager to hear more. She interrupted occasionally to ask, "*Dios mío*, did I tell you *that*?" She added a detail: One of the women she'd told me about, a woman who birthed a foot-first baby with only one foot presenting, apparently *hadn't even known she was pregnant!* She laughed when I got to the part about the would-be boyfriend who wanted a kiss. "*¡Madre mía!* Did I tell you *that*?"

I asked what had happened with that relationship.

"Oh, nothing came of it," she said, with a dismissive sweep of her hand.

On the bus, on the way back to the city, I wondered what choices women of modern Mexico would make if the cost of care were not a factor. There was a time when birthing with a midwife was the only affordable option for the poor. A woman would have had to be relatively wealthy to afford a Cesarean birth or a vaginal birth with modern interventions. Now the situation is reversed. Now, a wide array of interventions (but not pain relief for a vaginal delivery) are available, mandatory even, for the poor, while only the rich can afford to give birth in one of the private clinics that might support women in having a more natural experience.

Lena Gets a New Dress

I'd brought a new dress for Lena, the midwife who'd helped me give birth to my imaginary baby. The dress I'd found was black, with a print of tiny white flowers. It had a full skirt, a big lace collar, and a zipper up the back. I'd shortened it, using a picture of Lena standing next to me to gauge the length.

Could Lena still be alive? She'd been so frail and thin when I met her six years earlier. She would be ninety years old now.

I made my way to her village, found her house, and knocked on the door. And she answered! It took her a moment to remember who I was, but when she did—*¡qué milagro!*—she remembered all the details of the previous visit. She sparkled with happy energy. *¡Qué milagro, qué milagro, qué milagro!* I had never felt so welcomed.

She looked more girlish than ever, with the same impish glint in her eyes and with pink ribbons tied into floppy bows at the end of her short, white braids. She massaged my belly again. She held my hand. She reminded me not to tie the cord too soon. She repeated again and again that she couldn't believe I had come back. *Qué milagro.*

When she opened my gift, she looked up at me confused. "It's a dress," I said. "For you. Why don't you try it on?" She studied the zipper as if it were a high-tech invention, and I showed her how to operate it. She went into the house and returned wearing the dress, still open at the back, and had me secure the zipper. The dress looked beautiful on her. The fit was perfect; the style was right.

"I'll wear it on my birthday'" she said.

Daughter and Granddaughter

Let Paulita be still alive too, I prayed as I reached out to knock at the blue gate in front of her house. Paulita had been suffering from kidney failure when I first met her. She'd predicted that she'd be gone before I returned to Oaxaca.

A boy about fifteen answered.

"Is Paulita here?" I asked.

"No," he said. Just no.

"Will she be back soon?"

"No."

I didn't know what to say in the face of his dismissive attitude. Finally, he volunteered that she had died. I asked if he was her grandson, and he said that he was.

"Oh, well I'm sorry," I said. I didn't know what else to say, so I turned to leave. I heard the gate clink shut behind me as I walked away.

Heading for the highway where I would catch a bus back to the city, I felt bereft and lost. The connection I'd made with Paulita during the afternoon I spent with her had been important to me. I'd tacked a picture of her onto the bulletin board in my office when I came back from that previous trip, and I'd gazed at it often during the past six years, searching for inspiration, looking for meaning in the stories I'd been told, and struggling to believe that others would want to hear them. The cold, brief conversation I'd had with her grandson wasn't enough; I needed to know

[Opposite page] Lena wearing her new dress.

more or say more or be allowed to express how the news of Paulita's death had affected me. And so I returned to the house and knocked on the blue gate again.

"Is your mother here?" I asked the teenager when he cracked open the gate.

"No."

I tried to pin him down as to when she might be home, but all he could tell me was that it wouldn't be soon, so it seemed there was no point in waiting, and I couldn't imagine making the trip to the village again, not without some hope that I might receive a warmer welcome than I was getting from him.

"Could you give me a phone number I might use to reach her?" I asked finally. Cell phones were suddenly everywhere in Mexico, even in the villages of Oaxaca. It was likely that someone in the family would have one.

The boy's father, Paulita's son-in-law, appeared at the gate, looking almost as unfriendly as the teenager. I told him I'd met Paulita six years ago and that I would like to talk with his wife. My mention of a previous visit seemed to register with him. Maybe he'd heard about that visit. He gave me a phone number and told me to call his wife that evening.

His wife, Leticia, answered when I called a few hours later. She remembered my previous visit, and she wanted to see me. She reminded me that she and I had met briefly when I was there before. She said that Paulita had died a few months after my visit. Her voice broke as she told me that the time she spent with me had been important to Paulita. She begged me to come back so we could talk, and we agreed to meet the following afternoon.

I asked if they'd received the photos I took of Paulita, which I'd mailed to them after my first visit. They had not.

I would be able to show her the pictures—I had them with me on my laptop—but I wanted to give her copies she could keep, so I spent the next morning walking all over the city of Oaxaca trying to find a business that could make prints while I waited. It was Sunday—most stores were closed—but I finally found a store offering print-while-you-wait photo service. The store was just closing when I got there, but the owner agreed to stay open a bit longer, just for me, and he helped me through what was supposed to be a do-it-yourself process.

So I had the prints with me when I knocked again on the blue gate a few hours later. I was invited into the same room I'd sat in with Paulita on that first visit, and I sat on the same narrow bed. Leticia and her daughter Magalí sat on the other bed facing me.

I asked them about Paulita's life and her work, wanting to fill in details I'd missed when I was there the first time. They knew the answers to everything I asked. How many brothers and sisters had Paulita had? Four. Had she used *el tacto*? Yes, when the woman said she wanted to push. Did she tie a band around the woman's waist to help her push? Yes. Did she use fundal pressure? No.

Both women had helped Paulita in her work, and Leticia would have continued working as a midwife, but the demand was dwindling by the time Paulita died. Still, women continued to come to her for belly massages. Magalí was attending the University of Oaxaca, studying medicine.

I handed them the pictures and waited quietly while the two women leafed slowly through them, murmuring to each other, wiping away tears. They said that Paulita had been depressed before my first visit—she'd known she was dying—but the afternoon spent with me had cheered her up. She had talked about it often afterward. She marveled that someone *from so far away* had thought her life and work were important. She had said more than once, "No one has ever been interested before."

Magalí asked about my writing. "It made Grandma so happy to think that you might put her story in a book," she said.

I told her I hadn't finished the book yet, but I'd written the story of my visit with Paulita. When I offered to read it to them, they eagerly accepted. So I opened my notebook and read, translating as I had for Silvia.

Again there was that deep stillness as I read. They cried again, silently, and I did too, but as I approached the part of the story when the doctor smears poop on Paulita's face, both women began to smile in anticipation. They remembered hearing about that incident. They loved that I'd included it. They were still smiling as I prepared to leave.

Magalí drove me back to the city in her father's pickup truck. I asked her what she planned to do after medical school, and she said she didn't know. I suggested she might like to carry on her grandmother's work.

That possibility had not occurred to her. She was excited by the idea. I pointed out that the women who most needed her services were the poor.

"I could help them," she said. I could picture it: a woman, a neighbor who was a doctor and who trusted birth as Abuelita Paulita had trusted birth, helping women in the village have their babies with dignity. Magalí could picture it too.

***

It was spring when I made that last trip to Oaxaca. A year later, in the spring again, I returned to Zihuatanejo and revisited midwives there. They seemed like old friends now; they greeted me like old friends. I learned that three of the midwives I'd met in Guerrero had died: Doña Chucha, the one whose father had been the first midwife in the family, Mariana, the one who'd had her baby on a rock, and Isabel, the crotchety midwife I'd given the hearing aid to. (But happily, according to her granddaughter Sandra, Isabel had worn the hearing aid until the end of her life.) And when I got home I learned that the midwife Elena in Tulum (Antonia's mother) had also died.

A year later, I attended a *congreso* in Mexico City entitled *Nacer en Paz: Herramientas y Alternativas Ante la Violencia Obstetrica* (To Be Born in Peace: Tools and Alternatives to Counter Obstetrical Violence), held by the Asociación Mexicana de Partería. There I saw old friends and met young women who are taking on the fight for dignity and sanctity in birth in Mexico. I went back to the village in Puebla where I had fallen in love with Mexico fifty years before and walked the not-quite-forgotten streets—they were paved now—thinking about the changes that had taken place in Mexico and the ways I had been changed myself by my half-century-long love affair with this complex country.

I decided I would have an altar for the Day of the Dead that fall. My altar would honor the midwives I knew were gone—Julia, Paulita, Doña Chucha, Isabel, Mariana, and Elena—and others who had died without my knowing. It would be for all the traditional midwives of Mexico, living or dead, for my great grandmother, whose stories had been lost, and for me. I wanted the spirits of the midwives to be as present and tangible in my life as the spirits of dead grandmothers had been to Margarita's granddaughter in Huajuapan.

And so, when I returned from that trip, I planted marigolds. I felt the spirits of the midwives with me as I watered and weeded the flowers all summer long and then, at the end of October, as I gathered the materials for my altar. On the morning of the Day of the Dead, I prepared my altar, draping my old rebozo across the mantel over my fireplace and arranging my pinard horn and other mementos of my travels on top. I added candles, oranges, beer, leftover candy from Halloween, all the marigolds I could find in a fading fall garden, and, finally, pictures of the midwives who had shared their lives and their stories with me.

That evening I lit the candles and stood before the altar, offering prayers of thanks for all that the midwives had given me. I had yearned for a connection to Mexico, to the old Mexico I remembered, a connec-

Judy's Day of the Dead altar.

tion based on commonality and sisterhood, and they had given me that. I had wanted something practical I could do to help ease back labor, and they had shown me the rebozo procedure. I had wanted to learn some mystical secret about how to ease childbirth, and they had shown me their secret. It wasn't something they could "teach" me or pass along like another "trick of the trade," but they had allowed me to see it. It was faith: faith in the ability of God/Nature/Woman to perform the miracle of bringing new life into the world—faith that came from experience, not teachings, faith that had its roots in an ancient wisdom that was innate before modern medicine came along to challenge it.

Most of all, I had wanted to hear their stories. And they had shared their stories. They had shared them, and they had trusted me to honor them.

I thanked them for what they had given me and for what they had given the world. I thanked them on behalf of all the women whose bellies they touched, all the women whose lives they touched, all the women to whom they had whispered *you can do it*, all the women who had seen, with their guidance, that they *could* do it. I thanked them for showing us, by the examples of their magnificent lives, *what women can do.*

Epilogue

Hope for a New Midwifery in Mexico

"Nothing is as certain to start a social movement as a pendulum swing this far on the wrong side of the scientific evidence." —*Robbie Davis-Floyd (2007, 9), writing about the extreme level of intervention in childbirth*

"Every minute another woman dies in childbirth. We can save these women by getting midwives in their communities. By investing in midwives, governments can achieve universal access to reproductive health. . . . There is an urgent need for 334 thousand midwives around the world." —*Thoraya Ahmed Obaid (2008), United Nations Population Fund Executive Director*

"Recently [2012], newborn and maternal deaths among [indigenous women] have received attention at the highest levels within the Mexican government. . . . As part of this attention, the federal government has, for the first time in 2011, provided funding to eight of Mexico's 32 states to hire midwives to serve indigenous communities. The federal government also approved funds for scholarships for women who want to go to the CASA midwifery school [at the time, the only government accredited midwifery school in Mexico]. A CASA graduate was hired by the [federal government] to promote professional midwifery throughout the country . . . and Mexico's National Public Health Institute published a book of studies that recommends that the country open more midwifery schools using CASA's curriculum." —*Dr. Rick Martinez (2012)*

Judy with students from the Escuela de Parteras Profesionales del Estado de Guerrero at a conference, *Nacer en Paz: Herramientas y Alternativas Ante la Violencia Obstetrica* (To Be Born in Peace: Tools and Alternatives to Counter Obstetrical Violence), held by the Asociación Mexicana de Partería in Mexico City in November 2014.

"Mexico is re-making its centuries-old tradition of midwifery. These days the majority of babies are born in hospitals, but that hasn't helped reduce the number of maternal deaths. So health officials are now betting a new kind of midwife, one trained in a clinical setting, may be a solution. The southern Mexican state of Guerrero opened a school in August [2012] where these midwives are being trained.... Many [of the students] are ... the daughters, granddaughters or nieces of traditional midwives [and they are bilingual, speaking both Spanish and the indigenous language of their villages]. This is the first government-funded public school in Mexico.... The students' curriculum marries traditional midwifery with modern medicine. They learn the old arts like massaging bellies with long shawls while also studying gynecology, obstetrics and basic nursing. When they graduate in four years, they'll have a license and be able to work in urban hospitals and rural clinics.... Nationwide reform is a long way ahead. But the students in Guerrero will not give up easily. They know better than anyone the hardships that confront their communities and how they can help. In that way traditions begun long ago will endure." —*Mónica Ortiz Uribe (2013), reporting for NPR*

> "The Asociación Mexicana de Partería [Mexican Association of Midwifery] . . . is an organization . . . founded in 2011 [with support from the Macarthur Foundation] that works to strengthen the profession of midwifery in Mexico. . . . [We aim] to represent midwifery in Mexico, to promote the education and training of new midwives, and to influence the framing of legislation and public policy. . . . [We] respect, honor and support traditional midwifery as a fundamental and vibrant reality and we strive to learn and integrate its knowledge into current practice. We recognize the richness of the diverse practices and cultures of the traditional midwives throughout our country and value the legacy of indigenous midwifery as a privilege that we enjoy in Mexico thanks to our history and culture. We work to preserve, reclaim, document and disseminate the knowledge of midwives of diverse cultures, traditions and regions of Mexico." —*Website of the Asociación Mexicana de Partería, translated by me (2012)*

Change will be slow. The new midwifery school, the new policies, and the new *asociación* haven't yet significantly impacted the birthing scene in a nation that has over two million births per year, but it is a beginning. And it's heartening to see that a new midwifery in Mexico will build on, not replace, the wisdom of the traditional midwives who went before.

References

Almaguer González, José Alejandro, Hernán García Ramírez, and Vicente Vargas Vite. 2010. "La Violencia Obstétrica, Una Forma de Patriarcado en las Instituciones de Salud" [(Domestic Violence, a Form of Patriarchy in Our Institutions of Health]. *Género y Salud en Cifras* [Gender and Health] September–December.

Andersson, Ola, Lena Hellstrom-Westas, Dan Andersson, and Magnus Domellof. 2011. "Effect of Delayed Versus Early Umbilical Cord Clamping on Neonatal Outcomes and Iron Status at 4 Months: A Randomised Controlled Trial." *BMJ* 343:d7157. http://www.ncbi.nlm.nih.gov/pubmed/22089242.

Argüello, Isabel. 2011. "México, Incapaz de Disminuir Indices de Mortalidad Maternal" [Mexico, Incapable of Lowering Maternal Mortality Indexes]. *Red Voltaire* [Voltaire Network], May 16. http://www.voltairenet.org/article169882.html.

Asociación Mexicana de Partería [Mexican Association of Midwifery]. 2012. http://www.parteriamexicana.com.

Avila, Elena. 1999. *Woman Who Glows in the Dark*. New York: Jeremy P. Tarcher/Putnam.

Castro Martin, Teresa. 2002. "Consensual Unions in Latin America: Persistence of a Dual Nuptiality System." *Journal of Comparative Family Studies* 33 (1): 35–55.

CDC. 2005. "QuickStats: Total and Primary Cesarean Rate and Vaginal Birth after Previous Cesarean (VBAC) Rate, United States, 1989–2003." *Morbidity and Mortality Weekly Report* 50 (02): 46. Accessed February 24, 2015. http://www.cdc.gov/mmwr/preview/mmwrhtml/mm5402a5.htm.

Centro Nacional de Excelencia Tecnológica en Salud. 2014. *Vigilancia y Manejo del Trabajo de Parto en Embarazo de Bajo Riezgo* (Vigilance and Management of Labor in Low-Risk Pregnancies). Mexico City: Secretaria de Salud

Davis-Floyd, Robbie. 2000. "Anthropological Perspectives on Global Issues in Midwifery." *Midwifery Today*, no. 53: 68–69.

———. 2004. *Birth as an American Rite of Passage.* 2nd. ed. Berkeley: University of California Press.

———. 2007. "Changing Childbirth: The Latin American Example." *Midwifery Today,* no. 84.

———. 2014, April. "Daughter of Time: The Postmodern Midwife." http://www.davis-floydpresents.com/uncategorized/daughter-of-the-postmodern-midwife/.

Drywater-Whitekiller, Virginia. 2011. "Bringing Back the Tobacco." *Cultural Survival Quarterly* 35 (3): 16–24.

Ehrenberg-Buchner, Stacy. 2013. "External Cephalic Version." *Medscape,* November 25. http://emedicine.medscape.com/article/1848353-overview.

Elharmeel, S. M. A, Y. Chaudhary, S. Tan, E. Scheermeyer, A. Hanafy, and M. L. van Driel. 2011. "Surgical Repair of Spontaneous Perineal Tears that Occur during Childbirth versus No Intervention." *Cochrane Database of Systematic Reviews* 8, Art. No.: CD008534. DOI: 10.1002/14651858.CD008534.pub2.

Eng, Nick. 2014 "Enorgulleciendo a Nuestras Madres: Reduciendo la Mortalidad Materna en México" [Pride in Our Mothers: Reducing Maternal Mortality in Mexico]. Datos.Gob.MX, July 15. http://datos.gob.mx/historias/salud/reduciendo-mortalidad-materna.html.

Estadísticas Demográficas 2011. 2013. Aguascalientes, Mexico: Instituto Nacional de Estadística y Geografia. http://www.inegi.org.mx/prod_serv/contenidos/espanol/bvinegi/productos/continuas/vitales/demograficas/2011/cua_est_dem2011.pdf.

Figuera, Yolotl. 2013. "Yolotl Figuera." In *Nacer en el Ombligo de la Luna: Historias por un Nacimiento Humanizado* [To be Born in the Navel of the World: Stories for Humanized Birth], edited by Karina Falcón. Mexico City: Caliope Humana.

Goldsmith, Judith. 1990. *Childbirth Wisdom from the World's Oldest Societies.* Brookline, MA: East West Health Books.

Gonzales, Patrisia. 2012. *Red Medicine.* Tucson: University of Arizona Press.

Gonzalez-Perez, Guillermo, María Vega-Lopez, Carlos Cabrera-Pivaral, Armando Muñoz, and Ana Valle. 2001. Cesarean Sections in Mexico: Are There Too Many? *Health Policy and Planning* 16 (1): 62–67.

Hajdu, Steven, and Manjunath Vadmal. 2010. "The Use of Tobacco." *Annals of Clinical & Laboratory Science* 40 (2): 178–81.

Hutton, Eileen, and Eman Hassan. 2007. "Late vs. Early Clamping of the Umbilical Cord in Full-Term Neonates: Systematic Review and Meta-Analysis of Controlled Trials." *Journal of the American Medical Association* 297 (11): 1541–1542.

Jelliffe, Derrick, and John Bennett. 1962. "World-Wide Care of the Mother and Newborn Child." *Clinical Obstetrics and Gynecology* 5: 64–84.

Jordan, Brigitte. 1993. *Birth in Four Cultures.* 4th ed. Long Grove, IL: Waveland Press.

———. 1984 "External Cephalic Version as an Alternative to Breech Delivery and Cesarean Section." *Soc. Sci. Med.* 18 (8): 637–651.

Leboyer, Frederick. 2002. *Birth without Violence.* 4th ed. Rochester, VT: Healing Arts Press.

Malkin, Elisabeth. 2011. "Mexico's Universal Healthcare Is a Work in Progress." *New York Times*, January 30.

Martin, Joyce, Brady Hamilton, Michelle Osterman, Sally Curtin, and T. J. Matthews. 2013. "Births: Final Data for 2012." *National Vital Statistics Reports* 62 (9). http://www.cdc.gov/nchs/data/nvsr/nvsr62/nvsr62_09.pdf.

Martinez, Rick. 2012. "Midwives, a Crucial Part of Caring for the Women of Mexico." *Huffington Post Impact*, March 7. http://www.huffingtonpost.com/dr-rick-martinez/midwives-a-crucial-part-of-women_b_1326910.html.

Obaid, Thoraya Ahmed. 2008. "International Day of the Midwife." The Partnership for Maternal, Newborn & Child Health. http://www.who.int/pmnch/media/events/2008/midwifeday/en/.

Odent, Michel. 2003. "Champagne and the Fetus Ejection Reflex." *Midwifery Today*, no. 65.

Ortiz Uribe, Mónica. 2013. "Mexico Training Midwives in Hope of Preventing Maternal Deaths. *KPBS*, January 3. http://woodchoppers/news/2013/jan/03/mexico-training-midwives-hope-preventing-maternal-/.

Pérez Amador, Julieta, and Albert Esteve Palos. 2012. "Explosión y Expansión de las Uniones Libres en México" [Explosion and Expansion of Free Unions in Mexico]. *Coyuntura Demográfica* 2: 41–44.

Rogoff, Barbara. 2011. *Developing Destinies, A Mayan Midwife and Town*. New York: Oxford University Press.

Rojas Alba, Horacio. 1996. "Temazcal: The Traditional Mexican Sweat Bath." *Tlahui-Medic*, no. 2. http://www.tlahui.com/temaz1.html.

Suárez, Leticia, Elvia de la Vara, Aremis Villalobos, and Lourdes Flores. 2012. "Salud Reproductiva" [Reproductive Health]. In *Encuesta Nacional de Salud y Nutrición 2012*, edited by Juan Pablo Gutiérrez, Juan Rivera, Teresa Shamah, Carlos Oropeza, and Mauricio Hernández Ávila. Cuernavaca, México: Instituto Nacional de Salud Pública (MX).

Tully, Gail. n.d. *Spinning Babies: Easier Childbirth with Fetal Positioning*. Accessed December 6, 2014. http://spinningbabies.com/techniques/bodywork-and-professional-help.

Villagran, Lauren. 2013. "Is Birth the Old-Fashioned Way on Its Way Out in Mexico?" *Christian Science Monitor*, April 10.

Wagner, Marsden. 2006. *Born in the USA*. Berkeley: University of California Press.

WHO. 1985. "Appropriate Technology for Birth." *Lancet* 2: 436–437.

Woolley, Robert. 1995. "Benefits and Risks of Episiotomy: A Review of the English-Language Literature Since 1980." *Obstet Gynecol Surv* 50 (11): 806–820.

Zarembo, Alan. 2001. "The New Latin Labor." *Newsweek* (Pacific Edition) March 26, 40.